Further prais

'A smart, entertaining and winningly astringent
look at a very important topic'
WILLIAM GIBSON

'I used to think the dimmer switch was the best
anti-ageing product, but in this wise and witty book Mayer
proves that ageing is a thing of the past'
KATHY LETTE

'Catherine Mayer has most acutely struck a nerve that few, if any of us,
want to admit to. Our mental and physical ages are on divergent
tracks. Age in society is changing beneath our feet. Her exploration of
the complex consequences proves extraordinarily revealing'
JON SNOW

'This spooky sounding condition turns out to be very nice,
I'm definitely hoping I've got it. What is even better is the sheer
entertainment value of Catherine Mayer's witty language,
wealth of ideas and facts, and interviews that range
from the delightful to the sinister'
MATTHEW COLLINGS

amortality

THE PLEASURES AND PERILS
OF LIVING AGELESSLY

CATHERINE MAYER

Vermilion
LONDON

1 3 5 7 9 10 8 6 4 2

This edition published 2011
First published in 2011 by Vermilion, an imprint of Ebury Publishing
A Random House Group company

The Random House Group Limited Reg. No. 954009

Addresses for companies within the Random House Group can be found at
www.randomhouse.co.uk

A CIP catalogue record for this book is available from the British Library

The Random House Group Limited supports The Forest Stewardship Council (FSC),
the leading international forest certification organisation. All our titles that are printed on
Greenpeace-approved FSC-certified paper carry the FSC logo. Our paper procurement
policy can be found at www.rbooks.co.uk/environment

Mixed Sources
Product group from well-managed
forests and other controlled sources
www.fsc.org Cert no. TT-COC-2139
FSC © 1996 Forest Stewardship Council

Designed and set by seagulls.net

Printed in the UK by CPI Mackays, Chatham, ME5 8TD

ISBN 9780091939366

To buy books by your favourite authors and register for offers visit www.rbooks.co.uk

DISCLAIMER: The information in this book has been compiled by way of general
guidance in relation to the specific subjects addressed, but is not a substitute and not to be
relied on for medical, healthcare, pharmaceutical or other professional advice on specific
circumstances and in specific locations. Please consult your GP before changing, stopping
or starting any medical treatment. So far as the author is aware the information given is
correct and up to date as at 2010. Practice, laws and regulations all change, and the reader
should obtain up-to-date professional advice on any such issues. The author and publishers
disclaim, as far as the law allows, any liability arising directly or indirectly from
the use, or misuse, of the information contained in this book.

For Andy, with all my love, always.

In memory of Richard Flint.
All those moments will be lost in time, like tears in rain.
But not quite yet.

contents

introduction

'All the world's a stage,
And all the men and women merely players,
They have their exits and their entrances,
And one man in his time plays many parts,
His acts being seven ages.'
William Shakespeare, *As You Like It*

'I feel just as hungry today as I did the day I left home.'
Madonna

'The real challenge comes when you know there really is the chance of discovering something never before seen.'
Sport Diving: the British Sub-Aqua Club Diving Manual

TRANSITIONS CAN BE AWKWARD, and the start of a dive is no exception. There's a clumsy thunk into the water, the race to dump air from a billowing jacket, and then the descent, all the while trying to pop ears to reduce pressure and clearing the mask that inevitably mists like a lecher's glasses. This brief, ungainly struggle is the price of entry to a seductive parallel universe of dissolving certainties and unfamiliar rules. After a few metres, reds and yellows turn to shades of blue; further down and gases that are harmless on the surface become intoxicating or even toxic. Beyond a certain depth, the action that seems to promise safety – the return to the surface – is fraught with risk. Too quick an ascent can kill. My father was well beyond that point when a weight slipped from his integrated jacket and spiralled downwards into the gloom.

We had arrived at the quayside that morning to discover our Red Sea pleasure boat laden with US soldiers on leave from peacekeeping duties in the Gulf. The platoon's NCO – his pumped-up pectorals instantly earned him the nickname Sergeant Pufferfish – proved to be a seasoned diver. His charges were novices. A 19-year-old private from Arkansas, paired with my 70-year-old father for the safety check and first dive of the day, failed to secure the weights that are essential in controlling a diver's surfacing speed.

The mishap illustrated another rule that the sea subverts: on dry land a healthy teenager will invariably outperform a septuagenarian in any physical exercise. Underneath the waves, age is as fluid as water. Confronted with a problem, the soldier lost control of his buoyancy, flailing like a fish in a net, while the older man calmly recalibrated their dive plan, communicating the change in the limited vocabulary of scuba sign language. Only once we were back on board was the natural order restored, as the senior, an emeritus professor, grouched about the teen and the teen stretched out in the heat of the afternoon, blithely unaware of the animus he'd attracted.[1]

But the natural order is itself in flux. My father still dives in his eighties. At his age we're conditioned to expect to be in the sunset of our lives, not waiting for the sun to set so we can wriggle back into neoprene and take a night dive. People are living longer, sometimes much longer. Across the developed world the average lifetime has lengthened by 30 years since the beginning of the 20th century. The fastest-growing segment of the world population is the very old, with the number of centenarians up from a few thousand in 1950 to 340,000 in 2010 and projected to reach nearly 6 million by 2050.[2]

YOU MIGHT HAVE THOUGHT we'd use all that extra time to squeeze in a few additional stages of life – from the seven ages of man observed by Shakespeare when life expectancy at birth was below 40 to maybe 10, 12, 15 stages now that a man born in Stratford-upon-Avon, the playwright's home town, looks forward to an average span of 76.9 years.[3] Here's the crazy, counterintuitive thing: the ages of man are actually eliding. Youth used to be our last hurrah before the onset of maturity and eventual dotage, each milestone – childhood, adolescence, young adulthood, middle age, retirement, golden years, decline – benchmarked against a series of culturally determined expectations. Those expectations are now swirling and re-forming like shoals of glassfish catching the currents.

What that means is that the premises on which our governments legislate are outdated. Our economies are based on data that no longer applies. There is a profound disconnect between how we imagine life and how it actually unfolds.

If you doubt these statements, think how hard it is to answer the following questions: What's the best age to have children? Or to settle down with a life partner? Or to retire? When might a woman consider herself middle-aged? Does that differ for a man, and will hitting 40 or 50 or 60 inevitably plunge him into a midlife crisis?

It's not only that we don't grow old as we used to. There's a mutability to our assumptions about the first decades of life, too. The age of criminal responsibility – the age at which we deem children legally responsible for criminal actions – ranges from 7 (Nigeria, Switzerland, South Africa) to 10 (Australia, England and Wales, New Zealand) to 13 (France) to 14 (China, Germany, Italy) to 15 (swathes of Scandinavia, New York, South Carolina) to 16 (Japan, Spain, Texas) and right up to 18 (Belgium, Luxembourg and most US states).[4] The age of consent is almost as elastic, stretching from 13 to 18 in Europe. What legislators decide and what teenagers actually do rarely correlates. Almost 40 per cent of Britons have had sex by the age of 15, compared to around 25 per cent in Germany and Italy, 20 per cent in France and only 17 per cent in Spain, which has the lowest age of consent in Europe.[5] Brits not only tend to become sexually active before other Europeans but are also much more likely to have been drunk two or more times between the ages of 11 and 15.[6] These are 'adult behaviours'. Does that suggest British kids mature earlier or later than their continental counterparts?

The meanings of age have become elusive; visual clues untrustworthy. Children dress like louche adults. Their parents slouch around in hoodies and trainers. An epidemic of obesity, often among poorer populations but spreading up the economic scale, is helping to conceal generational differences under layers of fat – and threatening to curb increases in longevity as childhood diabetes spirals upwards. At the same time, rising phalanxes of Dorian Grays rely on exercise, diet and cosmetic procedures to remain transcendentally youthful. Glowing teens and twenty-somethings are propelled by some of those same procedures into a semblance of premature ageing, their sculpted, frozen faces timeless rather than fresh, their improbable bosoms matronly.

And there's another reason our perceptions of age have come adrift: the disappearance of death in the developed world. We observe it in anatomical close-up on news bulletins and in slasher movies and, if moved to satisfy prurient or atavistic impulses, one can always find death on the web. But no matter how authentic the experience, it's somebody else's experience. If we're lucky we may be in the middle of our lives before we see death close up and then it's usually medicalised, relegated to the corner of a ward, tucked behind screens. There's a comforting banality in the construction of those screens with their pastel florals and squeaking wheels. Even so, the first death of a family member or friend shocks us to the core because nothing has prepared us for the detail – the visceral struggle of a body resisting extinction, the finality, the numbing negotiations with hospital authorities and funeral homes and tax offices that crowd out grief. Polite societies don't dwell on death; we're expected to dab our eyes and get on with the business of living. In the absence of legitimised outlets, our orphan emotions attach to public bereavements, lining the streets of Wootton Bassett, depositing flowers at the gates of Kensington Palace and composing Facebook tributes for total strangers.

As for our own fate: we like to think we're in command. When we're in robust good health, we say things like 'if I'm ever paralysed in an accident, pull the plug' or 'if I lose my marbles, have me put down'. The Swiss-based organisation Dignitas, founded in 1998, charges a joining fee and yearly subscription to its members in return for helping them to die in as much physical and mental comfort as possible; by 2009, 1,041 members had ended their lives with the organisation's support according to one estimate.[7] EXIT-Deutsche Schweiz, another euthanasia advocacy and assistance group in Switzerland, claims some 200 such interventions every year. Many more of us flirt with the idea of do-it-yourself options. 'I tell my husband if it comes to the point where I no longer have quality of life "just put a plastic bag over my head",' an elegant publisher in her seventies confesses at a posh lunch, minutes after we've been introduced. Her husband nods and smiles. A doctor says he's made a deal with his children: 'When I get feeble and can't take care of myself, take me to a log cabin in the mountains and let me forage for myself. I don't want somebody taking care of me. I want to stay vigorous until I can't do it and then do what the Eskimos do, leave me on the ice floe, build me an igloo and leave me on the ice floe but don't take care of me, please.'

Assisted suicide is becoming just another lifestyle choice, at least in the abstract, and it's surprisingly easy to imagine morbidity and death can be indefinitely deferred. Science has already added decades to our lives and is surely on the verge of unlocking the secrets of immortality. That last point may seem fanciful but, as I discover, a growing number of scientists, brilliant men such as Ray Kurzweil, assure us that if we live long enough, we'll live for ever.

In this new age of age confusion, one phenomenon blurs definitions of age more than any other: the significant – and burgeoning – numbers of people who live agelessly. They rarely ask themselves if their behaviour is age appropriate because that concept has little meaning for them. They don't structure their lives around the inevitability of decline and death because they prefer to ignore it. They continue to chase aspirations, covet new products, marry, divorce, spawn, learn, work, assume all options are open, from youth into old age. These are amortals and this book is the first anatomy of the species.

RICHARD FLINT DIED AT 47. A degenerative condition called cerebellar ataxia imprisoned this most vital of beings in the kind of emaciated and unresponsive body we associate with the very old. At his funeral, friends discussed their good fortune in having coincided with him in all-too-brief time and space. Amortal to his bones, Richard features in a later chapter on amortality and religion. But he puts in a fleeting appearance at this stage as the author of a phrase he often used, before he lost the power of speech, to squelch any interruptions: 'I speak with complete authority because I'm making it up as I go along.' I write with the same incontrovertible authority as the author of the first definition of amortality, for a *TIME* magazine cover package called '10 Ideas Changing the World Right Now'.[8] The defining characteristic of amortals, I explained, is that they 'live in the same way, at the same pitch, doing and consuming much the same things, from late teens right up until death'.

I coined the term. I did not invent the phenomenon, which was familiar to many readers, as their passionate responses made clear. There were joyful letters and emails ('Finally a classification that fits me'). One correspondent complained that the piece pointed out the obvious. Amortality *is* obvious – if you know where to look. But the condition remains largely unacknowledged and only partially understood. Conventional wisdom still assumes the human life course follows road maps, each age ushering in a new, and set, phase. The US writer Gail Sheehy, for example, has spent decades charting the stages of adulthood. Her 1976 bestseller *Passages: Predictable Crises in Adult Life* deployed an image from the undersea world to describe how each developmental change left a person vulnerable and ready to grow. 'The lobster grows by developing and shedding a series of hard, protective shells. Each time it expands from within, the confining shell must be sloughed off.'[9]

Consider this contrasting marine image, used by a 59-year-old English bass-player-turned-property lawyer, David Battiscombe:

> If somebody said tomorrow I had to stop practising the law and do something else it wouldn't faze me in the least. And I think whenever I stop doing this I would expect to do something else, probably something completely different. I don't know what, but I find change rejuvenating. The principle of change. I'm with Chairman Mao on permanent revolution. It's the old Woody Allen dead shark thing, you can't stay still. That's just the kiss of death. A shark if it stops moving, dies. It's when Woody talks to Annie Hall and says I think this relationship, we need to talk about it. I think what we've got on our hands is a dead shark.

During extensive research and more than 100 hours of interviews for this book, the living, if metaphorical, shark swam into view several times as amortals sought to explain their impulse to keep moving. The lobster sheds its shell because of internal changes. A shark appears immutable as it swims through different environments.

Battiscombe took up running in 2009 and plans to complete the London marathon in 2011, a few months shy of his 60th birthday. Other amortals might mark that milestone with a different kind of marathon, a celebratory bender that leaves them mewling and puking like infants. We tend to dismiss both behaviours as typical of baby-boomers, and indeed they are. As a group, boomers have been conspicuous in challenging shibboleths about age. The postwar boomer bulge encompasses hippies and counter-culturalists and shock-headed punks who never imagined they would one day wake up to find themselves in danger of being marginalised by the youth-oriented culture they helped to create.

Bill Clinton fizzed with suppressed anger as he campaigned for his wife in 2008. The former leader of the free world didn't seem quite ready to slip into a supporting role of grey eminence. Yet not all boomers notice their predicament. Amortality more usually manifests not as heightened age awareness, but as age-blindness. When Battiscombe runs, he's not consciously racing against the dying of the light. At the end of his fifties, he happens to have found a new hobby, one that feeds his competitive nature. Some boomers hook up with younger partners in repudiation of age; others hook up with younger partners because they simply don't notice the age gap. Some boomers dress to look young; many dress young because it doesn't occur to them to adapt their style with the passing years. Nor are amortal impulses confined to baby-boomers. Though prevalent among boomers, amortality has reached a tipping point and is spreading through all the generations faster than norovirus in a nursing home.

MIGHT YOU BE AMORTAL? The quiz on page 265 will help you to identify the telltale symptoms of the pathology. Psychographics also offers up a helpful checklist for diagnosing the condition. Amortality is a social epidemic, defined by attitudes, values and behaviours, and is not restricted to generational cohorts, classes or locations. It is a syndrome and an observable phenomenon.

Largely benign in impact, amortality is not without its risks and is malignant in certain forms. This book will identify its dangers as well as its benefits. There are degrees of amortality, and the amortals portrayed in these pages represent both its stronger and more dilute expressions. It is culturally, not genetically, transmitted. A by-product of prosperity, it influences behaviours across the socio-economic spectrum and from youth to old age. For a dystopian vision of amortality you have only to watch hypersexualised teens competing with hypersexualised sexagenarians on any of the talent shows that have become Saturday night television staples.

The svengali behind many of these shows – and often sitting in sardonic judgement in front of camera too – is Simon Cowell, who is on the evidence of his own utterances one kind of amortal archetype. 'All the things I used to like as a kid I still like,' he told an interviewer.[10] 'Genuinely my tastes haven't changed at all ... I'm an old soul ... I do lead a relatively normal life, the difference being that I am totally and utterly consumed by my work to the point almost of an obsession.'

The evergreen Cowell – Botox, he once said, is a routine, 'like cleaning my teeth' – has more than a touch of the Peter Pan about him. He has fathered no children. His plans to marry, after his first-time engagement aged 50, show no signs of reaching a speedy fruition. Death is unconscionable to him. 'I can't go to funerals and stuff like that. I find it very difficult to deal with that kind of reality. I shut myself off totally because it affects me so badly,' he confided in the same interview, an intimate chat in front of a small live audience and some 6 million viewers.

Amortals like Cowell may appear marooned in Neverland but they are only part of the story. Amortality signifies an increasing trend to live the same way throughout life, however that life is lived, and for as long as possible. The geek prodigies of Silicon Valley such as Facebook founder Mark Zuckerberg represent one manifestation of the younger end of the amortal spectrum; their icon and inspiration is the changeless Bill Gates. There are beefy amortals and skinny types, smooth-skinned and shrivelled amortals, gay and straight amortals, amortals from different ethnic, cultural and religious backgrounds, although some cultures and religions inoculate far more effectively than others against amortality.

Amortals of greater vintages include Hugh Hefner. 'The big surprise for me is that age is just a number. It's a number without meaning,' *Playboy's* founding publisher philosophised, aged 81. 'A person who dies at 40 – through cancer, a car accident, what have you – how old is that person, really, at 38? He's near the end of his life, whether he knows it or not. And what about a person who dies at 100? How old is that person, really, at 78?'[11] In July 2010, aged 84, Hefner, still the owner of a substantial block of shares in the company he founded, entered a spirited bidding war for a further tranche of stock, competing for the prize with the owners of *Penthouse* magazine. On Christmas Eve of the same year, Hefner tweeted news of his engagement to 24-year-old self-described 'Playmate and recording artist' Crystal Harris. Speaking to the *News of the World* six months earlier, Harris said that the 60-year age gulf between her and her beau seemed immaterial. 'A lot of people talk about the age difference between Hef and I, but I don't see the age difference at all. If anything, I feel like I'm the adult and Hef's the kid,' she said.

Mick Jagger is another avatar of extended youth. 'I think you should just keep going while you can, doing what you like,' he observed at 66, ignoring his pronouncement in May 1975 that he'd rather be dead than still be singing *Satisfaction* at – or presumably long after – 45.[12] The actor Richard Wilson became the personification of grumpy old age as Victor Meldrew in the sitcom *One Foot in the Grave*. In real life he's as ageless as Jagger. 'I find myself looking at people and thinking, oh, look at that poor old man, and I realise that they're probably younger than me,' says Wilson, 73. 'Because my image of myself is not of an old man, I get quite shocked when people call me an old man.' When he was first offered the part of Meldrew, he turned it down. 'I didn't see myself playing older people yet.'

Amortals, like vampires, can be formed at any juncture. And, diverse as they are, they're tough to spot. They don't recoil from garlic, and crosses hold little iconic power for them. Unlike the bloodsuckers of the *Twilight* quartet their skin doesn't glitter conspicuously in sunlight. Nevertheless they share with these seductive monsters some significant characteristics. The current resurgence of the vampire genre in books and films and television is no coincidence. The sexed-up, socialised vampires of *Twilight*, *True Blood* and *The Vampire Diaries* represent a perfect ideal of amortality: ageless, adventurous, always at the centre of events.

One persistent problem: even socialised vampires are prey to anti - social urges. Nothing banishes those pesky intimations of mortality more effectively than illicit sex or emotional drama or some high-octane combination of the two. Amortals are experts at generating distractions. In January 2010, a few months before Dennis Hopper's death from prostate cancer, the actor filed for divorce from his fifth wife. 'Who would have ever thought I'd be getting a divorce in this state?' Hopper marvelled during a final interview, with *Vanity Fair*.[13]

Woody Allen's private life has not been devoid of cliffhangers that presumably helped keep the director's mind from metaphysics. In his creative endeavours he obsessively mines the comic potential of mortal fear. 'I don't want to achieve immortality through my work,' he famously quipped. 'I want to achieve it through not dying.' But that's not really a gag. Allen has organised his existence to minimise the intrusion of death. He never rests. He has turned out a film a year for 40 years and performs regularly with a jazz band. As he told an interviewer: 'When you're worried about this joke, and this costume, and this wig, and that location and the dailies, you're not worried about death and the brevity of life.'[14]

'FOR ME BOREDOM is a gateway to a melancholy. It's not the black dog but it's a sort of vast, empty sadness. It's triggered by evening twilight and it's triggered by morbidities and by being alone a bit too long. So I keep mani-acally active because if there's any down time I sit there guilty I'm not doing something. Anything. But ultimately all that rushing around becomes exhausting and not particularly satisfying. Except the music. So that's it, and then there's the relief that finally one day that just won't happen. That's quite comforting, you know.'

The speaker tells me he can stare death in the eye. He's seen enough of it over the years, in African famines and wars and AIDS clinics, but also at the heart of his family: the deaths of his mother, when he was six; of his ex-wife; and of his father, which he realised must come soon when we met to discuss amortality, and indeed followed a bare two months later. A mere three weeks after his dad's death his sister died suddenly and shockingly. He coped, made arrangements. But there's his perpetual motion. If he but pauses, what then?

Perpetual motion is a hallmark of amortality, but Bob Geldof's forward momentum is powerful enough to flatten buildings; those foolish enough to stand in his way carry tyre marks on their backs. His force of will launched Band Aid and Live Aid, creating a new model of public response to humanitarian disaster and a new model of celebrity interaction with the world. He has built up a considerable and cleverly strategised media empire. He tours incessantly, giving speeches and gigging. He keeps lobbying too, although the word 'lobbying' doesn't properly convey the violence of his assaults on the body politic. His primary focus remains the relationship between wealthy countries and the developing world, but he also argues for fathers' rights.

The Friday we've earmarked for our discussion is comparatively leisurely for Geldof, without family commitments or travel plans or high-level meetings, but our conversation is frequently interrupted, as all conversations with Geldof inevitably are, by calls — not meandering, shooting-the-breeze calls, but updates on projects and endless requests for his endorsement or his attendance or his wisdom. The previous day he has attended the funeral of rock impresario Malcolm McLaren and met up with many of his contemporaries in the music business. He remarks that old punks, unlike mainstream rockers, show the years: 'They haven't worn well, I must say.' He pauses. 'But then they weren't meant to really, were they? There was a sort of anti-vanity going on, so good for them.'

He's doing rather better, and despite the trademark dishevelment puts a modicum of effort into his health and appearance, though not, he says, to the extent of exercising: 'You look in the mirror and you go, fuck! That's weird: I'm old. And you start trying to manage that. I fully accept that I'm getting older, have no problem with it … you know, should I go jogging? Are my knees beginning to hurt? That's so fucking weird. What the fuck? Why is my stomach getting bigger? That's ridiculous. And I purposefully wear my pants tight because I will not relent, I'm not getting a bigger waistband. My trousers will remain the same. My stomach will just have to shrink, albeit somehow without the bore of something as lame as a diet. Of course I could send them round to the dry cleaner to get a little insert or something, because I kind of think, it's fruitless, it's pointless, to do jogging and the sit-ups and all the other bollocks. Pity you can't lose weight by reading. The Geldof Reading Diet. That would work.'

Geldof is an amortal but his impulse towards agelessness wars with an instinct to assert and explore his age. His last album but one was titled *Sex, Age and Death*. A key track on his latest album, *How to Compose Popular Songs that will Sell*, is 'Systematic 6-Pack', subtitled '58½'; the lyrics go 'time has the last laugh / you're 58½.' 'That's how old I am,' he says. This is what being that age sounds like to me. He could earn a decent crust by re-forming his old group the Boomtown Rats but, he says, 'I quite literally could not. Quite literally couldn't. Couldn't, couldn't, couldn't. Write me the cheque for 10 million, couldn't do it. Because we can't be a bunch of fat, balding, late-50-year-olds pantomiming the songs we wrote when we were 21 about being 21 … I can do some of them now with my own band, but only the ones that work in the context of the newer songs and still maintain a relevance and I am the determinant of that relevance. Not the audience.' During the years since the Rats topped the charts with 'I Don't Like Mondays', he's mutated from the angry young man swearing about dying children to one of the eponymous *Grumpy Old Men* of the television series of the same name. He spends 'life in a grump … You can't stand it any more, you can't tolerate the bollocks, like a cop coming along, fresh-faced, 19, and saying "step out of your car". Go fuck off. You just assume, "I've lived a life, I'll just drive off." "I'll arrest you." "Fine, do what you like, I don't care"; it's that too.'

'I don't understand the point where anger becomes charming and gets sanitised into grumpiness. I'm not raging against the dying of the light,' he adds. 'I'm raging at the same things I always have been. I'm not going gently into the dark night. I never went gently into the bright day either. There is about me an unfortunate consistency of anger and desire

hange. Sometimes that animus works and sometimes it's just tire-
some for all concerned, myself included.'

Yes, look a little deeper and what's really changed? Geldof has always
been supremely grumpy, always had the impulse to brawl about ideas. 'I
feel myself at my best when I most disappoint people, that's where I'm
comfortable in my skin,' he says. If he's asked to behave nicely, to
schmooze a head of state during a lobbying initiative, for example, that's
a red rag to his bullish spirit. ('Don't say it to me because I'm like "I'm
supposed to be dependent on you" and then I'm like a child. It's pathetic.')

Nor does he envisage cutting back any time soon on his ceaseless activity. '[When] I'm 70, and I pick up the phone and I'm talking to some young
spark of 30 who's at the top of his game, will he pay any attention to me?
No, but if I was still, say, having hit TV shows or hit records or still politically active in the proper sense, still arguing and being listened to, then
they probably would. So age disappears in direct proportion to the vitality
of your ideas.'

Like many amortals, he has no intention of ceding the stage, but he's
aware of the challenge that represents in a culture inclined to consign its
older members to obscurity. He speaks of the 'atomisation of society
where the old disappear. And they disappear because we don't want to be
confronted by the inevitable. Recently we've just ignored the possibility
of death and that is because were we to recognise it, the acknowledgement
of oblivion renders all ambition absurd.'

RETIREMENT ISN'T A PROPOSITION that appeals to amortals unless life after
work promises to be busier and better than the life that went before. And
the impulse to keep working isn't such a bad thing, given the changing
profile of the world's population. By 2050, a fifth of humanity will be 60
or older. In Europe, already the greyest region of the world, the 60-pluses
are projected to make up 37 per cent of the population (that compares to
10 per cent in Africa). There will be astounding numbers of the 60-and-

overs in China (437 million), India (324 million), America (107 million), Indonesia (70 million) and Brazil (58 million). In some countries, two-fifths of citizens will be in their seventh decade or beyond.[15]

One of those countries will be Greece. Its debt crisis, in early 2010, reverberated across the world, as financial confidence tumbled and the Eurozone struggled to prevent the contagion from spreading. Among the austerity measures the Greek government proposed as it negotiated a bail-out package was raising its retirement age, from 53 to 67.

Angry Greeks immediately flooded the streets to protest an outrage that threatened their right to be paid to do nothing for an average of 27 years. (Despite having the highest smoking rate in the world, the average Greek life span hovers around 80 years.[16]) France, another nation of long-livers where public sector workers retire on 75 per cent of final salary, convulsed with fury after President Nicolas Sarkozy moved to lift the retirement age from 60 to 62. A series of protests in 2010 brought the country to a noisy standstill as millions of demonstrators clogged the thoroughfares, their numbers swelled as students from schools and colleges inveighed against a distant future. 'This is the most unfair reform decided by the president,' railed François Hollande of the French Socialist party.

It's not clear how Monsieur Hollande imagines the expanding ranks of France's *retraités* will be funded in future. What is evident is that not all of today's sixty-somethings are old in the sense they used to be. In September 2010, scientists from the International Institute for Applied Systems Analysis (IIASA) in Austria, Stony Brook University in the US and the Vienna Institute of Demography published a proposal in the magazine *Science* to replace the old 'age dependency ratio' used by the United Nations with a more sensitive method of assessing population needs.[17] 'When using indicators that assume fixed chronological ages, it's assumed that there will be no progress in factors such as remaining life expectancies and in disability rates. But many age-specific characteristics have not remained fixed and are not expected to remain constant in the future,' said one of the report's authors.

A key point, inevitably lost in clashes between different interest groups whenever governments instigate reviews of retirement age, is that subsidising elderly populations to be unproductive can be, frankly, unproductive. That's not simply because of the tax burden on people in work. Studies show that retirement is sometimes bad for the people it supposedly benefits.

Otto von Bismarck forged a united Germany from a tumult of bellicose states. He is also widely credited with the introduction of the world's first national pension, in 1889. The British government followed suit in 1908. The intended beneficiaries of both schemes were those 70 and over (in those days the unambiguously old).

The idea of retirement as a golden era of leisure, the reward for a lifetime of grafting, was cooked up in the crucible of postwar affluence and increasing longevity. In 1960 an American building tycoon called Del Webb opened the world's first retirement community, Sun City in Phoenix, where residents, not unlike that mythical bird, could enjoy a new lease of life at the end of their lives. Today there are more than 50 Del Webb communities for the 55-pluses across America. The residents I interviewed during a May 2010 visit to Sun City Shadow Hills in California exuded an almost indecent degree of contentment.

They were also among the busiest people I've ever met, squeezing a lunch of barbecued salmon and salad between myriad social engagements, fitness classes, bike rides and communal activities. Retirement has been successfully re-imagined at Sun City not as a cessation of work but as a long whirl of absorbing activity, which for some residents still includes a paid occupation.

Here's someone else who re-imagined retirement – into a new iteration of professional life. After reluctantly leaving her job at the Royal Court Theatre only when her employers discovered she was well beyond pensionable age, she went on to establish a freelance public relations consultancy:

My life is interesting. My life is full. My life is varied. It involves all different age groups. The other day I was washing my hair in the shower and they were blabbing on the *Today* programme about the problems with whether Gordon Brown or David Cameron are going to be able to afford to take care of the old, the elderly, so that people will not have to sell all their worldly possessions to go into homes and the rest of it. And I was half listening, half washing and I suddenly thought, I'm an elderly person and this is about me, but I don't feel any connection to it at all. I'm listening to it and I'm listening to them saying all these things about our older population, and I thought I'm 76 years old and I don't feel anything that connects me to this conversation.

And it isn't a money thing because financially I'm the least secure I've ever been in my adult life, by far the least secure, so it isn't that I can go, oh well, I've got enough money. It's really that I don't feel like an elderly person, I don't have any connect in my brain so when they're talking I think grey, elderly people. I often look at people on the tube and idly wonder whether they're older or younger than I am, because I just don't feel any connection to my numeric age. I used to worry quite a lot about what people would think when I turned up to do jobs, because you know, the expectation, but I've completely got over that. I just think well, I am who I am and it doesn't seem to bother anyone. Nobody has ever said, 'Gosh, do you think you're up to this?' Never, never, never.

The speaker is my mother. This is not a memoir, but in researching and writing this book I've drawn liberally on the experience of growing up as an amortal in an amortal family. Though I'm based in the UK and also travelled to France, Germany and Italy in search of amortality, much of my research took place in America, both the source and the fulcrum for many tumultuous changes around age and ageing. It is also my birthplace and the birthplace of amortality.

IT'S HARD TO SAY when I first noticed that my family was *different*. Though friends' mums favoured elasticated waistbands to accommodate thickening middles, I ascribed my mother's lithe contours to her American genes. We had arrived in London at the tail-end of the 1960s. Some sections of the capital were swinging – in several senses of that word, as it turns out – but the rest of the country adhered to older values and conventions. If you were middle-aged – and if you were a woman, middle age started with the birth of your first child – you dressed and behaved middle-aged. The mothers served austere meals, spam with sliced tomatoes and Heinz salad cream, and subsumed their interests to the family project. The Americans I knew stood out: vivid, ambitious for themselves as well as their kids. In those days, we ate better than Brits too – not more, just higher-quality food.

I thought all grandmothers from the New World must comport themselves as mine did: travelling widely, drinking deeply, thinking freely. Both my grandfathers had died before I was born, one imagined from exhaustion. Their widows continued to run full tilt at life until they could run no more, some time in their late nineties. (We've never been sure exactly when my maternal grandmother was born. Grandma Ruth may have already been in her forties when she met my grandfather, then in his twenties. After her death, we found her passport, date of birth determinedly crossed out.)

The daughter of an impoverished family of Huguenot descent, Ruth was a thoroughly unsuitable match for my Jewish grandfather, as far as his parents were concerned. Judaism is transmitted through the female line, so my half-Jewish mother is not, officially, Jewish and although my atheist father is by birth wholly Jewish, making my sisters and me three-quarters Jewish – too Jewish for anti-Semites to count us as non-Jews – we can never in the eyes of some orthodox Jews be Jews. 'Ruth was the absolute beauty of the family, everyone agreed on that,' says my mother, who has pieced together her family history from sources more reliable than her mother.

She escaped to New York and had this incredible career where she sang classical and popular, she knew Gershwin, she knew André Kostelanetz, she opened the Radio City Music Hall as a [member of the singing duo, the] Glenn Sister[s]. She was in *Strike Up The Band* and Gershwin thought she was brilliant. And then she met my dad. He had the opposite lifestyle, rich Jewish family, and briefly worked in local radio and they sent him to New York to see what was on and he saw the Glenn Sisters.

And when my father's parents met Ruth they literally sat down and did a deal with her. They said they would accept her as a daughter-in-law, but that she must never tell a living soul that she'd ever been in show business and no member of her family must ever set foot in Chicago.

My paternal grandmother, Grandma Jane, was hardly a model of convention either, a novelist, whose heroines dared to challenge narrow ideas of propriety and whose own indomitable spirit overcame many of the barriers that might have circumscribed her life. She survived a car crash at 90, correcting the state trooper who sought to comfort her as she was being cut from the wreckage for mistakenly asking what an old lady 'of 91' was doing driving on her own in such icy Chicago weather, and confounding the surgeons who first predicted she would die from her injuries, then that she would never walk again. A couple of years later, she marched unaided into a starchy restaurant, where an overattentive waiter fussed around her, addressing his questions to me as if she might be too enfeebled by age to answer for herself. Jane leaned across the table and in a sibilant stage whisper wondered aloud, 'What do you think this nice young man would do if I asked him to fuck off?'

My father, a theatre historian and expert on early film, takes a similar delight in shocking the shockable and jousting with any authority he can find. He produced his eleventh book at 81 and is currently mulling over the subject of the next. Most phone calls with my mother start with her reeling off a laundry list of social engagements or detailing her expanding roster of clients. When she was diagnosed with colorectal cancer in 2003, she declined the irreversible colostomy her specialist recommended, agreeing only to the chemo- and radiotherapies that appear to have killed the tumour. Explaining her risky decision to her daughters, she lifted her shirt, displaying a washboard abdomen. 'This is part of my identity,' she said.

Genes don't make us amortal; our socialisation does that. As this book will make clear, the elements of that socialisation are changing. Traditional forms of authority, including family elders, are ceding dominance to a makeshift cast of public figures and a globalised range of cultural influences. Amortal parents like mine shape their offspring not only through the values they pass on, but those they fail to impart.

Most of my family works in entertainment. It's an industry that commodifies the desire for distraction, and it's rammed with people whose greatest talent is to distract themselves. Hollywood is the home of amortality and the music industry is amortality's outreach programme. At music festivals, prepubescents and silver-haired hippies stomp and sway to sets by musicians of similarly disparate ages. 'I told the wife I was taking the kids camping,' one Glastonbury regular told me as we waited in a fug of beer and joyously unwashed humanity for my husband's band to appear. 'I just didn't tell her where.'

My work might look weightier from the outside, especially when I'm literally weighed down by body armour. But news journalism is another obvious career choice for an amortal. A job that's ostensibly about thinking and analysing, its breathless pace ensures there's rarely time to think about death or analyse where one is in life. Occasional trips to war zones only serve to reinforce the illusion that mortality is something that happens to other people.

Amortals don't go gentle. At 97, Grandma Jane had no intention of going at all. She was outraged by the realisation that her iron will wasn't enough to keep her body functioning. When her breathing grew laboured, she used the emergency buzzer to summon the nurses, who barrelled into the room as if there still might be something they could do to alleviate her mortality. 'You see. I'm still a somebody,' she rasped, amused by the frenzied activity she had unleashed.

IF MY GRANDMOTHER had lived just a few days longer, she would have seen on the screen suspended above her hospital bed images of a passenger jet slicing into the North Tower of the World Trade Center and then, barely 17 minutes later, a second airliner blasting the South Tower and any surviving hopes that the first impact had been a terrible accident. These events are widely viewed as defining our time: an expression of rising tensions between cultures, ideologies, socio-economic and geographical polarities, an exemplar of the new, non-negotiable terror, a trigger for wars and a test that revealed weaknesses in the democracies and institutions that scrambled to respond. The consequences are still playing out, but there was a sense even as the buildings blazed and crumbled that the world had changed irrevocably. That would have been a familiar feeling for my grandmother, whose life encompassed two world wars, the Holocaust, Vietnam, Hiroshima and space flight, the Russian revolution and social revolutions, unprecedented economic prosperity and serial developments in communications technology. These phenomena impacted singly and collectively not only on the nature of the society Jane inhabited, but also on received ideas about the way individuals should inhabit that society.

Grandma was ahead of many of her contemporaries in shrugging off some of these received ideas. An early amortal, she not only seemed timeless but out of her time, surfing each wave with insouciance, greeting each development with curiosity. The longer people live, the more likely they will fall into nostalgia, regretting things lost rather than gained, mired in a mythologised past instead of savouring the present or planning for the future. I never once heard Jane deprecate modern life or wring her hands over its trajectory. Amortals look forwards; they rarely glance back, as we'll see when we visit amortals at home, in love, exploring religions or their psyches, in the workplace and the marketplace. Yet to understand amortality – its transformative power and deepening significance – we first need to do just that, to review the distance we've travelled in a remarkably short time and the forces that propelled us to this point.

Before we embark on this whistle-stop tour, you might wish to pause and take the test at the back of this book: *Are You Amortal?* It will tell you whether you are reading a guide to a strange new species – or your biography.

part one

into the void
THE AGE OF AGE CONFUSION

'You saw your whole life. You ricocheted
The length of your Alpha career.'
Ted Hughes, 'The Shot'

'An act of derring-do in which a person jumps from a high
platform, such as a bridge, attached (usually by the legs) to a
bungee cord, which is set to a length that will halt the drop
before the person reaches the surface of the earth or the water.'
Merriam—Webster Dictionary

'How beauteous mankind is. O brave new world
That has such people in it.'
William Shakespeare, *The Tempest*

IF ONE PLACE ON EARTH has vanquished nature and stopped the clocks, it
is Las Vegas. Built on land without water or any reliable resource apart
from the blazing sun, the resort entombs visitors in the permanent, cool,
jangling dusk of hotel casinos. Its skyscape positions Ancient Egypt close
to Renaissance Venice and *fin de siècle* Paris. I had come to this confected
city to find out if the Cenegenics Medical Institute, 'the world's largest age

management practice', could subvert the laws of human biology with similar ease. First I had to locate Cenegenics, and though you might think it would be easy to spot a building described by its incumbents as 'quite a lot like the White House', the cab driver took more than a few passes before we were able to pick out the right White House from the rows of White Houses that have sprouted in the Nevada desert.

That's the Vegas paradox: despite the mind-boggling range of architectural styles and eras represented, there's a remarkable uniformity to it all. The residents are similarly homogenous, perma-tanned and toned and sporting a uniface common to both genders and across the income range, from bellhops to casino owners. The uniface is defined by absences; its eyebrows have been plucked, threaded or waxed into submission; its fine little nose is free from bumps and bulges; its full lips part to reveal perfect teeth. Above all, it looks neither young nor old. It is ageless.

Amortality – this book and the phenomenon it describes – is about much, much more than the desire to resist ageing, or the technology that promises to help us to do so. Ageless living is reshaping our lives in profound ways, transforming how we approach work, leisure, family, love, youth and old age and everything that comes in between. From the personal sphere to public life, amortals are upturning conventions and challenging and changing the status quo, often by accident rather than design.

We'll consider those changes and their repercussions in detail, and meet a compelling cast of amortals on the way. But we begin in Vegas, and not just because the city is home to Cenegenics and a showcase for the growing global appetite for cosmetic interventions. Divorced from history and any recognisable cultural continuum, the resort sets its own rules about what constitutes normality. Across increasing swathes of the developed world a similar and widening disconnect is fuelling the rise of amortality. Untethered from the past, our assumptions about age and ageing are floating free. Before we can make sense of amortality, we must identify the winds that are speeding its progress.

EIGHTY PER CENT of Cenegenics patients are men who come in search of Life. That's Dr Jeffry Life (his real name), the star of a press and internet campaign in which the physician wears snug shorts and a vest with scooped armholes of a kind popular in Greenwich Village. His face is avuncular. His body is that of Mr Universe in his prime. The copy reads:

70 Years Old and Still Going Strong. Happy Birthday, Dr Life!
Find out more about the Cenegenics® programme, a unique and balanced combination of nutrition, exercise and hormone optimisation, when clinically indicated.
Benefits May Include:
- Decreased Risk of Age-Related Disease
- Improved Muscle Tone
- Decreased Body Fat
- Reduced Abdominal Fat
- Increased Energy
- Increased Sex Drive
- Sharper Thinking

Cenegenics doesn't promise to extend the human span, but to extend our prime. Its physicians are embodiments – unibodiments one might say – of that promise.

After two days at the clinic, I encounter Dr Life in the flesh, though there's disappointingly little flesh on display as he goes about his doctoring in a biscuit-coloured suit. His colleague Dr Beth Traylor, looking at just shy of 52 like the luscious younger sister of America's favourite actress-turned-health-guru, Suzanne Somers, tells me she moved from ordinary general practice to Cenegenics after a hysterectomy set her researching alternatives to conventional hormone replacement therapy. 'I turned things around in terms of how I feel, energy wise,' she says. 'I mean, obviously the symptoms have completely resolved at this point but more than that – and it's not just about not having hot flashes

– having the energy to do this which, it's really become, it's become a passion for me. I really enjoy it and I've become quite the proselytiser … I remember when I was 20, oh my gosh, I thought somebody of 51, that was really old. And they looked old. At least, they looked old to me then. And I think so much of the cosmeceutical aspects of it that have changed people's perceptions of ageing. Most folks I know are not allowing themselves to age gracefully.'

During my consultation with another Cenegenics medic, Dr Jeffrey Leake, 56, he flicks through a series of Powerpoint charts intended to give an overview of the science of ageing and slips in a picture of himself, *sans* jacket and shirt or much of anything else apart from swimming trunks. His honed physique, Leake tells me, has been achieved by following the Cenegenics precepts: healthy eating, exercise and a little of the 21st-century hocus-pocus that his colleague Dr Traylor holds responsible for her renewed wellbeing – hormone optimisation. Our hormones can be rebalanced to recreate the natural vibrancy of youth, he explains. It's an enticing sales pitch.

THE FIRST CONSULTATION at Cenegenics involves detailed blood work and a day of scans and tests, and usually costs $3,400. (I accepted a free consultation from Cenegenics; my blood was drawn in London a month before my visit and air-freighted for analysis in Utah; Cenegenics also paid the shipping costs.) Subsequent consultations and supplies of medicines and supplements typically add up to around $1,000 per month.

The more estranged we are from nature – and Vegas is testimony to the irretrievable breakdown of our relationship with the natural world – the more we assume nature to be benign. We buy 'natural' products and programmes that pledge to help us maintain or regain our 'natural' state of perpetual vigour. In a bloated, ageing population, 'natural' thinness and youth are scarce commodities. As their market value soars, so consumers are willing to spend more to acquire them.

Maria White, 54, a human resources consultant from Southern California, has been a Cenegenics patient since 2005. She possesses the body of an adolescent or an athlete, all lean muscle and no visible fat. Her smile is as bright as the Las Vegas Strip. 'Happiness they say comes from within and it does, it comes from within and I feel that [because of] what I've done for myself inwardly, because all of my organs that are inside of me are working at 100 per cent capacity,' she declares.

> I am using a lot of [Cenegenics] supplements and medications that they recommend … I have heard a lot of negative things about taking a hormone replacement, you know, and my response is well, I've done my research on all the things I'm putting in my body and I am comfortable with what I'm doing. I realise there may be some statistics that show there might be some danger but the percentages are so low in my particular case that I'm not worried whatsoever.
>
> I think I look a little younger than my age. Most people compliment me, most people guess me in my late thirties or early forties and I don't feel old at all. I'm not old, I mean 54 is not old but by yesterday's standards, by my grandmother's standards, 54 was old. I remember seeing a picture of my grandmother when she was in her fifties and either she looks a whole lot older or I look a lot younger because I don't resemble her in any way in that sense. The ageing process, I feel that I've worked hard to maintain more of a youthful attitude and appearance. I feel I look younger, yes I do.

Unlike many Cenegenics patients, White was already in good shape when she signed up for the full programme. She made the investment in order to achieve 'optimal' fitness. 'We all put priorities on our health and our wellness,' she says, 'and if you look at it from that perspective if you're not at your very best how can you possibly be your best to your spouse, to your family, to your profession?'

YOU CAN SPOT THEM in the clinics and casinos of Las Vegas and the high-end boutiques of Beverly Hills and New York's Upper East Side, dining at St Tropez's Club 55 or exerting themselves expressionlessly in Pilates classes: men and women whose taut faces bespeak a desire to make the best of themselves.

A facelift is a brutal process, in which skin is separated from the underlying fat and muscle, deep tissues ratcheted tighter, excess skin hacked off and the whole caboodle stapled or stitched back together. In the early days of such surgery the results were often brutal too, producing latter-day equivalents of Dr Frankenstein's monster, living symbols of the scientific hubris that seeking to outwit time represents. Such outcomes helped to stem America's appetite for facelifts, with demand declining by 23 per cent in the decade to 2009 according to the American Society of Plastic Surgeons.[18] Europe saw a similar decline from a lower base in the same period.[19]

Let nobody mistake this for a sign that the Western world might be growing comfortable in its saggy skin. In the same period, cosmetic procedures boomed, with US patient numbers for the less invasive technique of laser skin resurfacing rising by 154 per cent and Botox surging by 509 per cent, a figure guaranteed to raise eyebrows if only that were still possible.[20] Men are increasingly opting for the knife and the needle, especially drawn to male breast reductions (gynaecomastia), brow lifts, tummy tucks, Botox and microdermabrasion. US surgeons also saw increases among male patients asking for buttock lifts, cheek implants, surgical lip augmentations and lower body lifts.[21] European men are following suit.[22]

Americans are so used to the effects of routine cosmetic dentistry that a mouthful of English teeth can stop Los Angeles traffic. Even in Europe we're all becoming so attuned to the aesthetic of lifted, sculpted faces that at some point the unadulterated visage will begin to stand out, for the wrong reasons. And facelift techniques have improved beyond recognition. At his Upper East Side practice surgeon Dr Sam Rizk (pronounced 'risk') flicks through a portfolio of before-and-after shots. There's no sign of the telltale G-force effect that used to stretch faces into the rictus of astronauts during takeoff. Pillow faces, the surgical equivalent of over-stuffing a sofa, are also absent. Rizk's patients simply look fresher and younger, artificial only in their lack of imperfections. You really wouldn't know they'd been lifted. He says volume – but not too much volume – is the key:

> If I lifted a 100-year-old patient, he's still going to look 100. There's no volume. And that's where stem-cell fat grafting comes in. Fat grafting has been the single largest part in my practice with the deep-plane face lifts … My face lifts are really volume reposition-ing movements. The more jowl that I can get into the cheek the more natural the patient looks. The closer I get to the skin the more stretched the patient looks. Stretch looks fake.
>
> I'm able to go under the jowl fat pad and reposition this fat pad back into the cheek area. So that gives cheek volume. That cheek volume is very important for the beautiful look.

He tells me I could look beautiful too, after a necklift ($11,000) and a rhinoplasty ($8,000) to banish the hint of a hook that denies my nose Roman majesty. He points out that my brow is exceptionally low, but he can fix it for a further $5,000. 'I actually like a very low brow, I'm one of the few surgeons who don't recommend brow lifts. So [if] I recommend the brow lift, that means the brow needs to be done.'

He is wearing scrubs and has just performed two rhinoplasties, the second teamed with a laser resurfacing of the patient's skin. Still in the recovery room, the semi-conscious patient looks ghastly, her raw face smothered in something viscous, her nose bloody. As Rizk enters the room, she raises herself up on one elbow. 'Doctor, you're a genius,' she says.

NO EXAMINATION OF THE TREND to living agelessly can be divorced from a discussion of the scientific techniques that are helping us to do so. Cosmetic procedures are the most commonly deployed. (How many people you know have avoided at least one minor bout of cosmetic dentistry, a tooth saved rather than pulled, for example?) The chapter on amortal family examines how advances in reproductive technology that enable us to have children later in life more easily are actually encouraging us to have fewer children altogether. The final section of the book surveys the science of ageing, looks at the Cenegenics regimen and other programmes and treatments already available, and considers the prospects for medically gifted immortality. But our cultural attitudes to age and ageing – including the not insignificant matter of how we define ageing gracefully – have been impacted not so much by the realities of that science as by diffuse and swirling notions about that science and by a huge industry purporting to offer us the option to defer or stop ageing.

These ideas would not have so much purchase if many of the trusted voices in private and public life had not been stilled or discredited. Many of us now live, to greater or lesser degrees, in virtual Las Vegases, environments devoid of history and shorn of landmarks that might provide orientation for what to expect and what is expected of us as the years pass.

The precepts and strictures of age-appropriate behaviour that used to be reliably drummed into us by parents and teachers no longer hold sway. Their legacy remains in our uneasy laughter at 'mutton dressed as lamb' and the little voices in our heads that say things like 'act your age, not your shoe size' (an expression likely to confound the literal-minded in continental Europe where adult shoe sizes start at 32). Yet while some of us may have grown up with these 'traditional' views of age, they were never as deep-rooted as we assumed and are easily toppled, as we shall see.

Childhood itself is a comparatively recent construct. Neil Postman, an American academic and communications theorist who wrote on the erosion of childhood in the late 20th century, linked the recognition of childhood to the 15th-century invention of the printing press, a development of such profound impact that it forced a reappraisal of the social order. Communications technologies alter not only what we think about, but the thinking process and the society or space in which thoughts develop. 'One creates a machine for a particular and limited purpose. But once the machine is built, we discover – sometimes to our horror, usually to our discomfort, always to our surprise – that it has ideas of its own; that it is quite capable not only of changing our habits but … of changing our habits of mind,' Postman explained.[23] He called this law of unpredictable consequences the Frankenstein Syndrome, and listed among the unpredictable consequences of the printing press the 'intensified sense of the self … the seed that led eventually to the flowering of childhood'.[24]

By the 17th and 18th centuries, thinkers such as John Locke and Jean-Jacques Rousseau were articulating the special and separate role of children in society – a distinction, as Postman pointed out, that came under pressure in the industrialising economies of the 18th century: 'With the growth of large industrial cities and the need for factory and mine workers, the special nature of children was subordinated to their utility as a source of cheap labour.'[25] A variant of that pattern continues as Western countries sentimentalise children while sating their appetite for budget imports made by children in the sweatshops of poorer countries.

Teenagers are, conceptually speaking, younger than children. They didn't arrive on the scene until 1944, when American marketing men devised a label for 14- to 18-year-olds with dollars in their pockets. In September that same year came the launch of *Seventeen*, a US magazine aimed at girls of that age group. 'I love being seventeen,' mused one reader. 'Wish I could stay just this age for a while. Seventeen is the perfect spot between that strange state called adolescence, which means you are going somewhere, and adulthood, which means that you are on the downgrade.'[26]

Adulthood itself is a nebulous concept. The word first made it into the *Oxford English Dictionary* in 1870, and most languages don't have a specific word for it at all.[27] As all of these constructed stages of life blur and merge further, childhood sliding into adolescence and adolescence into adult-hood, older amortals show no signs of buying the line about being on the downgrade. You need only to watch the school run in the morning to see how that shift is reconfiguring the traditional nuclear family into ever-more complex constellations of siblings and half-siblings and step-siblings, and widening the age gap between parents and the children they're deliv-ering to the gates.

'Some scholars call this "a decoupling of the life course",' writes soci-ology professor James Côté in *Arrested Adulthood*, his jeremiad about the cult of youth: 'People attempting to enter "adulthood", as well as "adults" themselves, find that they have fewer cultural restrictions on their choices than existed in the past but they also have fewer cultural patterns to follow to govern their lives.'[28]

In the 60s, feminism and the Pill transformed work and home life, as more women joined the labour force and had fewer children. Divorce rates rose while the church, champion of marriage – indeed, its inventor – lost traction. The size of families in every industrialised country has continued to fall; the most marked increases have been in single-parent households and people living on their own. In England and Wales, one in 10 babies were born into single-parent households in 2009; more than a third of all households are home to only two people; just 2 per cent of households are made up of six or more members.[29 30] A poll conducted by the Washington-based Pew Research Center in 2007 found that children had slipped from third to eighth place on Americans' list of the ingredients that make a successful marriage, behind sharing household chores, good housing, adequate income, a happy sexual relationship and faithfulness.[31]

The family unit isn't simply shrinking: it's dispersing. Children move away for work, for education, for love. In retirement, their parents assign a substantially lower priority to staying close to their children than to considerations about the cost of living, healthcare provision, recreational amenities, networking opportunities and a sunnier climate, according to a 2010 survey of American baby-boomers.[32] In their youth, many of these boomers challenged parental authority. As parents, they've been reluctant to assume authority.

Changes of this magnitude in the family, 'an institution of such fundamental importance, were likely to have far-reaching psychological repercussions', observed historian Christopher Lasch in his 1979 tract, *The Culture of Narcissism*. These repercussions, he believed, encompassed a retuning of the collective American psyche, as psychiatrists reported an increase in patients with narcissistic personality disorders: 'If these observations were to be taken seriously, the upshot, it seemed to me, was not that American society was "sick" or that Americans were all candidates for a mental asylum but that normal people now displayed many of the same personality traits that appeared, in more extreme form, in pathological narcissism.'

We often imagine narcissists to be marinated in self-love. That's a misunderstanding – narcissists often suffer from low self-esteem – but they view the world as an extension, or reflection, of themselves, altering the image they present to the world in an attempt to secure the external validation they crave. In a world of mirrors, externals matter. The desire for eternal youth is as old as the hills but the fetishisation of youth has reached an apogee in the world Lasch observed unfolding.

He continues: 'Freud always stressed the continuity between the normal and the abnormal, and it therefore seemed reasonable, to a Freudian, to expect that clinical descriptions of narcissistic disorders would tell us something about the typical personality structure in a society dominated by large bureaucratic organisations and mass media, in which families no longer played an important role in the transmission of culture and people accordingly had little sense of connection to the past.'[33]

The vast majority of amortals are not narcissists but they are products of a society that, as Lasch noted, normalised certain narcissistic traits as it decoupled from the past. That past included firm concepts of age and induction into a faith that provided further guidance on how to behave, so the loss of this socialisation deals a double blow to those concepts of age. Religion – not its occasional, take-it-or-leave-it strains, but the more potent varieties that bind adherents into self-reinforcing communities of values – can still provide an effective vaccine against amortality, instilling rigid notions of behaviour at different ages and stages, and providing narratives, sometimes bracingly harsh, sometimes comforting, about what happens at the end of life – and beyond it. But such faiths are on the wane.

MY ORIGINAL DEFINITION of amortality was limited, for editorial reasons, to 770 words. *TIME* was conceived in 1923 to deliver exactly that commodity – time – to prospective readers dubbed 'Busy Man and Busy Woman' by founding publisher Henry Luce. As life spans have increased, so too have ways to fill each additional second. Busier Man and Busier Woman – and busyness is a hallmark of amortality – expect news magazines to deliver ideas and information with brio. Newspapers and online outlets, under even greater pressure in this regard, are often more condensed still. The *New York Times* blog 'Schott's Vocab' rendered down my original, mildly discursive treatise to this 15-word definition of amortality: 'A state of hopeful agelessness wherein one acts the same from adolescence to the grave.'

This compression, though elegant, misses one of amortality's most conspicuous features: its exponents' habit of ignoring the grave until it yawns beneath them. It can be easier to do this if clerics are kept at bay. A 19th-century bestseller boasted the catchy title *The Pious Christian's Daily Preparation for Death and Eternity*. A headmaster of the elite Catholic school Ampleforth, only half-joking, described his job as 'preparing the boys for death'.

The irony, of course, is that Christianity stresses mortality in order to enhance the attractiveness of its alternative: eternal life. In *Aubade*, his searing poem about fear of death, Philip Larkin finds no comfort in the teachings of 'That vast moth-eaten musical brocade / Created to pretend we never die'. But religion does help to reconcile believers to physical mortality, though over tea and homemade walnut cake at Lambeth Palace, Rowan

Williams, the Archbishop of Canterbury, and Timothy Radcliffe, a Catholic priest and Dominican friar, gently attempted to refine my understanding of how this works:

> Williams: 'The significance of religion is not that religious people can face death more equably because they know it's not the end. A religious person who knows their business will know that it is the end in a very important sense.
>
> 'It's not just going to be more of the same, whatever else there is, and the significance of faith therefore is not just minimising the gap. It is possible to let go and look and face the truth.'
>
> Radcliffe: 'We don't believe in the afterlife. We believe in eternal life and eternal life begins now when you love and forgive and reach out.'

As the chapter on amortal belief will show, amortals are experts at recasting religions to match their psychological needs. Indeed – with apologies to Williams and Radcliffe – that's a trick Christians have always known, transmogrifying the profundity of eternal life into visions of a heaven populated with everyone who has gone before, from distant ancestors and much-missed loved ones to Princess Diana.

But church congregations have been thinning out for years and their decline is accelerating. The American Religious Identification Survey, published in March 2009, found that numbers of non-believers had almost doubled since 1990, to 15 per cent. 'The challenge to Christianity ... does not come from other religions but from a rejection of all forms of organised religion,' concluded the report's authors.[34] This trend is echoed across Europe, where agnosticism and atheism are the fastest-growing belief systems. (Islam is also notching up substantial gains, but its adherents still account for just 2 per cent of the US population, and 10 per cent in France, which has the largest Muslim contingent in Western Europe.)

GOD HASN'T BEEN THE ONLY major figure to see His power ebb. Politicians and civic leaders are in bad odour too. There's a line graph entitled *Public Trust in Government: 1958–2010* that can be found on the Pew Research Center website.[35] At the start of this graph, during Dwight Eisenhower's administration, the percentage of respondents expressing trust in their representatives in Washington rises from around 76 per cent to hover just below 80 per cent during Lyndon Johnson's presidency, when it begins a precipitate descent. There's a brief respite, during the Reagan years, followed by briefer upticks during Bushes W.H. and W., but the downward trend continues, dipping to 20 per cent and below since Obama took office. The Dublin-based European Union organisation Eurofound registered falls in levels of trust in government and national parliaments across the continent from 2007 to 2009. Longer-term studies show that, in Europe as in America, trust has been eroding for decades.

Over the same period, the media, which often presented itself as a proxy for familial or moral authority, began expanding rapidly, at first consolidating power, then atomising into a galaxy of outlets and delivery methods. Today's press sometimes still affects the voice of morality, but its real driver is competition for eyes and ears, and nothing sells like scandal, celebrity or ideally a cocktail of the two. The age of deference might have survived Profumo and Watergate. It couldn't withstand the unforgiving detail of Monicagate, Squidgygate, Duckhousegate or the seemingly endless revelations of sexual abuse, and conspiracies to conceal sexual abuse, by members of the clergy. But coverage of those scandals in the traditional media seems almost courtly compared to today's instant, unmediated exchanges of news and noise online.

The internet has blown up the foundations of our old, familiar analogue world, though many of us are too busy social-networking to notice. I met William Gibson on Twitter, which he inhabits as @GreatDismal. Gibson's short story *Burning Chrome*, published in 1982, coined the term 'cyberspace' and anticipated the 'mass consensual hallucination' of the web, and his work has continued to anticipate and explore Postman's Frankenstein

Syndrome, the unexpected consequences of technology. Eventually Gibson accepted that the conversation I wished to pursue, about amortality, couldn't be compressed into 140-character tweets. Over a landline – one that passes deep under the Atlantic – he put forward the following view on age and the wired world:

At 62 my cohorts are starting to notice that they are probably going to die. For most people my age that's been sort of hypothetical. Maybe something will happen, you know, the rapture will come or maybe they'll invent something. These same people who are currently starting to accept their own mortality with whatever grace or lack thereof are also much more functional than people their age would have been 50 years ago. The roles of age-specific behaviours are stretching and spreading in lots of different ways. People stay younger longer; some people are able to stay childish longer or pursue interests that would have seemed not age appropriate before.

Younger people are doing it too. If you're good with the language and have an internet connection you can sort of be any age you want to be. A precocious teenager can strike up conversations with anyone and explore anything it's possible to explore with words alone, on the internet.

I'm not very physically modified yet. I still have all my own teeth but all my teeth are permanently fastened to my head. That technology didn't exist in my father's day. In the same way I've artificially been made immune to a number of previously dangerous diseases and I have multiplying bifocals that are really thin and you can't tell they're bifocals.

Otherwise I'm just kind of like an unaltered old guy except that I'm massively augmented by the internet. And so is everyone else. I have this enormous 24-hour-a-day instantly accessible prosthetic memory that goes far beyond anything my own memory could have done. I can look anything up, I can crowd-source, I have total strangers all over the world providing me with little tidbits of novelty in a constant 24-hour-a-day stream that I use to navigate in my novelistic way. None of that is anything I would have imagined in the 1970s or even at the beginning of the 80s. I never thought that I would be able to have a telephone-like object in my pocket that would allow me to look up anything in the biggest, if sloppiest, encyclopaedia that the world has ever known.

And that's peculiar. We take it so much for granted already and yet it's so strange. It's changed everything, and we've changed with it and now we can't really get a handle on how new that is.

Anyone can be massively augmented, like Gibson, by the internet, although a surprising number of otherwise intelligent people prefer to rail against it, as if the internet were the router of all evil. It's hard to remember how journalists lived without it; how we researched and checked stories, made arrangements, filed copy. These days the internet is the starting point for most research and the easiest way to communicate – at least until technology goes wrong or a repressive regime erects digital blockades. During Iran's green revolution, Twitter, the best news aggregator around if you work out how to use it, more than proved its value as a way to bypass censors.

But like the other phenomena this book will chart – plummeting birth rates and a surge in later-life pregnancies, for example – the point, in this context, is not whether the internet is a force for good or evil, but simply that it exists. The web has irrevocably changed not only what we debate and how, and the context in which we do so, but also *what we do*. And in an age in which the old methods of cultural transmission have weakened, it's the most powerful transmitter for information, disinformation, attitudes and opinions.

Sometimes the internet helps to subvert tyranny. At other times it looks like mob rule. The skewerings of traditional authority figures are the *autos da fé* of our age; reputations are trashed and public institutions held up for ridicule. If these institutions hadn't helped to forfeit our trust, if church and state still commanded our unthinking respect, we wouldn't be so receptive to the insistent chatter of the worldwide web. In the absence of credible authorities, we increasingly take our cues from incredible sources: celebrities and snake oil salesmen. But there's another reason for our confusion about age in particular. Scientists number among the few 'experts' we're still prepared to believe, most of the time. And not even scientists – indeed, especially not scientists – can agree on the causes of ageing or the possibility of an antidote.

WHEN A FRIAR IS DYING, he's invited to come and die with the rest of the brethren, says Timothy Radcliffe. This is as much for the benefit of the young friars as for the soon-to-be departed. 'It's a very important part of the formation, that they get used to death in their twenties if not earlier. When the time comes for somebody to die we ring the bell and we all gather round and we sing a particular *salve regina*. We sing it with them – there. Occasionally a brother will sort of sit up and say, "Oh, I don't think I'm going quite yet."'

I DON'T THINK I'M GOING QUITE YET. That would make a good bumper sticker for amortals. My friend Charlotte offered to send me a bumper sticker she'd seen in Australia: *I REFUSE TO GET OLD.* Slogans like this used to be ironic in intent. Nowadays we adopt them as mission statements.

'I'm still feeling invulnerable, immortal, like a teenager,' 36-year-old Andy Garfield, a Californian composer of film and TV scores, confides. He admits he does things that might shorten his life – 'like eating badly' – but isn't entirely convinced his life will ever end. 'I literally assume that technology in the next 60, 70 years will probably reach the point where there'll be quantum computers and the kind of technology where your brain could be scanned and your consciousness transferred to a computer of infinite computational power and then your consciousness could continue on virtually and then you might even have an avatar kind of situation where your computer consciousness controls some sort of android,' he says.

At a birthday dinner for a London gallerist, I find myself next to a famous art dealer who tells me of mega-wealthy collectors who are secretly spending even more attempting to have their organs cloned in a laboratory than they habitually invest in paintings and sculptures. They've undergone extensive testing to predict which body parts might fail first and want to be sure to have the necessary replacements at the ready. 'We'll all be doing this soon,' remarks the dealer.

Variants of this idea – that scientists stand on the brink of delivering immortality in one form or another, or at least giving us another few hundred years – are widespread. They are at odds with much of mainstream science. In 1961, the year of my birth, a microbiologist called Leonard Hayflick made a depressing discovery with direct relevance to how long any of us may expect to live. Hayflick found that most human cells are able to divide only a limited number of times and the older the cells – and their human source – the fewer times that will be.[36] The inescapable conclusion is that all cells eventually become senescent and no matter whether we get through life without contracting a single disease, we'll die when enough of our cells cease dividing. Although our life expectancy has continued since its big leaps in the late 19th and 20th centuries to increase at a more moderate pace, by two to five years per decade in the developed world, Hayflick is gloomy about the possibilities for unabated life extension. His law – it's known as the Hayflick limit – in his view dooms us to a maximum of around 120 years. The world's verifiably longest-lived person, Jeanne Calment, died at 122 in 1997.

Hayflick may have answered why we die. For anyone who accepts that we are the products of an evolutionary process (and I'll take the liberty of assuming that's most readers), the obvious question is why natural selection has not gradually eradicated processes and mutations that lead to ageing and death.

A brilliant zoologist called Peter Medawar gave a lecture in 1951 that began to address this second question. His conjecture was that natural selection favours the characteristics that enable an organism to reproduce its genes irrespective of the havoc some of those same genes may wreak in later life. Another biologist, George Williams, went on to suggest that the deterioration that we experience in the period after our reproductive peak may be caused by some of the same characteristics that give us an advantage earlier in life. That theory is known as 'antagonistic pleiotropy'.

The blind watchmaker – evolutionary biologist Richard Dawkins's term for natural selection – turned his blind eye to Richard Flint; the genes that inflict cerebellar ataxia continue to be passed on because they don't impede the ability to reproduce (the first symptoms of Richard's form of ataxia typically first put in an appearance in the thirties or forties, after peak reproductive age).

Watching Richard die inexorably gave me some small insight into the challenges that keeping someone alive in a failing body might present. Aubrey de Grey believes those challenges are surmountable, by intervening at cellular level to conduct repairs and maintenence. One of the world's leading advocates of 'the fight against ageing and death', de Grey tells me he's doing 'God's work, however that might be defined, helping to alleviate suffering'. Indeed, nursing a pint of Old Speckled Hen in a riverside pub, he offers another twist on religious dogma. It would be unchristian, he suggests, to reject the possibility of eternal life *before* death. His mission is to defeat ageing.

A Briton, based in Cambridge, he is the chief science officer of the US-registered SENS Foundation (mission: 'to develop, promote and ensure widespread access to regenerative medicine solutions to the disabilities and diseases of ageing'). The acronym stands for Strategies for Engineered Negligible Senescence, defined as 'an integrated set of medical techniques designed to restore youthful molecular and cellular structure to aged tissues and organs'. Regenerative medicine will be able to keep humans biologically young indefinitely, says de Grey:

In biological terms what we have is a situation where the human body is this ridiculously complicated machine of which we have very, very, very poor understanding. Understanding of how metabolism works, how the body works, is just pathetically incomplete. And if you try to mess with an operation like that, you try to in some way optimise the process, you're going to fuck up. You're going to have a whole bunch of other side effects and on balance you're going to do more harm than good. Any biologist will agree about that. It's fundamentally why gerontologists have come to this very pessimistic conclusion that there's basically nothing we can do about ageing for the foreseeable future.

The repair and maintenance approach doesn't do that. The repair and maintenance approach says we'll let the metabolism create these various types of molecular damage at the natural rate. So actually we don't have to interfere in the metabolism at all, we just have to interfere in the by-products of the metabolism, the side effects of metabolism that are accumulating slowly throughout life, and get in and repair them before they get to a level of abundance that causes the metabolism to start working less well. We're essentially going in and saying, OK, all we have to do is characterise these particular side effects that are accumulating and figure out how to fix them and we can target those things and simply stay out of the way of this stuff that we don't understand.

The repair and maintenance approach underpins de Grey's SENS Foundation. In 2005, Jason Pontin, the editor-in-chief of the prestigious magazine *Technology Review*, published by the Massachusetts Institute of Technology (MIT), launched a $20,000 prize open to any molecular biologist who could prove that the idea of SENS was 'so wrong it was unworthy of learned debate'.[37]

An expatriate Brit, Pontin first coincided with de Grey at an English public school where both were pupils. 'Anyone who tells you that there are people who are alive today who will live for a thousand years is not a scientific figure but is a leader of a religious movement,' he says. And his old schoolmate de Grey, with his long beard and gaunt frame, could be mistaken for a latter-day prophet, or a member of ZZ Top. (De Grey admits the beard is 'a bit of a trademark' and 'has a certain value in emphasising my unmaterialistic motivations'.)

Pontin assembled five judges to review entries, including Nathan Myhrvold, the co-founder and chief executive of venture capital company Intellectual Ventures and the former chief technology officer of Microsoft, and Craig Venter, the founder and president of the Venter Institute, who led the effort to map the human genome and in May 2010 announced a truly godlike achievement, the creation of 'synthetic life' in his laboratory.

There were five submissions for the prize, three of which met the criteria for entry, but no winners. Myhrvold, summarising the judges' deliberations, wrote:

> The scientific process requires evidence through independent experimentation or observation in order to accord credibility to a hypothesis. SENS is a collection of hypotheses that have mostly not been subjected to that process and thus cannot rise to the level of being scientifically verified. However, by the same token, the ideas of SENS have not been conclusively disproved.
>
> SENS exists in a middle ground of yet-to-be-tested ideas that some people may find intriguing but which others are free to doubt.[38]

Many members of the mainstream scientific and medical community remain sceptical about the possibilities for radical life extension and frustrated by the difficulties of shooting down propositions so lofty and interdependent that they can't easily be tested. A disproportionate number of immortalists have emerged from one scientific discipline: computer science (de Grey, for example, graduated from Cambridge University in computer science in 1985).[39] The digital world can seem a long way from the happenstance and unpredictability of laboratory experimentation.

Another leading immortalist — or 'futurist' to use the term most commonly suffixed to his name — Ray Kurzweil (BSc in computer science and literature, MIT, 1970) puts his faith in nanotechnology, the development of machines tinier than atoms that could be deployed in the human body to repair the ravages of time that are responsible for ageing. He believes that scientific progress is exponential, not linear, so progress is accelerating in great convulsive leaps and bounds. Provided we live long enough to avail ourselves of the sorts of regenerative techniques that have de Grey excited, we'll survive longer still, to the moment of singularity when 'the pace of technological change will be so rapid, its impact so deep, that human life will be irreversibly transformed'.[40] Machines and men will merge, Kurzweil argues, augmenting human intelligence with the processing capacity of computers.

Kurzweil's impressive record as an inventor (he developed the first flatbed scanners, optical character-recognition software, print-to-speech and speech-recognition technologies, as well as making fine keyboards found in many music studios), together with his unnerving habit of issuing outlandish predictions that later prove true, mean that only the foolhardy would dismiss his forecasts of transhumanism out of hand. He understood, only a little later than William Gibson, the massive transformative power of the internet. Bill Gates has called him 'the best person I know at predicting artificial intelligence'.[41] An apparent blooper — Kurzweil prophesied the use of self-driving cars by the end of the 1990s — may have been premature, but that doesn't mean he's not prescient. October 2009 saw the launch of an EU-funded research project called Sartre (Safe Road Trains for the Environment) that envisages platoons of six to eight cars able to make motorway journeys controlled solely by the lead driver. Self-parking cars have been on the market since 2003.[42]

Like de Grey, Kurzweil has signed up to have his head cryonically frozen just in case he has the misfortune to die before the techniques have been developed to keep him alive. That hints not only at a willingness to overlook barriers to successful cryonics that mainstream science insists are insurmountable, but also at a surprising plasticity in Kurzweil's sense of where his identity resides. My comment to this effect elicits another Kurzweilian prediction: 'People really factor their body into their identity: I'm a skinny teenage girl or I'm this big guy who's overweight. It's very much part of their identity but it's just their body and we'll have a different perception of that when we can have different bodies, which we'll be able to have actually very quickly, just like any video game.'

As for cryonics, Kurzweil says he's not 'super-enthusiastic' and that refrigeration is just a back-up plan. He is perched on a sofa in his office in Wellesley, in the affluent outer reaches of Boston, surrounded by the accretion of a successful life – awards, photos with people more successful still, posters for two films centred on Kurzweil: *Transcendent Man*, a documentary about Kurzweil and *The Singularity is Near*, a blend of fact and fiction written and co-directed by Kurzweil. 'I have enough trouble pursuing my interests while I'm alive and kicking,' he says. 'It's hard to imagine doing that when you're frozen but proponents of it say it's better than the alternative. You can argue what the likelihood is that you can keep anything going without your active involvement for the decades it would require, but it's a back-up plan. Really my plan is to avoid dying, I think that's the best approach.'

For Kurzweil – 'I'm 62; biologically more like 41' – that effort involves a Spartan diet, exercise and handfuls of vitamins and supplements. He fears he may have inherited a propensity for the heart disease that killed his father at 58; he himself developed type 2 diabetes in his thirties. (His surname, with a spooky resonance, seems to be derived from two German words *kurz* – short – and *Weile* – while.) He takes around 150 supplements daily. That's 100 less than a few years ago, but only because the capsules now offer better bioavailability.

Kurzweil fumbles in his pocket for his afternoon supplements as he describes a project very like composer Andy Garfield's vision of the digital afterlife. He aims to 'bring back' his father by creating a paternal avatar programmed with his dad's identity salvaged from boxes of his personal papers. Given Kurzweil's distaste for death it's surprising how much of his life centres around it. This apparent contradiction, as I find, is not uncommon among the ranks of amortals. Energetic, proactive, productive, ageless, amortals are open to all ideas but one. We often expend considerable energy and ingenuity in attempting to blot out intimations of mortality but our very efforts often summon up the apparitions we seek to banish.

Pontin, despite his scepticism about de Grey's work, is sympathetic to the impulses that would seem to fuel it. 'My wife when I talk about my fear of death thinks that I'm just nuts,' says the *Technology Review* editor:

> She says, 'But everyone dies.' I think that most people can't see it – it's a form of blindness. And if we could see it we would be immobilised by terror. And the only way I can live my life is by averting my eyes from it. There's a whole new theory in psychology. It says that enormous elements of human activity – politics, corporate activity, or some scientific activity like anti-ageing research – can be understood as terror avoidance.[43]
>
> You have to think like a hero to accept your mortality and look at it, and I can only do that intermittently. Only intermittently can I truly stare at the sun and see that I am a living organism, possessed of consciousness for a tiny portion, with two eternities of darkness on either side. But most of the time I try not to think about it, and some of the time I'm like Larkin, in that famous poem *Aubade*, where he talks about the mind blanking at the glare. It's a beautiful poem. It's the most perfect expression of the fear of death.

MERRIAM-WEBSTER DEFINES SCIENCE as 'the state of knowing; knowledge as distinguished from ignorance or misunderstanding'. As trust in most authorities has crumbled, scientists have largely retained the faith of the wider public. We tend to assume scientific endeavours – and the underlying motivations that drive them – are rational.

So they are. There's the rational desire to solve problems and puzzles and find out more about the world. There's the rational desire to obtain funding for further research, perhaps even make money. And in some cases, there's the rational desire to defer ageing and death, in oneself and one's family.

Biologists have long known that caloric restriction can prolong life in yeast, flies and rats. David Sinclair, an alumnus of MIT, now at Harvard University, decided to figure out a way of mimicking the effects of such a diet without the need for a punitive regimen. A compound called resveratrol, a molecule found in red grapes, seemed to do just that. Sinclair theorised that resveratrol activates sirtuins, enzymes that are switched on by restricting calories consumed and are involved in regulating the metabolism.[44] When Sinclair found resveratrol lengthened the life span of yeast he decided to start popping the pills himself. 'I'm a scientist so occasionally I experiment on myself as well. I started taking resveratrol as soon as we had tested it on yeast cells,' he told a BBC documentary. 'Looking back that was a little mad. We didn't know if it was toxic. It might even have caused cancer.' He added: 'Fortunately, as we now know, resveratrol is as far as we can tell relatively safe. My wife started taking resveratrol. My family does. Now I don't endorse [resveratrol]. It's still an investigational molecule. But I felt the science was strong enough for me to take that risk. And I know what's going to happen if I don't take it.'[45]

Exactly that calculation – we know what's going to happen if we don't figure out how to stop what's going to happen – drives the multi-billion-pound, multifaceted global immortality industry that is devoted to combating ageing and death or exploiting our passionate desire to do so. At one end of this industry are the tightly regulated pharmaceuticals companies. Scientists often turn to the private sector to expand their research in ways academic institutions cannot support. Sinclair went into partnership with a venture capitalist to found Sirtris Pharmaceuticals, and set about trying to develop synthetic, and more powerful, sirtuin activators. A report published in the magazine *Nature* in 2007 suggested that three compounds were able not only to trigger the desired response, but in one case might improve insulin sensitivity, suggesting a possible treatment for type 2 diabetes.[46] The next year, Sinclair sold Sirtris Pharmaceuticals to GlaxoSmithKline for $720 million, and some Sirtris drugs progressed to the second stage of clinical trials.

But a study in the January 2010 edition of the *Journal of Biological Chemistry* raised doubts about resveratrol and the other Sirtris compounds designed to mimic its effects.[47] 'The enthusiasm for resveratrol ... seems to have been premature,' Richard Miller of the University of Michigan Geriatrics Center in Ann Arbor told *Nature* magazine.[48] When the business magazine *Forbes* asked Glaxo's chief executive Andrew Whitty about these concerns, he insisted, 'We feel good about where we stand today.' He added: 'There's no doubt there's risk in pharmaceuticals, and there should be. If you make 30 per cent returns it should be a risky business. If you don't want risk, go be a grocery store and make 6 per cent.'[49] Later that year, Glaxo abandoned trials of one Sirtris compound, SRT501, amid fears that it might increase kidney damage in cancer patients. Two other compounds are still in development.[50]

BRINGING DRUGS TO MARKET is a notoriously lengthy and expensive process that sees many apparently promising treatments fall by the wayside during rigorous testing. The immortality industry bypasses such disappointments by promoting a raft of products and devices that are not subject to such strict controls.

Online and in every department store and supermarket, in private clinics and high street chemists, we're offered unguents and potions, procedures and miracle cures, devices and cod philosophies, proprietary diets and a host of vitamins and supplements that promise to make us thinner, healthier and younger. Many of these products and treatments are beyond the purse of the people who buy them anyway. The best ones deliver improvements in health or appearance, though not infrequently by promoting lifestyle changes that might have been possible without signing up for costly programmes. The worst are snake oil.

Snake oil can be harmless; the sales pitches rarely are. Salesmen exacerbate insecurities and raise false hopes. Sometimes their wares turn out to be damaging too. The Pap-Ion Magnetic Inductor, PAP-IMI for short, was widely deployed in America under the guise of a clinical study into the pain-relieving properties of its pulsed electromagnetic waves. Its inventor, a Greek mathematician called Panos Pappas, also claimed it cures AIDS and cancer and banishes many of the effects of ageing, including reducing wrinkles 'by as much as 20 years' and 'reversing' grey hair. The comical-looking gadget – its display panel resembles a cartoon face – was banned by America's Food and Drug Administration amid mounting evidence that it wasn't simply ineffective but potentially dangerous.[51] Pappas still markets the devices from his base in Athens. 'I'm not sure the world is ready to understand the PAP-IMI,' he told the *Seattle Times.* 'It goes beyond known human knowledge.'

You might think where our health is concerned we'd choose to remain within the bounds of what Donald Rumsfeld called the 'known knowns' rather than venturing into the known unknowns or, worse yet, Rumsfeldian unknown unknowns. But faith in science and technology, like religion, is for many unscientifically minded types exactly that: faith. We don't understand how it works but we trust that it does. Once we've made that leap, it's easy to take another: to believe people who tell us they are pushing the envelope and that their critics are dullards like us. We might not realise that most scientists work in teams and submit their work for peer review. And of course we've learned to disbelieve the establishment, which bolsters our willingness to give renegades a fair hearing.

An article by Robert Park, a physics professor, originally published in the *Chronicle of Higher Education* and later posted on www.quackwatch.org, a website devoted to exposing the false and dangerous claims made for health products and treatments, offers this useful list of seven ways to spot dubious science[52]:

1. The discoverer pitches the claim directly to the media.
2. The discoverer says that a powerful establishment is trying to suppress his or her work.
3. The scientific effect involved is always at the very limit of detection.
4. Evidence for a discovery is anecdotal.
5. The discoverer says a belief is credible because it has endured for centuries.
6. The discoverer has worked in isolation.
7. The discoverer must propose new laws of nature to explain an observation.

But dubious science isn't the preserve of individuals peddling weird machines and specious serums on the fringes. Our daily lives are infused with dubious science deployed by the marketing departments of multinationals to push their products. Boffins loom large in the romantic mythologies of the cosmetics business. At the Crème de la Mer franchise in Selfridges, a doe-eyed sales assistant called Laura explains that a scientist called Dr Max Huber created the brand. Badly scarred in a lab accident, he tested out different unguents to reduce his disfigurement and devised this gooey miracle. 'It's got kelps in it,' Laura says. She doesn't know the nature of the experiment that went so horribly wrong, but the company's website reveals that the cream's invention really was rocket science.

Forty years ago, aerospace physicist Dr Max Huber set out to help smooth the appearance of the scars he suffered in a lab accident. Pioneering the use of sea kelp in skincare and mastering the art of bio-fermentation, he created Miracle Broth™ – the seaborne elixir that powers the legendary Crème de la Mer. It took twelve years and thousands of experiments to perfect, but the transformational results made it well worth the wait. Formulated with Miracle Broth™, renowned for its renewing energies, this potent, nutrient-rich crème helps soothe, nourish and renew the look of skin.

The smallest pot of Crème de la Mer moisturising cream, 30 ml, will set me back £92 and keep me going for two months, says Laura. There are larger pots that appear to represent better value for money – right up to £950 for 500 ml. But mightn't the cream go off? No, says the helpful Laura. It's made by bio-fermentation and so it improves with age. That seems an alien concept in the cosmetics hall at Selfridges, where every second slogan promises to delay age, interrupt it, vanquish it, destroy it.

Just a few feet away from the Crème de la Mer stand, tucked underneath the escalators that dominate the hall, a display showcases a range of cosmetics by a company called Ren. The sales assistant has taken an early lunch break and her colleague from Eve Lom doesn't feel she can do justice to the science behind the products. What's caught my eye is a slim dispenser emblazoned with the phrase Sirtuin Phytohormone Replenishing Cream. Sirtuins are the focus of David Sinclair's research. Found in just about every organism, researchers aren't entirely clear what sirtuins do, although they appear to be involved in helping cells to survive when the food supply is cut off or curtailed. Alternatively there's this definition on the Ren website: 'Sirtuin from rice increases skin cell life, promotes natural repair and enhanced activity of the anti-ageing bio actives.'

On the way to the food hall, another cosmetics sales assistant waits in ambush. There's a special 30 per cent offer on creams from Kimia, assistant Sarah says, and that's not to be sniffed at because 'Kimia possesses a magic force'. Does it stop ageing? 'Yes,' Sarah says. 'It actually reverses it.' The sales pitch is familiar: a doctor invented Kimia; the 'all-natural' products 'harness the forces of nature'. And the name? 'It means chemistry, in Hebrew.' The leaflet reveals that Kimia is manufactured on a business estate in Warrington. Magic indeed.

In the final section of this book I look in more depth at the science of ageing and try to distinguish the hopeful from the hokum. A trip to the cosmetics counter in your local department store will show you just how tricky that can be.

THE POINT IN TERMS of how this relates to amortality isn't about which face creams to use – though if I had a pound for every time I've been asked that question since embarking on research for this book, I'd be able to afford several buckets of Crème de la Mer – but where we get our information. As it happens, there is a solid source of information on cosmetics. Josephine Fairley (disclosure: a good friend), and her co-author, Sarah Stacey, recruited 2,400 women to test truckloads of so-called anti-ageing products and distilled the results into 2011's *The Anti-Ageing Beauty Bible*. But there are few such manuals for the bigger questions. Families and communities can no longer be relied on to transmit knowledge and attitudes; we brush aside religious teachings and shun the preachings of the state. Do we listen to Jason Pontin, Aubrey de Grey, Laura or Sarah at Selfridges? Well, yes, to all of these, and often without differentiating much between them. We're also swayed by people who lead by example – and who could be better placed to lead by example than someone with a ready-made following and guaranteed exposure: a celebrity.

Jack LaLanne, an American bodybuilder born in 1914, expanded seamlessly from his eponymous and astoundingly long-running TV fitness show into marketing products carrying the LaLanne imprimatur. 'I'm a personal consultant coming into your home every day,' he announced at his TV debut in 1951. He continued to visit American homes that way for the next 34 years, and for years after that as a purveyor of juicers. ('Do you wish you could look and feel young again? You can! By unlocking the power of natural juice with Jack LaLanne's power juicer!') Lalanne continued to put in appearances on the chatshow circuit until shortly before his death, aged 96, in January 2011. 'I can't die,' he used to say. 'It would ruin my image.'

Robert Atkins would surely have identified with that sentiment. His low-carbohydrate, high-protein diet made him rich; some ask if it also hastened his demise. After surviving a heart attack he denied was linked to his eating habits, he was killed by a fall on ice, aged 72, in 2003. His legacy was threatened after it transpired that the nutritionist had weighed in at 258 pounds when he died (his defenders claim he was bloated after two weeks in intensive care).

The risk to any celebrity health brand is that its poster boy or girl may undermine its image, by getting fat or old or dead. Such risks are more than offset by the marketing benefits of tapping into celebrity power, with all the added value and free publicity celebrity endorsement entails. When we see a famous actress apparently thriving on her health plan, we react like envious customers watching Meg Ryan's phoney orgasm: 'I'll have what she's having.' In Suzanne Somers's case that would be a version of the bio-identical hormone therapy favoured by Cenegenics' Dr Traylor that eschews prescription HRT drugs, instead deploying individually tailored combinations of hormone preparations that mimic hormones produced by the body and are designed to recreate a more youthful endocrinal balance.

Somers's career as an actress has long been eclipsed by a fitness empire that encompasses her branded ThighMaster toning system, a skin and hair care range, and a slew of books including *The Sexy Years* and *Slim and Sexy Forever*. Her most recent self-help manual, *Breakthrough*, published in 2008, promises to tell readers how to 'balance hormones through bio-identical (not synthetic, cancer-causing) hormone replacement, fix thyroid problems, sleep eight to nine hours each night without drugs, improve memory, detect diabetes early, prevent and manage cancer, restore hearing, preserve eyesight – and much more!'

Nor does she lack for celebrity assistance in carrying her message to consumers. Somers has guested on Oprah Winfrey's show; Winfrey's website carries plugs for two of Somers's books, *Breakthrough* and a 2006 paean to bio-identicals, *Ageless*. The film *Sex and the City 2* gave *Breakthrough* a further boost, with a plotline that saw the predatory Samantha devouring its advice. 'With Kim Cattrall playing Samantha, I couldn't ask for a better, albeit fictitious, publicist to let women know they have options when it comes to their health and tackling menopause,' noted Somers on her blog.

Estimates suggested at least a million American women were already using bio-identicals before Samantha's endorsement, despite warnings from the US Food and Drug Administration that such preparations are no safer than prescription drugs and may indeed carry higher risks since they are not subject to the FDA's rigorous evaluation processes.[53] The growth in the wider field of health maintenance products has been spectacular – worldwide sales of dietary and nutritional supplements alone soared by almost 40 per cent in the decade to 2008 – and the market is expected to prove largely immune to the economic slowdown.[54] Ray Kurzweil's personal consumption goes straight to his bottom line since he launched Ray & Terry's Longevity Products, a range of supplements, with Dr Terry Grossman, his co-author on *Transcend: Nine Steps to Living Well Forever*, a book full of advice to help readers stay young 'until we have even more knowledge to become even younger'.

'Believe me: I would be a dermatologist or own a vitamin store if I could do it all again,' says geriatrician Dr Harrison Bloom, a professor at the Mount Sinai School of Medicine in New York and a senior associate with the International Longevity Center-USA (ILC), a New York-based nonprofit organisation founded to promote healthy ageing. His colleague at the ILC, the organisation's founder and CEO Robert Butler, was more blunt, dismissing most dietary supplements as 'a way to make expensive urine'.

'STRICTLY SPEAKING, longevity is measured in numbers: it is the arithmetical accumulation of days, weeks, months and years that produces our chronological life,' Butler wrote in his last book, *The Longevity Prescription*. 'Yet ageing – or, more accurately, its converse, staying young – is in no small measure a state of mind that defies measurement.'

The prominent psychiatrist and gerontologist coined the term 'ageism' in 1968 when he was 41 and became by example his own most eloquent argument against age prejudice. He remained busy and productive until three days before his death in July 2010. He had recently accepted a professorship at Columbia University and told me less than a month before he died that he planned to work 'indefinitely'. A widower, he spoke of his delight at having fallen in love again. He exuded *joie de vivre*. His death, from leukaemia, was startling because it came without any visible preamble of increasing frailty of body or mind. In some ways it was the perfect exit, proof that it's possible, as Butler insisted, to live to the full until the last. But he seemed much too young to go. 'Robert Butler was only 83 when he died,' I noted in an obituary for *TIME*.

Butler campaigned on a number of age-related issues and helped to make Alzheimer's disease a research priority. His overarching concern was to promote healthy ageing. At his instigation, the ILC runs an annual week-long immersion seminar for journalists and writers, the Age Boom Academy, a series of talks and discussions with policy makers, researchers, clinicians, health care workers and other professionals involved in helping to run and plan for the ageing world. I attended the 2010 academy.

I was already deep into research for this book, and was aware that Butler's mantra of healthy ageing attracted its critics. Aubrey de Grey, for example, had launched into a passionate diatribe against the idea during our lengthy sojourn at his local pub earlier that year. 'People talk about "healthy ageing" but they mean it in the sense of stay healthy until you fall off a cliff at the age you otherwise would have done,' he said. 'This sounds terribly splendid, you know, it sounds like it might actually be a vote winner, but of course it's crap. It's not even particularly desirable.

Say you were to stay as you are at the moment, yet were actually aged 100. Are you going to be any keener to die than you are today?'

It's a typically plausible argument from de Grey, yet ignores the huge and urgent challenge facing policy makers. Our increased life spans have not been matched by corresponding increases in healthy years, the so-called health span. Indeed, underpinning America's unhinged debate on healthcare reform were these stark statistics:

- The US spends a higher percentage of its GDP on healthcare than any other industrialised country. About 70 per cent of healthcare costs relate to the treatment of chronic conditions.[55]
- More than 70 million Americans aged 50 and older suffer from at least one of the chronic conditions associated with age, such as Alzheimer's, arthritis, asthma, cancers, depression, diabetes, heart disease and osteoporosis.[56]
- 4 per cent of Americans suffer from five or more such chronic conditions.
- Almost a third of the entire Medicare budget, the US government-administered social insurance for 65-pluses, is spent on chronically ill patients in the last two years of their lives.

No civilised society would argue that the solution lies in cutting the money to the frail and the dying, although opponents of President Barack Obama tried to suggest that his reforms would do exactly that, through 'death panels' given the power to decide who merited continuing care and who did not. But a real priority for America and any country facing the prospect of an escalating older population – and that is every single country in the world, developing nations included – must be to figure out ways to keep us healthier for longer, ideally until the moment we die.

In the final section of this book, we'll look at high-tech options for remaining ageless to the last and the low-tech alternatives: a wholesome diet and exercise. But as Butler pointed out, staying young is also a state of mind. That isn't a platitude, as a Harvard psychology professor called Ellen Langer proved back in 1979. Her experiment, designed to see to what extent people can think themselves younger or older, started with the retrofit of an isolated hotel in New England. The fixtures and fittings were exchanged for 1959 period equivalents; the refrigerator stocked with food-stuffs available 20 years earlier; black-and-white televisions set to receive *The Phil Silvers Show* and Ed Sullivan. Then came the hotel guests: men in their seventies and eighties, instructed not to view this as an exercise in nostalgia but to pretend they had travelled back two decades in time.

This pretence proved decisive. A control group, taken from the same demographic, came to stay in the hotel after the first contingent had left. Their experience differed only in one key respect: they were allowed to acknowledge that this was an experiment and to reminisce about the world the retrofit evoked. In just a week, both groups chalked up physical and cognitive improvements; increased activity, sociability and mental stimulation benefited everyone. But the changes were much more pronounced among the time-travellers, who gained in dexterity and joint flexibility. Their gait grew surer and their posture straighter. They were sharper, too – and they looked younger.[57] (In September 2010, the BBC broadcast a series called *The Young Ones*, a re-creation of this experiment featuring aged celebrity participants, who achieved the anticipated improvements in physical and cognitive functions. The only surprise of the series was that it had taken television executives three decades to spot in Langer's seminal research the germ of a reality TV show.)

In a later study, Langer discovered that dressing old can make you feel and behave older. 'Clothing can be a trigger for ageing stereotypes,' she explained. 'Most people try to dress appropriately for their age, so clothing in effect becomes a cue for ingrained attitudes about age. But what if this cue disappeared? We found that people who routinely wear uniforms as part of their work life, compared with people who dress in street clothes, missed fewer days owing to illness or injury, had fewer doctors' visits and hospitalisations, and had fewer chronic diseases – even though they all had the same socio-economic status.'[58] The moral of the story: it's healthier to be mutton dressed as lamb than mutton dressed as mutton.

That may sound glib, but it goes to the heart of our conflicted views of age and ageing. Few people – amortal or otherwise – feel comfortable with the current views and definitions of age. There is widespread disquiet that many of the changes around age are related to a cultural dumbing down; that in failing to grow old as we used to, we're failing to grow up. That is partially true and amortality is partially to blame.

Amortals, as this book reveals, are fond of keeping things light, of skimming the surface, for fear of what we'd find at depth. We're experts at displacement activity. Motion without purpose; self-obsessed 'journeys' of self-discovery; a fixation with externals: these number among amortals' less attractive traits. Readers who approach the idea of ageless living with distaste, holding it up for inspection like a calorie-restricted laboratory rat, will view these symptoms as proof of the dangers of the syndrome.

Yet amortality is not invariably synonymous with arrested development. Amortals as a group are detached from societal expectations of chronological age. Some might live, like the fictional Elina Makropulos, at 42. Makropulos – EM – the tragic heroine of a Karel Capek play and Leos Janacek opera, becomes immortal at 42 after drinking an elixir of youth. Her plight ('her unending life has come to a state of boredom, indifference and coldness'[59]) moved the eminent British philosopher Bernard Williams to meditate on the implications of immortality. He remarked: 'If one pictures living forever as living as an embodied person in the world rather as it is, it will be a question, and not so trivial as may seem, of what age one eternally is. EM was 342; because for 300 years she had been 42. This choice (if it was a choice) I am personally, and at present, well disposed to salute – if one had to spend eternity at any age, that seems an admirable age to spend it at.'[60]

Moreover, all of us, women even more so than men, have solid reasons for resisting age. Forget vanity: it's a matter of economic survival.

As populations grow older and our perceptions of age alter even faster than its realities, you might expect the prejudice that Butler first gave a name to back in the 1960s to fall into disuse. Instead ageism – and the impediments to ageless living ageism creates – remain stronger than ever. Our cultures – by which, of course, I mean we ourselves – deify youth and disregard age in equal measure. Our economies need us to keep working beyond our fifties and sixties, yet employers routinely favour younger workers and discriminate against mature candidates. At 42, Makropulos might already find certain career paths closing to her. No wonder the immortality industry does so well. 'I have to have a dynamic and youthful image,' Donato Massimi, 60, told one of my colleagues as we researched an article about Europe's passion for plastic surgery. Massimi, a Rome-based businessman equipping spas and health centres, had undergone a facelift. He waved away his teenaged son's embarrassment. 'He's had a classical education,' he said.[61]

What happens in Vegas, stays in Vegas: in much of the rest of America and most of Europe cosmetic interventions still carry a social stigma, especially among the beneficiaries of classical educations and other members of the intellectual elite. Yet a failure to stay young-looking carries a greater penalty, especially in industries that involve a public, presentational component. During a period of leave I took to research and write this book, I was interviewed for a job in television news. My heart wasn't in it. Mostly I go on doing things I've been doing for years without noticing the passing of those years until a fleeting reflection in a shop window briefly nudges me out of my amortal rhythms. I look reasonably young for my age, thus far without any cosmetic interventions beyond four veneers on my front teeth (they became British citizens before I did). But since Dr Rizk suggested a brow lift, it's been hard to ignore the downward drift of my forehead, especially on the right side. It's not so bad if I remember to interrogate the mirror, brows lifted quizzically, eyes stretched wide, or sweep a hand back through my hair and drag a little of my loosening skin with it. Would it be possible to record every piece to camera in this pose?

SOME FOUR CENTURIES BC, Hippocrates devised potions to minimise wrinkles. Most representations of the founding father of medicine suggest he wasn't too concerned with maintaining a youthful appearance himself. His furrowed brow, receding hairline and bushy facial hair may conceivably have added to his authority in a society that venerated its elders.

More than two millennia later medicine still owes a debt to Hippocrates, but if he teleported into the present day he'd find that greybeards carry little sway in societies that banish even the slightly dogeared from view. Exceptional permissions to remain in the public eye beyond the first flush of youth or its expensively maintained appearance are granted in Anglo–Saxon countries to only a few individuals: authoritative (male) TV anchors, superannuated (male) rock stars, (male) movie legends, (male) light entertainers, Oprah Winfrey, Meryl Streep. Continental Europe has a better record on age diversity. Kristin Scott Thomas, bilingual in English and French, told the *Observer* that at 50 she is offered better and more varied roles in France. 'In America, when you get to 35 or 40, it's over,' she said: 'I don't know why that is. It's almost as though they find age a bit embarrassing. Often the roles I'm offered in England are melancholic women who are filled with regret for the past, regret for their fading beauty. I like playing women who have plenty of life still in them.'[62]

In the chapter on work, we'll look in more detail at the thought processes that lure film studios and broadcasters into neglecting older talent – and older audiences. Executives often come to regret their decisions but rarely to recognise their mistakes. In 2002, America's ABC attempted to lure David Letterman to the network. His chatshow was to have displaced ABC's flagship current affairs programme, *Nightline*. The news programme had a larger audience but broadcasters could expect to command $10,000 more per 30-second slot during Letterman than *Nightline*. The reason for this conundrum? 'Letterman draws younger viewers and so more advertisers' dollars, whereas news programmes are traditionally a magnet for Metamucil [laxative] ads,' explained James Poniewozik, my estimable colleague at *TIME,* as the controversy roiled.[63] *Nightline*'s supporters argued that the programme was more important than a chatshow. Nobody thought to challenge the idea that older viewers were interested only in current affairs and laxatives. Such assumptions obtain even now, no matter that the queues for first-day sales of iPads and iPhone 4s appeared as grizzled as a line of pensioners in a post office.

Age prejudice is rife across the media but the strains afflicting women are especially virulent. The BBC, in theory a non-commercial broadcaster but locked in a permanent ratings war to justify its taxpayer funding, ditched 66-year-old choreographer Arlene Phillips from the judging panel of *Strictly Come Dancing* in 2009, replacing her with the 30-year-old singer, Alesha Dixon, the winner of a previous series. Viewers reacted with outrage. Jay Hunt, the controller of BBC1, insisted that the move was 'about refreshing that [*Strictly*] brand'. She added: 'Is it about ageism? Absolutely not. It's not about bringing in a younger audience. The average age of the BBC1 viewer is 52, so why would I take older women off the channel?'

That excellent question still hangs in the air in the light of the unhappy departures not only of Phillips but also of a clutch of female BBC presenters in their forties and fifties, including Miriam O'Reilly, 53, who won her case against the BBC for ageism and sexism after she was dropped from the presenting line-up of the rural affairs programme, *Countryfile*. 'Words cannot describe how happy I feel. It's historic and it's going to have huge implications for all broadcasters,' she said after the verdict in January 2011.

A month earlier the series finale of *Strictly Come Dancing* could also claim to be historic, featuring, as it did, a 61-year-old competitor, comedienne-turned-psychologist Pamela Stephenson. She twice achieved flawless rounds but despite these maximum scores, Stephenson lost out in the finals to two younger competitors. The eventual winner was 27-year-old actress Kara Tointon and the runner-up was Matt Baker, 32, one of the crop of new presenters that replaced O'Reilly on *Countryfile*.

The male judges on *Strictly* are no spring chickens and Bruce Forsyth, at 82, continues to front the show with Tess Daly who, though literally half his age, might already expect to be approaching the twilight of her career. 'I don't want to grow old gracefully. I want to put up a bit of a fight,' said Forsyth.[64]

That's exactly what Selina Scott aspired to do. She worked for British and US broadcasters, anchoring ITV's *News at Ten* and the BBC's *Breakfast Time*, and notching up a clutch of high-profile roles at Sky and the American networks CBS and NBC. In 2008, aged 57, she successfully sued Britain's Channel Five for age discrimination. She later wrote that in her dealings with a range of broadcasters including Channel Five and the BBC she had experienced 'a disregarding, unthinking, almost casual maiming which leaves women like me with their confidence and career in tatters but which is done in a sly and at times almost unspoken and Machiavellian way. You are rarely told outright that you are not wanted. There is never a conversation. It seems to be conducted by whispers in corridors.'[65]

Scott co-authored a report into ageism and sexism at the BBC but found the political establishment unwilling to take up cudgels on the issue. Ageism isn't simply tolerated. It's woven into the fabric of our institutions. Media organisations continue to woo younger viewers, listeners and readers. Advertisers keep on chasing younger consumers although their numbers are dwindling and their resources are more limited than their older counterparts. Fallacious thinking about the power of youth goes unchallenged because the people who would challenge it have been sidelined. Older faces 'seem to be vanishing instead of increasing as in real life', noted a 10-year study of American television output. Researchers found that only 5.4 per cent of characters on primetime TV and 4 per cent on soaps were over 60.[66] Many of these conformed to dull stereotypes of soapland seniors: kindly neighbours, narrow-minded old gossips, comically cantankerous oldies.

IN THE FOLLOWING PAGES we'll meet amortals who puncture these stereo-types or subvert them, people of diverse ages and backgrounds, working in different fields, finding different expressions for their amortality. Here's one thing they all have in common: the power to change the world.

This book is not conceived as a polemic but as a guide to an uncharted phenomenon. Yet in that phenomenon there is an opportunity. Any substantial reordering of attitudes – and policy – needs catalysts, and amortality could be just the catalyst needed to transform the age of age confusion into the age of agelessness.

Unlike a natural disaster, the grey tsunami has been gathering force in full view; its progress can be predicted, its course and points of impact anticipated. It need not be a disaster at all. But a lack of political leadership and vision, the sway of corporate interests, competition for research fund-ing and health resources, and our collective and unthinking genuflection to youth are conspiring to inhibit preparations for the inevitable moment of impact.

Amortals, as they advance in years, hold the key to transforming perceptions of older people by diverting some of their restless energy into showing what older people can do and showing older people what they can be. 'Older adults are never free from time-dependent physiological changes, but they can be freed from the arbitrary constraints of socially constructed meanings of being older,' observed Duke University sociology professor George L. Maddox.[67] Amortals don't always accept the first part of this statement, but they are leading the charge against reductive defi-nitions of old age.

Agelessness isn't always desirable, and in subsequent chapters I do not shrink from exploring the problems of amortal life and the problems amortality causes. But the trend to ageless living is accelerating. You can't just close your eyes and wish us back in Kansas, amid kindly folk who obligingly conform to outdated expectations of age. There is a widening disconnect between the ages we are and the ages we feel. Until we accept that many social constructs of age are obsolete, the figures we look to for guidance may turn out to be as ineffectual and fraudulent as the Wizard of Oz.

All this change is unsettling but also fascinating. It's an exciting time to be alive; no wonder we seek to outrun death. When I grope for an image that best captures the constant, flickering movement, I find myself back underwater, diving with my father in the Red Sea. The ecosystem of age – how we experience different ages, how we evaluate and value them, how we organise our societies and laws around them – resembles the teeming life of a reef, intricately interdependent, each alteration in behaviours and attitudes, each medical breakthrough, each economic wave, affecting some other part of the living structure.

part two

1

the amortal family
BABY, YOU'RE OUT OF TIME

Eddy: 'I did tell you the facts of life, didn't I, sweetie?'
Saffy: 'If you mean that time you sat on my bed and shook me awake at two in the morning, stoned out of your brain, and slurred into my ear, "By the way, sweetie, people have it off," then yes, you told me the facts of life.'
Absolutely Fabulous, Season 2, Episode 6

'The family that plays together, stays together.'
Traditional saying

THE ROOM IS HUSHED, the blinds are drawn and only a few fingers of winter sun insert themselves through the metal slats. There's a conspiratorial air about this meeting, as if its participants were plotting insurrection – as indeed they are. These men and women have chosen to spend a chunk of their Saturday closeted in the upstairs room of a London clinic as a potential first step to joining a global radical movement.

They've come to the London Women's Clinic on Harley Street to learn about IVF and other forms of assisted fertility treatment. The clinic advertises on London's tube network with a pink and white poster campaign featuring cheery babies and a punning term for these information sessions you suspect made its parent cigar-chompingly proud: *inseminar*. On this March morning, the inseminar is led by Dr Kamal Ahuja, the clinic's scientific and managing director.

Ahuja sets out the long list of clinical options on offer to all attendees, starting with basic intrauterine insemination (IUI) at a cost of £550 and a further £850 for donor sperm, if needed. The Rolls-Royce of treatments combines IVF with ICSI – that's IntraCytoplasmic Sperm Injection, in which each egg is individually injected with selected sperm – and a single cycle adds up to more than £4,000. The success rate for IUI is 26 per cent for under-35s, going down to 5.5 per cent for those 42 and over, while ICSI results in pregnancy for 50 per cent of under-35s, dropping to 21 per cent of women aged 40 to 42. 'The body clock is ticking,' Ahuja tells his attentive audience, and they strain to listen through the hum of London traffic.

If only we could hear it, the ticking of the female body clock might sound like the reedy sighs of dying fairies. Women mark the passage of time in eggs: born with millions, by puberty our ovaries contain only 150,000 potential eggs, and none at menopause, explains Ahuja's colleague, Peter Bowen-Simpkins, in a separate conversation. 'From the moment you start your periods, you are continually losing eggs,' he says. 'It's called time cell death, it means every single one of those follicles has got a clock in it, and some will disappear when you're 13 and some will disappear when you're 53.'

Most women will have their last period in their early to mid-50s. The numbers of women who use fertility treatments to conceive after their menopause are rising, but these later-life madonnas are still of sufficient rarity to attract press attention – and censure. An Indian woman called Omkari Panwar lays claim to being the world's oldest mother. She gave birth to twins in 2008, at a putative age of 70, but has no certificate to prove her own birthdate. Several better-documented mothers, 66 at the birth of their children, are the official record holders. These included Maria del Carmen Bousada de Lara, a retired sales assistant from Cadiz in southern Spain. Her twin boys Pau and Christian were born in December 2006 and orphaned in July 2009, when the cancer diagnosed shortly after their birth killed their mother.

Bousada's fate – and her sons' – lends weight to the view that fertility treatment should be denied to patients beyond normal reproductive age. That view is based on the idea that biological age is a fixed entity. It is mutable.

Admittedly, women still find it progressively harder to conceive after 35; some studies also suggest that the quality of sperm declines with the passing years, lowering fertility and raising the risk of some genetic disorders.[68] Yet there are inklings that the female fertility span is extending in both directions, with girls menstruating younger, continuing a process that saw the average age of puberty decline from 14 years and 2 months at the beginning of the 20th century to 13 years and 7 months 30 years later.[69] Improved health may also be pushing back the menopause, by about a month a year.[70] Bowen-Simpkins, a consultant gynaecologist and the medical director of the London Women's Clinic, perceives a bigger shift than these figures would suggest. 'Today's 50-year-old is yesterday's 30-year-old,' he says.

> Fifty-year-old women now are fit and healthy; they look after themselves, they're eating so much better, by that age most of them have packed up smoking, and they've got a lot more knowledge about life in general …
>
> There was a woman here the other day, she came, absolutely beautifully dressed and she is Spanish, gorgeous woman, and she said she wanted a baby. I said, 'Tell me about your periods.' She said, 'They're absolutely regular.' Blood test, completely normal. She was 54. She looked about 40 maximum. And all her hormones were normal as well. She was ovulating …
>
> I'll never accept the argument that [fertility treatment for mothers over 50] is not natural. It's not natural to take somebody's appendix out; it's not natural to treat your cancer but we do, we have the ability and we do it.

Across Europe, the US and the industrialised world women are having babies later than ever before. Almost half of all births in England and Wales in 2009 were to women aged 30 or over, up from 28 per cent in 1988; in the same period the percentage of births to mothers aged 45 or over rose from 0.07 to 0.23.[71] In America, the birth rate for mothers aged 35 to 39 years has increased every year since 1978. The birth rate for mothers aged between 40 and 44 years has more than doubled since 1981, and has risen by more than 70 per cent since 1990.[72]

This trend is dizzying in its range of possible ramifications, and not just for those older mums and their offspring. Older parents of both sexes are more likely to have fertility problems. That means a higher incidence of only children, and conversely a higher incidence of multiple births among the recipients of some kinds of fertility treatment. IVF may even be skewing the balance of males to females. An Australian study discovered that certain forms of assisted fertility boosted the ratio of boys to girls, normally 105 to 100, to 128 to 100.[73]

Then there are the social consequences. The children of older parents often attract pity: they may find themselves at relatively young ages consigned to the role of carer for those parents or mourning their loss. Yet older parents often enjoy a more stable lifestyle and are more affluent than their younger counterparts. Children born as a result of gruelling and expensive fertility treatments can never doubt that they were wanted. A large-scale study in the US found older fathers to be more sensitive in their interactions with their babies and toddlers than younger dads.[74] Delaying starting a family can give women time to build a professional career.

As with the impact of the internet, the point in the context of a study of amortality is not whether the trend to having kids later is bad or good, but simply that it *is*. Behind shouty headlines ('This Woman of 72 Spent £30,000 on Six Courses of IVF ... and She's STILL Trying for a Baby', *Daily Mail*, 14 July 2009; 'Women of 55 Queuing at London Clinics for IVF', *London Evening Standard*, 26 February 2010) there's a quiet revolution in train.

Amortality is redrawing and dehomogenising the family unit in many and profound ways, as this chapter will reveal. As the nuclear family implodes, new, looser familial structures have emerged, in which fresh strands of family are often added through divorce and remarriage, and official family can be supplemented with an elective network.

Cenegenics patient Maria White has children; they just aren't her biological issue. 'I've always been very career-minded – even as a teenager I was driven to take on a career and just go with it,' she says. 'It was always my goal to be at the top of my field whatever I did and the idea of family just never became a priority. Fortunately for me I met a wonderful man who has four children and I'm able to enjoy parenting through his children and now grandchildren.'

Another woman – I'll refer to her as Ms Givings – thirty-something and thus far childless, is married to a man 16 years her senior. His three children from an earlier marriage are frequently in residence. Their step-mother has yet to be convinced that she wants to add to the brood. To conceive would require medical intervention – her husband had a vasectomy before they met. Even if Ms Givings follows the doctor's advice and starts a family soon, her progeny will be younger than their half-siblings by well over a decade. They would probably look quite different too – she is Hispanic, Mr Givings's first wife was northern European.

Celebrities are in the vanguard of the amortally driven transformation of family life, endorsing these changes through their work and their own adventures in family-building. *The Switch*, a film released in 2010, stars the childless, divorced 41-year-old actress Jennifer Aniston. She plays a childless, unmarried woman who uses donor sperm to impregnate herself. (Spoiler alert: in a heartwarming twist, her male best friend later reveals he replaced the donor sperm with his own seed and is the father of her child.) That followed hard on the heels of a Jennifer Lopez vehicle. A mother of twins in real life, in *The Back-up Plan* a 40-year-old Lopez portrays a woman who uses artificial insemination to become pregnant, fearing she's getting too old to wait for the man of her dreams to turn up and do the job. (Spoiler alert: she meets the man of her dreams *on the very same day* she gets herself clinically knocked-up.)

'A family doesn't always look like girl meets boy, they fall in love, they get married, they have a kid,' observed the singer Sheryl Crow.[75] Her own narrative went like this: girl meets world-famous cyclist Lance Armstrong, they fall in love, they break up, she is diagnosed with breast cancer, makes recovery, adopts one little boy, then another. There often seem to be multiple twists and turns to celebrities' real lives – or what passes for reality. At 38, Madonna gave birth to a daughter, Lourdes; she was just shy of 42 when she produced Rocco, half-brother to Lourdes, 49 when she adopted David in Malawi and 50 when she completed formalities to adopt a second Malawian child, Mercy. Elton John and his civil partner David Furnish became first-time parents to a son born to a surrogate mother in December 2010. 'It is too late for me [to become a father],' John had told an interviewer nine years earlier. 'Twenty years ago I would definitely have done it. [But] I don't want to be 70 when my daughter turns 16.' Instead, as the *Sunday Times* pointed out, the singer 'will be 79 when his son turns 16.'[76] John explained his change of heart to celebrity magazine *OK!*: 'David said "Well what about surrogacy?" I said "You know what? Why not?" I'm 62 at this point, but I feel 40. I said "We could give a child a wonderful home."'[77]

The royal highnesses of Romania, Prince Paul and Princess Lia, announced the birth of their first child in January 2010. The new father was 61, his wife 60. 'We were blessed by fine doctors, here in Romania, in the US and in Harley Street in London,' Princess Lia confided to the *Daily Mail*.[78] Model Cheryl Tiegs bore a son, aged 43, failed in her early fifties to become pregnant again and then had twins carried by a surrogate (implanted, Tiegs said, with her own eggs fertilised by her husband's sperm). 'You know, there's chronological age, there's biological age, and there's psychological age,' Tiegs told CNN's Larry King.[79]

> Tiegs: 'Chronological age, there's nothing you can do about, which is I'm 52. You set that number aside. Biological age, I

think because I've been taking care of myself for so long I know not just my reproductive organs, but my heart, you know, are much younger than … than what I am. It's not … it's nothing that I really recommend, which is waiting this long. I mean, it was not an easy process. But it certainly is possible. There was just a woman who gave birth at 64.'

King: 'But you were trying to give … you were trying to be pregnant, right?'

Tiegs: 'I was trying to be pregnant.'

King: 'Why at 52 did you want to be pregnant? That's risky.'

Tiegs: 'Well, I guess, but I just feel so strong.'

Assumptions about our ability to procreate at a time of our choosing are out of step with any natural or medically engineered extension of fertility, but technology is catching up. Centres such as the London Women's Clinic are cautious about accepting women over 50 for treatment. Although the Human Fertilisation and Embryology Authority (HFEA), the body that monitors British fertility clinics and any research involving human embryos, doesn't set an upper age limit, it could revoke the licence of any practitioner who fails to take into account the welfare of any child resulting from treatment. Clinics in less closely regulated parts of the world continue to push back the boundaries.

It's already possible to test a woman's ovarian reserve – to establish how many eggs she has left. Bowen-Simpkins predicts that the freezing process known as vitrification, available for the past few years to women undergoing medical treatment that may render them infertile, will sooner rather than later be used as a way to defer decision-making by enabling patients to bank their eggs for later use. Another technique, ovarian replanting, holds out hope of a major extension to reproductive life. Slices of ovarian tissue have been seeded on to the pelvic side wall and become functional. 'All still very new and exciting,' says Bowen-Simpkins: 'There have been pregnancies recently in 40-year-old women who put their ovary back and it starts to function. And she'll produce eggs. So there is no reason now in theory why a girl of 25 could not say, "I really don't want any kids now," so [she'd] pop down and have one ovary removed, as a day patient, put it in the freezer, come back when [she's] 40 and have it put back. So you now at 40 have a 25-year-old ovary. With another 25 years' potential of producing eggs in it. So you should go on menstruating until you're 65.'

AT THIS MOMENT of transformation, society – or at least a vocal cadre of moralists volunteering to act as society's guardians and interpreters – is united in disparaging the selfish and 'unnatural' maternity of older mothers. A backwards glance shows you how swiftly the moral compass spins.

Bowen-Simpkins has practised in the field he calls infertility work for close to 30 years. Early treatments usually involved stimulating the ovaries, often using a drug called Pergonal, originally derived from the urine of menopausal women. Nuns proved a reliable source. When the demand for their holy water outpaced the nuns' capacity to produce it, pharmaceuticals companies found new wellsprings of follicle-stimulating hormone. 'We didn't have the same sort of controls then, and there wasn't the HFEA and it was all done by the seat of our pants,' recalls Bowen-Simpkins.

The birth, in 1978, of the world's first 'test-tube baby' changed everything. Louise Brown was immaculately conceived in a British laboratory when an egg extracted from her mother was fertilised. The egg was grown for a couple of days in vitro, and then implanted in her mother's womb. The procedure had been developed with the aim of assisting young, married women whose fallopian tubes were damaged through disease or surgery.

In the absence of an equivalent procedure to address male infertility, the practice of artificial insemination by donor flourished, unregulated. 'I used to go across to the university next door to the hospital and say, "I want a six-foot blond with blue eyes today, please",' says Bowen-Simpkins.

'And he'd say, "Give me half an hour", and he'd bring over a warm specimen and I'd treat the woman on the spot. There were absolutely no checks at all. It was just like a blind date, you'd get a pot of semen instead of a bloke. But it was totally anonymous; that was the only rule there was.'

The next upheaval came in the shape of IntraCytoplasmic Sperm Injection, introduced in the 1990s, which enabled men with low sperm counts to father children. If the technique had become available 20 years earlier when assisted fertility was an option offered only to respectable marrieds, it might have inhibited the growth of artificial insemination. But by the time ICSI came on line, health authorities everywhere were struggling to regulate the booming sperm donor business that grew up to meet demand not only from couples with fertility problems but a new clientele: single women.

In the 1980s fertility practitioners registered a sudden influx of would-be mothers concerned they might become too old to start families if they waited for a suitable partner to show up. A piece I wrote about the phenomenon straddled two pages of the *Guardian*'s weekly women's section in January 1986. This was the era of growing awareness of the dangers of AIDS. Condoms, something of an anachronism among the middle classes since the arrival of the Pill, were making a reappearance in the impolite circles of one-night stands, and the chances of 'accidentally' getting knocked up were consequently slimmer. One interviewee, a financial journalist approaching her 30th birthday, told me about a prominent Member of Parliament whose graceless attempt at a chat-up routine consisted of flashing the rubbers he carried in the breast pocket of his suit as proof he was a modern man; the *Guardian* felt it unwise to include this anecdote in the printed piece.

Faced with physical barriers as well as social impediments to single parenthood, the journalist was drawing up a list of friends, some gay, others straight 'but not husband material', who might wish to be involved in parenting and whose genes seemed adequate to the task. She planned to proceed with haste but, unlike J-Lo in *The Back-up Plan*, fell in love before putting her scheme into action.

That plot twist eluded other would-be mothers of the time who instead swelled the patient list of fertility clinics. 'I can remember a head teacher coming along to see me [in the mid-1980s], and she was intelligent, a middle-class lady with a good income, and she was about 36, 37, and she said, "I want to have a baby",' Bowen-Simpkins recalls.

I said, 'Look, what about your husband?' And she said, 'I don't have one.' And I said, 'Have you thought about this? Having a baby by yourself?' And she said to me, 'Listen: at least a third of the kids in my school don't know who their father is. And you're saying to me I can't have a child. I'm a woman with a good income and I can support a child whereas these women can just go off and have a one-night stand and get pregnant.'

And she said, 'I refuse to do that. I don't want to just go and get shagged one night and have a baby, I would prefer it to be done properly and choose the sort of donor I get.'

And it made me suddenly sit up and think. Most of the donor banks were set up because of men who had poor sperm counts so that their partners or wives could use donor sperm. But then of course ICSI came along and took that away. So why have donor banks? Well, the real reason is because lots more single women were coming along – particularly in this clinic, because we've got the biggest donor bank in the country – and same-sex couples too. We see a lot of lesbian couples.

UNLESS YOU'VE BEEN READING John Wyndham or watching horror movies, you're hardly likely to imagine that the lovely swell of a pregnant belly conceals an alien creature unrelated to its carrier. Yet fertility treatments involving the use of donor eggs and sperm create such babies. And, like Midwich cuckoos, they're often outstandingly attractive and notably bright. Sperm donation no longer entails the kind of blind date recalled by Bowen-Simpkins; egg donors, although in shorter supply, are also carefully screened. Prospective parents are able to select donors likely to produce babies that look as if they might be their own flesh and blood, but the desire to build the best possible baby may also influence donor choices. Sperm banks often carry photographs of donors and list their academic achievements.

Because each element of the reproductive process carries a price tag and a sense that the most precious commodity of all – time – may be in short supply, fertility practitioners have tended to use drugs and treatments that result in a higher than average incidence of multiple births, even though multiple births carry higher risks for mother and baby. More than one embryo is often implanted during IVF to increase the chances of success. 'When we started the idea was that the more you put back, the more chance you would have of getting pregnant,' says Bowen-Simpkins. 'Then there was a great glut of twins and triplets being born, and the problems with that are prematurity and neurological damage. And then the HFEA said that we had to go down to two embryos, and now, by 2012, that we should voluntarily get the twinning rate down to 15 per cent. Which is still high: it's 1 in 80 in nature. But most of the clinics are running at 20 to 25 per cent.'

With all this technology to help us go forth and multiply, you might think we'd be multiplying faster than ever. Instead, the developed world has witnessed a vertiginous drop in birth rates, at its sharpest in Europe. Pulses of immigration – and, typically, higher birth rates among immigrant populations – have helped to disguise the continent's diminishing appetite for parenthood. Maintaining current population levels requires a birth rate of about 2.1 children per woman; Europe's average birth rate languishes at 1.5.

Russia's population is being squeezed at both ends of the age spectrum. Increases in longevity have been eroded by the turmoil following the collapse of the Soviet Union and high rates of alcoholism. Financial insecurity has also dampened desire for large families. In his state of the nation address in November 2010, the country's President Dmitri Medvedev called for measures including state subventions and free land for every third or subsequent child born. An innovative scheme to stimulate the birth rate has already been introduced in a region east of Moscow christened Ulyanovsk after its most famous procreative product, Vladimir Ilyich Ulyanov, aka Lenin. In Ulyanovsk, 12 September has been declared a public holiday, a day of conception. Babies born nine months after the holiday win their families prizes including fridges and cars.

France has long regarded child-bearing as a national service, awarding the Médaille de la Famille Française for fecundity. Four or five kids net proud parents a bronze, six or seven a silver, but only couples who serve France eight times or more – and are deemed to have made 'a constant effort' to raise their children 'in the best material and moral conditions' (and that means, within marriage) – will be invited to the Elysée Palace to receive a gold medal. No matter: the French birth rate, at 1.98 babies per woman, isn't high enough to halt the Republic's population decline. [80]

In 2009 Germany's federal office of statistics revealed a dip in the birth rate in the land of *Kinder, Küche, Kirche* (children, kitchen, church) – a drop of 3.6 per cent over the previous year – despite a raft of family-friendly policies including an allowance equal to 67 per cent of salary for a mother or father who stays home for the first year after their child is born.[81] The nation's family minister issued a statement: 'There are many reasons why couples don't have children. The economic crisis and job fears play a role. We have to help people combine work and family, especially in these difficult economic times.'

There are links between economic hardship and declining birth rates. Germany last saw a birth rate this low in 1946, amid the rubble of its insanely expansionary ambitions.[82] Russia's high abortion rate – the numbers of terminations in 2009 came close to equalling the numbers of live births in the country – in part reflects widespread anxieties about its shaky economy. During the Great Depression, America quickly revised its ideal of the family unit, with one-child families rising to 23 per cent of all households.[83] Big families in Anglo-Saxon countries are increasingly symbols of significant wealth or palpable poverty; people on moderate incomes are responding to the downturn by cutting household expenses – and household sizes. But Joshua Goldstein, executive director of the Max Planck Institute for Demographic Research in Rostock, proffers another explanation for the latest dip. 'Women are continuing to post-pone motherhood to an older age and this process of postponement is temporarily lowering the birth rate.'[84]

LARGER ANIMALS GENERALLY ENJOY longer life spans than smaller animals; elephants, whales and humans may be expected to outlive Chihuahuas. But there are interesting exceptions. One of these turned up in 2005 in remote Siberian woodlands. A Russian wildlife biologist called Alexander Khritankov – nicknamed 'Hagrid' by colleagues because, like Harry Potter's bulky mentor, he roams the forest – captured a bat that had been banded for observation 41 years earlier and thus 'had lived ten times longer than similarly sized mammals, such as mice, thereby outrageously defying a longevity pattern that almost seems a law of nature', as David Stipp recounts in *The Youth Pill*.[85] What Hagrid's bat had in common with other longer-lived creatures is low fertility. The correlation between fertility and life span seems to involve a trade-off between efficient reproduction and longer life. Bats tend only to have one pup per litter. Mice breed like rabbits, and pay the consequences by dying young.

Many amortals seem to have internalised the lessons of Hagrid's bat, reproducing sparingly – or not at all. This trend is intimately linked to the individualism that has supplanted collectivist impulses in Western societies. How individualism might relate to the female amortals' increas-ing hesitancy to reproduce is articulated by sociologist James Côté by way of an entertainingly splenetic sideswipe at the softest of soft targets, the uppercrust British columnist Petronella Wyatt. In his book *Arrested*

Adulthood Côté quotes a 1997 piece by Wyatt in which she speaks of the 'dubious advantages' of marriage for women and 'on the issue of children ... goes on to complain that they are part of a "prison" in which women risk losing their intelligence and looks'.[86] Wyatt's recommendation that women focus instead on professional success draws this response from Côté: 'This is but one snapshot of a growing number of Brave New Adults who apparently relish increased opportunities, but seem oblivious to notions of community and cooperation. Or perhaps Wyatt thinks people who are "below average intelligence and attractiveness" will take care of the children.'[87] If, like Côté and the French Government, you equate child-bearing with public-spirited community service, then amortality is doubly damned. Amortal women not only breed less, but amortals opting for parenthood often do so because they regard children as a route to their own fulfilment.

There's another 'selfish' reason for having kids, according to Brian Burke, an associate professor of psychology at Fort Lewis College in Colorado. In 2010, Burke published a meta-analysis, a study of studies, of research into terror management theory.[88] TMT is the theory Jason Pontin described as the belief that 'enormous elements of human activity ... can be understood as terror avoidance'. Here's Burke's more detailed explanation:

One of the main problems of being human is that we have the knowledge that we are going to die. A deer might realise, 'Oh, the lion's chasing me, I'd better get away,' but he's probably not going to be thinking a month down the road of 'Hmm, when winter comes maybe I'm going to die or maybe the lion will get me'. They're not thinking in the future of their own deaths in the way that humans are. We've evolved a mechanism to be able to manage that terror – the intense anxiety about the fact that we know we're going to die.

The terror management mechanism is really [in] two parts, it's a two-part anxiety buffer: we have to invest in a meaningful cultural worldview to protect us, so some sort of an immortality formula essentially, and second, if we're doing well in that culture, then we're protected from the terror of our own death …

One thing we find is that men and women tend to gravitate towards different types of worldview defences. Both men and women tend to use having kids, that's a literal and symbolic immortality thing. But women in certain cultures, for example Holland, are actually doing that less, because in Holland, it's very much more valued for women to have a career.

The basketball player Michael Jordan 'is only valuable in a culture that values putting an orange ball through a red hoop', says Burke. America idolises its basketball players; Jordan would find his cultural value reduced in Europe, which sets greater store by the ability to wallop a football into the back of a net. Burke continues: 'If your culture is wrong, then it doesn't matter if you're doing well within that culture. If basketball is ridiculous then it no longer serves its function, it's no longer buffering your anxiety. So basically all of our lives are spent trying to manage this terror and essentially investing in our culture and building ourselves up relative to the culture.'

Feminism wasn't created by the Pill, but would have unfolded differently without the Pill's revolutionary impact. The Pill helped to liberate women from unplanned pregnancies and a dodgy biological clock that was supposed to mark time in cycles of around 28 days but was often less than reliable; 'Employers, meanwhile, lost a primary excuse for closing their ranks to women,' wrote Nancy Gibbs in her retrospective analysis of the first 50 years of the Pill.[89] As feminism and post-feminism invested value in a range of activities for women that take place outside the home, home-making and child-rearing began to lose cachet. Maternity no longer has the same potency as a female terror management mechanism. There has been no equivalent social downgrading of fatherhood, so men are still shielded from their mortal fears by having kids.

If you find TMT plausible – and the amortal impulse to ward off intimations of mortality showed itself again and again in interviews for this book – it provides useful explanations for many manifestations of ageless living. Certainly if you apply TMT to the procreative history of the Spanish musician, Julio Iglesias, and his father, Julio Iglesias (remember: 'having kids [is] a literal and symbolic immortality thing'), you would have to conclude that they've been unusually diligent in banishing their night terrors.

Julio Senior was a gynaecologist and fertility expert. His first marriage produced two sons, Julio and Carlos, and ended in divorce. Late in an eventful life that included fighting on the unfashionable but victorious side in the Spanish Civil War and a two-week spell in 1982 as a hostage to the Basque separatist group ETA, Julio Senior met an American called Ronna Keitt. He proposed and, in 2004, became a father again, to their first child Jaime. Ronna was 40, Senior was 89; his eldest son was 61. Senior and Ronna's second child, Ruth, was born in 2006, seven months after Senior's 'unexpected' death, aged 90.

Senior's eldest child, and namesake, by that time was world famous. According to Julio Junior's official website, his singing career came about by accident, quite literally, after a car crash when he was 20 left him partially paralysed.

> Julio spent hours listening to the radio and writing poems. They were sad, romantic verses that questioned man's mission in life. Never did he think of becoming a singer.
>
> He began to sing to alleviate the nostalgia of having been an athlete who now was prostrate in a bed. He was learning to play the guitar, basic chords to dress his poems with music.
>
> His personal force, his will to live, and the great support of his family, especially of his father, who even abandoned his profession

during more than a year to help his son's rehabilitation, produced
a true miracle: Julio began to walk again.

The rest, as they say, is his story. According to the same official biography, 'Julio Iglesias is the most popular recording artist in the world. He
has sold more than 300 million albums, and has been the recipient of
more than 2,600 platinum and gold records in his illustrious musical
career, a figure that no other singer has ever managed to achieve in the
history of music.'

Since status and legacy lie at the heart of human activity, at least
according to terror management theory, Junior's achievements might
seem to be an adequate defence against fear of death. But he embraced
the protective powers of procreation with even more enthusiasm than
his dad. His first marriage produced three children. The eldest, a daughter nicknamed Chabeli, was born in 1971. A son arrived a year later and
with glutinous inevitability took on his father's and grandfather's Christian name: Julio. Enrique, who would go on to his own pop stardom,
was the last child of that union, born in 1975, three years before his
parents' separation.

Like father Julio Iglesias, like son Julio Iglesias: after a long intermis-
sion, Junior found a substantially younger partner and began to reproduce
again: baby Miguel arrived in 1997 and baby Rodrigo in 1999. The family
was augmented two years later by the arrival of twin girls, Victoria and
Cristina, and completed – although that may yet prove a false assumption
– in 2007, by Iglesias' fifth son, Guillermo.

CONTRAST THE STRENGTH of these paternal instincts with the wobbly
indecisiveness that ever more frequently characterises female attitudes to
having kids. A dialogue on Facebook between Ms Givings, the thirty-
something with an older husband, and several of her contemporaries
highlighted typical concerns. It starts with Ms Givings's status update:

'My doctor told me if I'm going to have a baby, I need to do it like … now. No pressure. Like I don't have other things to worry about.'

This drew the following responses:

Facebook Friend A: 'Oh wow! I'm thinking I'm in the same boat, girl. At least you have a hubby to help ya!'

Faceboook Friend B: 'Fuck, me too. I hate getting old!'

Ms Givings:

[to FBF A] 'True, but you know moms do all the hard work.'

[to FBF B] 'I know, right? How did I become that age when the clock starts ticking? Wasn't I just 22 like a few weeks ago?'

FBF B: 'There's so many of us in the age group that haven't made the decision yet but our bodies will make it for us. I really hate that I waited so long and now I probably don't get a choice in the matter.'

Ms Givings: 'It's just not fair. I still don't feel old enough to have kids or be responsible for them. Let alone the desire to give up my own life for someone I haven't met yet.'

Facebook Friend C: 'Word to everything you guys are saying.'

FBF A: 'I agree, but at the same time I think I'm ready. I've really been considering artificial insemination and throwing caution to the wind! It'll be hard but I've pretty much given up on finding a guy I can tolerate enough to marry (although that statement will probably bring one barging through my door), so I figure I'd better charge forward and see what happens.'

Facebook Friend D: 'There will never be a good time.'

Amortals approach family-building with the same age-blindness they display in other areas of life. They don't have a strong sense of *now is the right time to start a family*, because from the amortal perspective any time seems as auspicious or inconvenient as any other. There's always so much to cram into life. For amortal men, parenthood is a potentially fulfilling activity that can be squeezed into the schedule at any chronological age and with little real discomfort. For amortal women, children often look like roadblocks to potentially more fulfilling activities.

TEN YEARS AGO THREE WOMEN stood chest deep in the infinity pool of a holiday villa and discussed maternity. Water plays tricks with form and perspective, so from the limestone terrace it might not have been immediately apparent that the eldest of the women, in her early forties, was seven months pregnant. The second of the bathers, younger by a few years, was just embarking on a variant of the treatment that had helped her friend to conceive. She, too, would fall pregnant. Both gave birth to sons; further attempts at IVF failed. The third looked at her hands, shrivelled into old-lady claws after an hour's immersion in the cooling water, and wondered aloud whether she might start to regret her childlessness as time ran out on the biological option to have children. In recent years, I had watched friends succumb, one by one, to a syndrome Germans call *Torschlußpanik* – literally gate-shutting panic: the fear of closing doors. At 39 I feared the fear itself, the idea that I might suddenly be gripped by the anxiety that created such havoc in friends' lives. It never occurred to me that I might already be beyond the point when the gates slam shut.

Amortal women, deaf to the ticking of body clocks, blithely delay starting a family to ages that make fertility experts blench. They're lucky if a single child squeaks through the gates, much less two or more. As reality dawns, insouciance can give way to cycles more predictable than ovulation: disbelief, anger, despair. Amortal marriages come under strain as the quest to have a baby takes priority over the rest of life, often more so for one partner than another. The centre cannot always hold, things fall apart and couples split. Those fortunate enough to carry a child to term are often unable to repeat the trick, contributing to the upsurge of single-child households. Such households have doubled in numbers in America since the 1960s, to a fifth of all families, and in Britain account for more than a quarter of all family units.[90][91]

This profusion of only children should make the US and the UK very sick societies according to Granville Stanley Hall. A psychologist who came to prominence in the late 19th century, he famously declared that 'being an only child is a disease in itself'. He wasn't a man to brook argument. 'The exact sciences consist of a body of truth which all accept, and to which all experts strive to contribute,' he told a 1915 meeting of the American Psychoanalytical Association in New York.[92] His views of only children could hardly be described as exact science, but Hall's notion of the only child as a pampered and solipsistic social misfit remains pervasive almost a century later.

Yet evidence, provided in increments by a pair of academics called Denise Polit and Toni Falbo, who have researched only children for decades, suggests Hall was way off base. Their quantitative review of 141 studies of the personality characteristics of only children, published in 1987, found that singletons fared better in achievement motivation and personal adjustment than children in larger families.[93] In many other respects only children were indistinguishable from other kids, not least because traditional family structures aren't the only route to forming relationships with adults and contemporaries. 'Parent and peer contact can compensate for the lack of siblings,' Falbo told me.[94]

Nicola Jennings was adopted in London as a baby by a Jewish couple after they overturned a legal bid to stop the non-Semitic child being placed with Jews. The family upped sticks frequently – Nicky's father was a US diplomat – and Nicky remained without siblings and largely without long-term friendships until university, when she 'adopted' me and other friends, drawing us into her family and becoming an indispensable part of ours. After she married (one imagines it may not be entirely coincidental that her husband is the eldest of a very large family), she created her own family of three children, further binding me into the structure by making me the godless godmother of the eldest.

Prospective parents used to be encouraged to adopt babies within their own ethnic and religious groups. Nicky's 1961 adoption set a legal precedent that helped to erode such strictures in Britain. There are still those who frown on adoptions that depart from the earlier model, assuming, for example, a black child placed in a white family might encounter prejudice. But as mixed-race families edge from being exceptions towards the commonplace – 22 million of the 281 million US citizens surveyed in the 2000 Census described themselves as mixed race and both the US and UK have high rates of mixed marriages – such prohibitions are becoming rarer. Many Western countries have long since abandoned requirements that prospective parents are married or heterosexual in favour of more nebulous concepts designed to safeguard the wellbeing of the child.

One enduring prohibition relates to age. Many authorities set maximum permissible differentials between the age of the prospective parent and the prospective adoptee. In 2009 Elton John was blocked from adopting a Ukrainian toddler and his three-year-old brother. Not only does the Ukraine fail to recognise civil partnerships but its adoption law stipulates that prospective parents must be no more than 45 years older than the child they wish to adopt.

John and his partner Furnish instead found a surrogate mother in America to carry a donor egg inseminated by John or Furnish. (The latter told *OK!* 'We both contributed. For the time being we don't have a clue [who is the biological father]!')[95] Another route for older would-be parents is to adopt in one of a diminishing number of countries that takes a relaxed view of age and marital status. Madonna, twice divorced, single and 50 when she adopted daughter Mercy, acquired her youngest children in Malawi.

Madonna has four children – for now. That's small beer by the standards of celebrity amortals. As we've already seen, Julio Iglesias has fathered eight kids. Angelina Jolie and Brad Pitt are parents to three biological children and three adoptees, from Cambodia, Ethiopia and Vietnam. During a brief marriage to Frank Sinatra, Mia Farrow played stepmother to two children older than she was. She went on to construct her own litter of 15: three biological offspring with second husband André

Previn and three children adopted during that union, including Soon-Yi, who at 27 married Woody Allen, then 62, and the former lover of Farrow. Allen and Farrow had one biological son. During their relationship, Farrow adopted two further children, and after its dissolution collected another six.

Granville Stanley Hall would presumably have considered these forms of amortal family healthier than the one-child unit that is a more frequent outcome of amortality. Nicola Jennings does not in any way conform to Hall's preconception of the only child – indeed Nicky runs herself ragged looking after other people – but she suspects the absence of siblings left her oversensitive to the kind of rough-edged but benign communication common within families.

Being an only child also left her to care single-handedly for her parents – both became sick and died when she was still in her thirties. She was the significant carer for an elderly uncle, too. Elective family tends to elect out of such duties, as the growing numbers of only children of older amortal parents will discover. That may prove a harsh discovery for child-less amortals too.

A decade on from the conversation in the infinity pool, little has changed for me. I opted not to have children and must look elsewhere for legacy, terror management mechanisms, and help and companion-ship as and when I get sick or old or both. The gate-shutting panic never materialised. Then again, who's to say whether the gate is shut, as the Bowen-Simpkins of the world throw ever more wedges in its path. A number of acquaintances mistook my break from *TIME* to write this book for maternity leave.

The medical profession, by contrast, continues to assess me according to traditional measures. I've been going to the same family planning centre for years. At my last visit, the nurse told me that she could not prescribe the birth control pill I requested to someone of my age.

An accidental pregnancy would certainly test my resolve. My husband sometimes looks wistfully at the richly textured family life of friends. Yet his tolerance for children is limited and, like many childless couples, we enjoy the flexibility that childlessness confers. We know many amortals living agelessly without growing children to remind them of passing time or to circumscribe their movements according to school calendars; there are many more out there. Heterosexual and single-sex couples living without children – 49 per cent of all households – have become the most common form of family unit across the European Union.[96]

Some of those households are childless. Others are empty nests. But amortal parents are finding it's not always so easy to persuade their fledglings to fly.

NICKY AND I MET at university, aged 17. We both left home at the earliest opportunity, for different reasons. I was relieved to escape the car crash of my parents' marriage, at that stage in its final slow-motion somersault. Nicky wished to loosen the close embrace of her mother and father. (They had a tendency to fuss, in a sweet but stifling way, summed up by a chance encounter on a London street with Nicky's dad. 'Catherine!' he exclaimed. 'In London! And without a coat!')

Once we left home, staying in touch with parents involved letter writing or at the very least saving up coins and making the trek to a pay phone at a time when someone might reasonably be around to receive your call. I don't recall making the effort often or being expected to do so. Visits home were more problematic still, requiring fare money we didn't have or the patience to linger on hard shoulders holding up hand-made signs that proclaimed our desired destinations but may as well have read *CALLING ALL PERVERTS*. Higher education in Britain in those days was free and we also were given grants to cover living expenses, which we augmented with bar work or, in my case, toiling in the linen room of a Brighton hotel to erase the evidence of the resort's popularity among dirty weekenders. Our ties to our parents – financial, emotional, habitual – weren't severed, but they did slacken.

The technology developed to enable people to stay in touch at distance has made us fear distance. Seventeen-year-olds today routinely text or Facebook their parents to update them on their whereabouts, using mobiles and computers paid for by their parents. They drive cars provided by their parents and continue to take holidays with their parents.

And as they get older, there's little incentive to break away from a home that provides such generous material support and imposes so few rules in return. Over a third of Italian men aged 30 to 34 still live with their parents.[97] These *mammoni*, mothers' boys, are allowed to remain in a permanent, cocooned adolescence. But similar patterns are emerging in many different cultures and different family structures. Rising unemployment and a shortage of affordable accommodation lie at the root of this development. So does amortality.

My father, David Mayer, had a difficult relationship with his father (also called, with Iglesian predictability, David Mayer but widely known as Red in reference to hair he had long since lost before any surviving photos of him were taken). The gulf between them was generational and emotional, according to my father.

> I never had the kind of conversation with him that would have enabled a sense of his own achievement, let alone anybody else's. Thinking about him now, I would say he was deracinated, he didn't belong anywhere and he lived in his work. And didn't have a lot of friends, didn't have any kind of moral compass, didn't have strong political or social allegiances. I don't know what satisfaction he got from his family. I don't know any of these things.
>
> So what I've had to do in terms of my own life is to kind of make up a script that set a standard that I hoped he could acknowledge and accept and even applaud. That's something that none of you [children] has ever had to face, that sense of what you do not mattering. Not mattering to anybody.

You've had responses from your parents that tell you that you've done well, that not only have you done well, you've been good people. Which I think is important, that there has been a recognition of your moral and personal and cultural achievements.

Those who worry that amortal parents, focused on their own needs, attend insufficiently to the needs of their children would do well to remember the Victorian model that Grandpa Red represented. Some traditional models of parenthood offer greater emotional sustenance than the amortal version: the mothers of my school friends; Nicky's parents; Nicky herself.

But amortal parenting isn't necessarily such a bad option, and certainly not by comparison to the chilly formality that characterised my father's interactions with his father. Amortal parents love their children. They may be less certain how to nurture them. In another paradox of the modern world, that may keep their children living at home for longer. I left home during my parents' divorce. I did not leave home in order to seek freedoms that I already enjoyed at home. If there is a noticeable weakness to amortal parenting it is that amortal parents may be better friends to their children than they are parents.

THE PITFALLS OF AMORTAL PARENTING inspired one of the BBC's most successful sitcoms. *Absolutely Fabulous*, first broadcast in 1992, centres on the Monsoon household, home to public relations guru Edina 'Eddy' (Jennifer Saunders), her teenage daughter Saffron 'Saffy' (Julia Sawalha), and Eddy's mother (June Whitfield). This ménage is frequently invaded by Patsy Stone, a drug-addled fashion editor, played with *Grand Guignol* gusto by Joanna Lumley.

Saffy, it quickly transpires, is the only member of the family who carries out the functions traditionally expected of parents: she is the voice of reason and responsibility; the enforcer of rules and boundaries; the one person prepared to issue unpopular decrees for the greater good of the household. She has taken on this role because her perpetually adolescent mother is unwilling to do so and her serenely scatty grandmother is incapable of doing so. She is also the sole character to develop during each series, eventually maturing from impotent schoolgirl to empowered matriarch. Eddy and Patsy are timeless and unchanging, marking the years in empty bottles. Saunders wrote the series, at least in part basing the character of Eddy on her friend, the public relations guru Lynne Franks.

AbFab worked as comedy because it rang true. Teenagers often strive to differentiate themselves from their parents. But how to rebel against a rebel? Saffy's choice is one answer. Integrative psychotherapist and chartered psychologist Pauline Rennie Peyton cites a real-life example, sisters now in their late forties: 'They were brought up in a commune, a hippy sort of household where everyone got stoned. Mum was amortal, she was going to live forever. Mum would say, "Do you want a toke on a joint?" and these girls would say, "No thank you, we're doing our embroidery." So they rebelled in a way that was outrageous to their mother, by being absolutely straight.'

Lynne Franks's real-life son, Josh Howie, resorted not to embroidery but Judaism. His mother had at different times embraced Buddhism, taken the family to live with Native Americans and subjected the teenaged Josh to a rebirthing rite that, at least in his recollection, involved mother, son and mother's nubile female friend splashing naked in a hot tub as he tried to conceal his involuntary tumescence. Embarking on rabbinical studies served the dual purpose of endorsing the one religion his Jewish mother had rejected and being about as conservative a career choice as it's possible to imagine.

Yet to assume from this example that the children of amortal parents will inevitably define themselves against their parents is to underestimate the complexity of such relationships (and of amortality). Franks's other child, Jess, turned out 'a hippy child and she's running a yoga centre and teaching five rhythms; she followed, in a way, much more my lifestyle,' says Franks. Howie set out to be rebel and Rebbe: he is neither. Son and mother now inhabit overlapping professional spheres, in which their different brands of expressive impulse successfully keep them in the public eye. Franks, an amortal dynamo, has founded serial businesses since the public relations consultancy that first brought her to wider attention. When we meet she is planning the launch of B.Hive, a national network of women's business centres in collaboration with Regus, and has several other projects on the go, including 'a wellbeing TV concept with a global company' and a fashion and music event ahead of the London Olympics in 2012. She is herself a TV regular and in 2007 competed in the British reality show *I'm a Celebrity . . . Get Me Out of Here*. Howie aspires to be 'the Jewish Woody Allen', and is deftly turning his familial experiences into comedy gold. His 2010 one-man stand-up show *Gran Slam* recounted his experiences of lodging with his 87-year-old grandmother ('like *Cocoon* in reverse'), an arrangement made after his mother finally ousted him from her home, aged 28. Anyone who saw his 2008 show, *Chosen*, will have wondered why he needed any persuasion to leave. That depiction of life as the son of an amortal mother made for hilarious, and hilariously uncomfortable, viewing.

Moreover Howie is living as agelessly as his mother:

Something froze, or rather, I feel like I came to know myself. As human beings, we change and it's faster when you're younger – certainly it was for my generation. Where it finally started slowing down was in my late twenties. That is still how I feel. I've got interviews of me saying I'll never get married and people in long-term relationships are idiots and now you look at that and think, my God, what an absolute idiot. But I don't think there's much that I've said over the last five years that I would go, oh God, who was that guy? I'm still pretty much the same guy that I was at 29 or so . . .

I want to be buying comics when I'm in my eighties and I want to be into the music that I like. That old saying about the older you get the more you know about less and less. I hope I'll always have new hobbies and new interests but at the same time the interests that I have I don't want to be age confined.

At 34, Howie feels 29, and anticipates feeling 29 for years to come. Franks, rather like Mia Farrow and her Sinatra stepchildren, is younger than her son, at least in terms of psychological age. 'I find it extraordinary when I verbalise my age, not that I hide it, but it seems so weird,' she says. 'How old am I? 62. How old do I feel inside? About 27, max. More like 22. My generation, we're still going to music concerts, we're still going to festivals, we dance, we live the life that we've always lived.'

That baby-boomers still go to gigs is hardly news. Franks, vivid in silks, in her flat in the Bohemian enclave of Notting Hill, embodies many of the values and aspirations of the first wave of that cohort. But the way *Absolutely Fabulous* reimagined her relationship with her son through Eddy and Saffy echoes a wider assumption about how such relationships turn out, with the child becoming the adult and rejecting the agelessness of the parent. That's rarely the case. Amortals may not pass on their genes as reliably as non-amortals, but amortal parents frequently and unconsciously transmit amortality to their children.

One way they do this is by abandoning the hierarchical family model. 'Sometimes I'd like to tell [my stepchildren] off, but I don't want to cross that line so they think "silly cow". I really don't want to become what we all think of as a "stepmum". It's harder to be on a level with them as a younger woman. I want to be their friend,' said Danielle Lineker, the new, young wife of ex-footballer and pundit Gary, explaining her strategy of pre-emptive surrender of authority over his sons.[98]

Parenting, in its traditional guise, tends to involve setting boundaries. That can be tricky when amortal parents recognise no boundaries. Parents and children, afforded equal power, may also end up competing for the same prizes. 'It's an interesting thing for my generation,' says Howie.

There was this book I read, by Michel Houellebecq, *Atomised*. His protagonist is essentially someone like myself or a little bit older, but his mum and dad were 60s people.

The 60s generation, as he argues it, created youth culture as we know it today, an emphasis on youth as the all-important thing. And the problem is that generation can't give up the mantle.

And so now they're old themselves and they've dismissed their parents' generation, or at least seemingly took over from it, now they can't handle that there's a new generation coming through. I feel that tension with my parents. That they don't want to hand over, they're not willing to retire or to have the spotlight not be on them.

Waiting for amortal parents to step aside for younger generations – or to start to pass on any wealth they may have been fortunate enough to accrue sufficiently far in advance of dying to reduce inheritance tax liabilities – is a hiding to nothing. Revenue services do well from amortals whose distaste for acknowledging their mortality often extends to estate planning. Howie jokes in *Gran Slam* that he was only able to persuade his grandmother to stump up some of the deposit that finally enabled him to buy a place of his own by pointing out he'd be doing everything he could to keep her alive for seven years after banking the money; if she died before then, her gift would be taxable.

Amortals' failure to plan for their end-of-life needs may add to the burden on their children. Don't expect an amortal parent to move willingly into a nursing home – or to have saved up to pay for private care. But the same desire to keep busy that may leave their kids feeling a little neglected also makes them the most undemanding of parents, at least while they still have their health. I see my parents because I want to; sometimes I have to nag them to make time. Franks has just started a new business; she doesn't rely on her children to provide social contact. 'I feel like Doctor Who,' she says. 'I'm regenerating. I really feel like that at the moment, because I've got lots of things that I'm really enjoying.'

If age catches up – and this really is beyond her powers of imagination – she doubts her kids will act as carers, and looks to an elective family structure to provide any support she needs:

> My children and their generation, they look after themselves and their families. And God help me, that's all I can say. I just hope I've got enough money to put myself into some luxury hotel or it's off to Switzerland.
>
> You remember the movie *Cocoon*? Which I loved. That, to me, is all our dreams, really. Except that we don't have to get alien influence to get to that point.
>
> I have one friend who wants to take over a hotel and we'll all have one room in it. At that point you don't care about food, you take drugs, you have these young nurses come round with a silver platter and you open it up and take your drug of choice of the day and put on some James Brown and start dancing.

That's the amortal vision of life: one long party full of movement and distraction. And nothing provides movement and distraction more effectively than amortal love.

2

amortal love
STILL CRAZY AFTER ALL THESE YEARS

'But at my back I always hear
Time's winged chariot hurrying near
And yonder all before us lie
Deserts of vast eternity
Thy beauty shall no more be found
Nor, in thy marble vault, shall sound
My echoing song; then worms shall try
That long preserv'd virginity
And your quaint honour turn to dust
And into ashes all my lust
The grave's a fine and private place
But none I think do there embrace.'
Andrew Marvell, 'To His Coy Mistress'

'In the meantime we try
Try to forget that nothing lasts forever
No big deal, so give us all a feel.
Funny how it all falls away.'
Pulp, 'Help the Aged'

HIS FIRST LOVE WAS FRENCH, remote, beautiful. David Battiscombe at 15
still dwelt in a world of scraped knees and catapults and trees that called

out to be climbed. Cécile, a year older and a decade more self-assured, seemed utterly and irremediably out of his league when they first met at her school in a small market town north of Paris. *À coeur vaillant rien d'impossible*: when her class made a return exchange trip to Southampton, romance flared like teenage acne. 'On a sunny day we went down by the river bank and she kissed me,' he recalls. 'I was so shocked, but I thought it was the most extraordinary experience. I can still remember it. And we then had a passionate, but incredibly chaste, intense, emotional relationship, culminating in me standing on a hill in Dorset with her and promising to marry her when I was grown-up.'

He would grow up to renege on that promise. Cécile returned to France and sent him passionate letters drenched in perfume. ('My parents raised an eyebrow and I was so embarrassed that I tried to explain that they were from my French male exchange pen pal but he'd broken his wrist and had to get his sister to write the letters,' says Battiscombe. 'I don't really think my parents were taken in. I'd then scurry off with the letter into the bedroom to read it.') Ultimately no amount of fragrance or ink could sustain their long-distance relationship and the *affaire* petered out. Battiscombe still keeps a fading image of Cécile in a photo album that demonstrates how quickly he moved on, to further girlfriends, a glamorous first wife and a second wife of exceptional loveliness, the mother of his two sons.

Movement ranks high among Battiscombe's defining characteristics (remember: 'a shark if it stops moving, dies'). During the more than 40 years between bidding adieu to Cécile and the moment an email from his old flame pinged into Battiscombe's inbox, he'd been in perpetual motion, gliding through experiences and around obstacles with a flick of his heterocercal tail fin. As a young radical he found his way to higher education apparently blocked – admissions officers were unimpressed that he'd put a dent, with his right boot, in a car carrying then Minister for Education Margaret Thatcher – but he completed an external degree at the University of London instead. By the time he graduated, he was enjoying some success in a band, 'writing staggeringly pretentious songs as people did then, prog rock, lots of things involving demons and Tolkien references, long hair, big flared trousers and self-indulgent guitar solos, but we were good enough that we did attract some interest ... We were then sent on some crazy tours and supported people like the Bay City Rollers and Thin Lizzy. We started out as Solstice, then became Witches Brew and finally The Entire Population of China.'

The band went on to work with Sandie Shaw, a singer famous for winning Eurovision ('Puppet on a String') and performing barefoot. Battiscombe, by contrast, wore 'thigh-length gold boots with very high heels' together with skintight black trousers appliquéd with astral symbols and a spider's-web black T-shirt designed to display a torso that could have graced a Cenegenics advertisement. He might easily have spent a lifetime swimming in the warm shallows of the music industry but at the end of his twenties felt the urge to seek out greater depths:

> I decided to sell all my guitars, and went and studied law. I wanted something that was intellectually fulfilling and that I could look in the mirror and feel I was doing something that had integrity. I was naive enough to think that law was about justice, because a lot of aspiring lawyers do, and then they discover actually, overwhelmingly, it's a business ...
>
> I qualified as a lawyer when I was, I think, 32. I'm now 59 so I've now been practising for 27 years. And people are often amazed when they discover how old I am, because they all assume I'm much younger and I think that's because I've got less miles on the clock, I've been doing it for a shorter period.

Now a partner in a big London law firm, Battiscombe is easily Googled. After an exchange of emails, Cécile suggested they meet. In what he calls 'an excess of chivalry' and his wife gave another name – naivety – Battiscombe agreed to lunch in France. Cécile had selected the venue 'with an extraordinary amount of forethought, in a very ancient quarter of Paris, a 16th-century building … She said, "I thought you would like this," and I said yes, and she said, "But particularly," and I said, "Why?" It was in one of my letters I'd written when I was 15. I'd written, "I'm quite enjoying history at school." I thought that's very interesting, to be trying to divine from evidence from 40 years ago. She assumed I was still interested in history.'

AMORTALS ARE OFTEN INTERESTED in history — their own. To people living without a strong awareness of time, the past seems distant, an exotic country we scarcely believe we once inhabited. Emissaries from that country, arriving with gratifying messages about our importance in that country and how little has changed — and how little *we* have changed — can expect a warm reception, at least at first. Battiscombe was intrigued and flattered by Cécile's interest: 'She was the only person I knew from when I was that young,' he explains. 'She's worn well in a sense that she was blessed with a very good bone structure. She was a beautiful woman. She looks as I would have expected her to look given the passage of time.'

During the meal she produced a sheaf of letters he had written and photographs documenting their teenage encounters. She seemed surprised that he had told his wife of their planned tryst. She had not informed her husband. 'She said everyone should have a secret garden,' says Battiscombe.

The lunch ended like their teenage relationship, chastely, but such reunions often lead to more turbulent outcomes. The ease with which old loves reconnect has increased dramatically thanks to search engines such as Google and social networking sites such as Facebook. One lawyer told the *Daily Telegraph* that 20 per cent of divorce petitions processed by his firm cite Facebook as the agent of marital breakdown.[99] That percentage may be lower for traditional law firms: the lawyer quoted heads a web-based divorce outfit and it's reasonable to suppose that people who have used the internet to get into trouble might turn to the internet to get out of trouble.

Nevertheless, there's plenty of anecdotal evidence about illicit relationships kindled and conducted online.

Such adventures aren't exclusive to amortals, but amortals are more than usually susceptible to their appeal. To understand why amortals are fools for love, we must also address broader questions about love and sex in industrialised societies. Why do we continue to marry even as the institutions and social conventions promoting marriage lose force? Is it realistic to promise to forsake all others when our life spans have more than doubled since the early Christian church declared marriage to be insoluble, except by death? And since we are no longer that fussed about having kids – and given that babies can be made without a man and a woman being present at the moment of conception – what, if anything, besides sex, do we want out of sex?

LOVE AND MARRIAGE go together like a horse and carriage, especially when celebrities marry. Katie Price emerged from a pumpkin-shaped horse-drawn carriage at her wedding to Peter Andre. Trudie Styler dispensed with the wheels and rode a white steed at her nuptials to Sting.

Styler and Sting have defied an unwritten law of celebrity marriage that states the flashier the ceremony, the shorter the union. Not so Price and Andre, whose acrimonious split generated at least as much publicity as their cartoonishly fairytale nuptials. No matter: the pumpkin carriage reputedly remains in constant demand from brides eager to emulate Price's style, if not her marital record, and costs £20,000 for a quick trot to the church and back, as much as the not inconsiderable price tag of the average British wedding. (Brits splash out proportionately more on their big day than Americans, whose average spend of $23,000 nevertheless represents more than five months of the median household income in the US.)[100]

Celebrities are the most effective sales force of our age and they're as committed as ever to the institution of marriage. It's the institution of being married that has palled. These trends are reflected in the wider community. There's more focus than ever on the wedding day as the dreary surfeit of wedding-themed reality shows broadcast across Europe and America testifies. But in the US only about half of all adults are married, a 10 per cent drop since the 1970s, and half of those marriages are likely to end in divorce within the first 15 years.[101 102] In Europe the picture is similar.[103] When figures published in 2010 showed a decline in divorce rates in Britain for the fifth consecutive year, proponents of marriage trumpeted the statistics as a vote for married life. There are likelier interpretations. 'Our experience is that fewer couples are divorcing because fewer are marrying,' divorce lawyer Ayesha Vardag told the BBC.[104]

Efforts by organised religions to promote marriage have been undermined by a broad social acceptance of cohabitation and illegitimacy – and by the weakening hold of those same religions. The authors of the 2010 British Social Attitudes survey highlighted Europe's 'widespread acceptance of non-traditional family arrangements, such as having a child out of marriage'. Younger Americans no longer see a wedding as a necessary prelude to sex or starting a family. A 2007 survey of US attitudes noted that 'younger adults attach far less moral stigma than do their elders to out-of-wedlock births and cohabitation without marriage. They engage in these behaviours at rates unprecedented in US history.'[105]

Indeed, the phenomenon of children born to unmarried mothers has become so commonplace – representing almost four in ten (36.8 per cent) births, according to the same survey – as to scarcely merit attention, unless, of course, the unmarried mother is the teenaged daughter of a gun-toting avatar of tub-thumping, church-going, old-fashioned morality. At the height of the 2008 US election campaign, vice-presidential candidate Sarah Palin and her husband revealed that their 17-year-old daughter Bristol had come to them 'with news that we as parents knew would make her grow up faster than we had ever planned'. Yet America seemed more intrigued by the baby's name (Tripp Easton Mitchell Palin) than the fact that the stork had delivered a tangible, wriggling bundle of evidence of changing mores to its conservative heartland.

As recently as 1990, a survey found that Americans considered the raising of children to be a key role of marriage. By 2007 respondents had revised their priorities, seeing marriage primarily as a route to the 'mutual happiness and fulfilment' of the couple. A majority also agreed with the following statement: 'Divorce is painful, but preferable to maintaining an unhappy marriage.'[106]

That's because now more than ever, we believe in love and being in love – 'whatever "in love" means', as Prince Charles demurred when a journalist used the L-word and Diana endorsed it. We live in an era of consumptive romantics – not doomed Violettas (or Dianas), but lovers primed to buy their relationships like partworks in expensively commodified increments: from celebrity-style engagement ring through celebrity-style wedding to celebrity-style honeymoon. When romance fails the erstwhile partners move on, pausing only to request the return of the ring or the division of the marital spoils.

Longer life spans – and lengthened sex spans – give us more time to hunt for that elusive soul mate, or to sow our wild oats. Just under half of American high school students aged 14 to 18 admit to sexual experience.[107] In Britain close to 40 per cent of 15-year-olds are sexually active, emulating not just their peers but their idols.[108] Drew Pinsky, known to American listeners and viewers as 'Dr Drew', the host of programmes such as the syndicated radio show *Loveline* and VH1 blockbusters *Celebrity Rehab with Dr Drew* and *Sex Rehab with Dr Drew*, might seem in danger of lobbing stones through his glass house in embarking on a critique of celebrity culture. Nevertheless, his book *The Mirror Effect* makes a strong case for the way in which the Britney–Paris–Lindsay–Miley culture helps to sexualise kids earlier and endorse their sexual behaviour:

> Hypersexuality is occurring with increasing frequency among younger teens and even preteens who eagerly imitate their favourite teen stars. These celebrities, often in their late teens, may initially tone down their own sexuality to preserve a tamer

persona for a younger audience. However in their private lives (and the more famous the celebrity, the less private their lives can be), these celebrities often engage in adult behaviours, even beyond those appropriate for their age.

When these types of behaviours – drinking, using drugs, dressing provocatively, engaging in a string of brief relationships – surface in the entertainment media, young fans may be enticed by the behaviour and begin looking for ways to mirror it back in their own lives.[109]

Children grow up in cultures marinated in sex and sexual imagery; they are also inculcated with consumer-driven romanticism. It's not surprising they're almost as befuddled as their parents. On one thing, however, everyone below 50 agrees: passion is the province of the young.

Well, no – and nowadays less so than ever. A survey conducted in Sweden in 1996 addressed a subject that had largely been ignored or misunderstood by the medical profession: the sexuality of elderly men. Researchers concluded that sex remained of importance to men even after they reached their seventies and eighties.

> The results of the present study leave little doubt that intact sexual function is common among elderly men, even among those 70–80 years old. Only 17% of all men regarded sex as a trivial part of their life. Among those with intact sexual function, a substantial number regarded it [as] important to preserve their current sexual capacity. Moreover, it is clear that waning sexual function distressed a substantial proportion of the men.[110]

Unbeknown to the Swedish researchers and their anxious subjects, scientists working for the drug company Pfizer had discovered only a few years earlier that the compound called Sildenafil, originally in development as a treatment for angina, had unexpected side effects. It became available for prescription in 1998 in a distinctive blue tablet form under the brand name Viagra.

Amortality was already on the rise (not least thanks to feminism and the Pill) when Viagra and rival oral treatments for erectile dysfunction, vardenafil (Levitra) and tadalafil (Cialis) made an appearance; they speeded amortality's growth and altered its trajectory. Men inclined to agelessness had often been rudely reminded of the ageing process in the bedroom. Viagra and its ilk – the only recreational drugs legitimately prescribed by doctors – banished such unwelcome reminders.

Endowed with a new confidence that age could not wither them, men who might once have considered themselves out of the game no longer did so. Not long after Viagra became available, and especially once it became easy to buy online without prescription (or the precaution of knowing its provenance or undergoing any medical checks for suitability), women started to confess to a freshly minted crop of relationship problems. Used to occasional sex with their long-term partners, they were suddenly confronted with insatiable gymnasts demanding to be pleasured with alarming frequency. And there was a rise in infidelity among men who no longer feared humiliation and, at least in one instance revealed during off-the-record interviews for this chapter, by a woman turned off by the mechanistic athleticism awaiting her in the marital bed. The repercussions for women is also a subject addressed by American comedienne Wanda Sykes in *I'ma Be Me*, her 2009 special for the US channel HBO: 'You know who I feel sorry for? I feel sorry for these little old ladies who have been married 50, 60 years and these last two, three years all they've been doing is waiting for that dick to break, they just been waiting for that dick to die ... And then he goes and gets that pill.'

One interviewee, in his forties, went and got that pill. The erectile dysfunction treatment meant freedom from 'a really serious impotence problem' that had troubled him throughout his life. His wife, he says, used to take great pride in being able to stimulate him 'enough so that I was just about able to have a normal sex life' and was initially resistant to her husband receiving chemical assistance. But they now agree, he says, that the drug has turned their sex life 'from good into supernaturally wonderful'. It has also enabled him to act on his belief that 'monogamy is unnatural ... I think that sex is just like anything else that friends might choose to do together and it's not an indication that my wife, in any way, fails to give me anything, that my wife is not enough. I've got enough friends, but that doesn't stop me making more friends. That's the way I look at it ... I actually started to explore having other lovers only fairly recently, less than two years ago, so now I'm exploring using these drugs and they work very well for me.'

VIAGRA WORKS VERY WELL for men, and not very well, if at all, for women. That fits with widely held assumptions about the differences between male and female sexuality. 'I was reading the other day about the drugs companies trying to find the Viagra for women and if only they could find it, you know, it would be like winning the lottery,' says Justine Roddick. 'It makes me laugh because for men, an erection, it's a physical thing. For a woman to get turned on it's so cerebral. It's a thought process, it's like a lot of women don't even realise they actually want sex until they're actually having sex. It takes women a lot longer to come than it does for men because our minds need to hook into it whereas a man's mind is always practically there.'

The proprietor of a Los Angeles erotic boutique, Coco de Mer, Roddick's livelihood depends on her ability to understand human sexuality and to anticipate its needs. That is becoming more difficult as amortality narrows the gap between male and female sexuality. The cerebral dimension to sex is as important to male amortals as it is to their female counterparts. And female amortals are taking on attitudes to sex that are traditionally associated with men.

To understand these trends, let's return to the question of what we might hope to get out of sex. The textbook answer remains reproduction, at least for non-humans. 'Sex is a marketplace for natural selection,' writes geneticist Steve Jones in *Almost Like a Whale*, his brilliant updating of Darwin's *The Origin of Species*. As Jones explains, in that marketplace, there are entrenched reasons for gender differences. In the struggle to pass on genes and to bring to adulthood the offspring carrying those genes, two entirely different models of behaviour serve males and females best: 'It pays all males to be lazy, selfish and debauched, while any female is better off with an active, helpful and faithful spouse.'[111]

In the post-reproductive human sphere, it pays all of us to be lazy, selfish and debauched, especially if we can find an active, helpful and faithful spouse to look after us. And the reasons we seek out sexual opportunities, whether we are male or female, range from the obvious to the abstruse, from the instinctive to the incredible. We have sex to express love and to feel love. We have sex for pure pleasure or, like the wives of Viagra-fuelled husbands, out of duty. Or, like one interviewee, 'because everyone kept telling me how eligible he was'.

Among the reasons another interviewee gives for having sex is that 'it is very good for you ... it's good exercise, it's good mental exercise, it ticks all the boxes'. Wilhelm Reich, a protégé of Sigmund Freud, emphatically agreed. Orgasm released a cosmic energy called orgone, he said; if pent up in the body, it would turn to destructive anxiety. He called the capacity to experience that release 'orgastic potency'.

A quick trawl on Amazon for books about sex reveals a large market for manuals to boost orgastic potency. Simone de Beauvoir's *The Second Sex* finds itself an unlikely bedfellow of the following: *Sinful Sex: the Uninhibited Guide to Erotic Pleasure, Sizzling Sex: the Sex Doctor's 250 Hottest Tips, Tricks and Techniques, Sex 365: A Position for Every Day, Make Your Own Sex Toys: 50 Quick and Easy Do-It-Yourself Projects* and many similarly helpful titles, all moaning for attention. *Shag Yourself Slim: the Most Enjoyable Way to Lose Weight* by 'Imah Goer' combines two latter-day obsessions. The subtext of all these books and much else in our cultures, from pornography to gossip porn, the barely regulated coverage of tangled celebrity lives, is that everybody else is doing it more, and better, than you are.

Who knows: that might be true. But for those brought up to think sex is dirty or aberrant or embarrassing – and such ideas remain pervasive despite the waning powers of the institutions that helped to promote them – it's also confusing. We're damned if we do do it and damned if we don't do it. It's hardly surprising if many people are bewildered or ambivalent about sex. Proponents of terror management theory suggest an additional, deeper reason for conflicting attitudes to sex – the act which, after all, may culminate in *la petite mort* reminds us we are animals and, as such, mortal.

'If humans manage the terror associated with death by clinging to a symbolic cultural view of reality, then reminders of one's corporeal animal nature would threaten the efficacy of this anxiety-buffering mechanism,' say the authors of the study *Understanding Human Ambivalence about Sex*. 'From the perspective of TMT, then, the uneasiness surrounding sex is a result of existential implications of sexual behaviour for beings that cope with the threat of death by living their lives on an abstract symbolic plane.'[112]

Chastity would be the obvious way to avoid being reminded of death. But the study suggests that we have developed alternative strategies:

Sex, because of its very strong positive appeal, is often trans-formed by embracing it as part of a profound and uniquely human emotional experience: romantic love. Love transforms sex from an animal act to a symbolic human experience, thereby making it a highly meaningful part of one's [cultural worldview] and obscuring its threatening links to animality and mortality. Indeed, research has shown that sex and love often accompany one another ... [and] that close relationships can actually serve a death-anxiety buffering function.

In addition to romantic love, there are other ways in which sex can be elevated to an abstract level of meaning beyond its physical nature ... for example, sexual prowess can serve as a source of self-esteem, sexual pleasure can be used as a pathway to spiritual enlightenment, and we would even argue that some of the so-called sexual deviations can be understood as making sex less animalistic by making it more ritualistic or transforming the source of arousal from the body to an inanimate object, such as a high-heeled shoe.[113]

Leaving aside the idea that research was necessary to show that 'sex and love often accompany one another', TMT once again sounds plausible and provides possible explanations for amortal behaviour, not least the conspicuous amortal facility for weaving emotional dramas and sexual intrigues. Not for amortals the appeal of the no-strings shag buddy. Sex appeals to amortals when it has many strings – or possibly silken ribbons – attached. Amortals, male and female, not only find ways to endow sex with multi-layered meanings that remove it from the animal sphere with its reminders of mortality: they expertly use love and sex to distract themselves from mortality.

Unfortunately for their long-suffering partners, this means amortals may be prone to adventuring. Although few truly believe in God, amortals will unblushingly genuflect to the power of love ('it was bigger than both of us'; 'you have to follow your heart'). As the philosopher John Gray points out, the idea of sinning, even for the godless, adds intensity to any sexual activity: 'Post-Christians deny themselves the pleasures of guilt. They blush at using a queasy conscience to flavour their stale pleasures. As a result, they are notably lacking in *joie de vivre*. Among those who have once been Christians, pleasure can be intense only if it is mixed with the sensation of acting immorally.'[114]

The sensation of acting immorally can be heightened by discovery, and there's another reason that amortals' secret gardens don't always stay secret. What could provide a better distraction from age and death than finding oneself the centre of a conflagration of lust and jealousy? That impulse is one of the wellsprings of midlife crises – although the phrase itself is misleading, since such crises often occur well before the midlife point as calculated on our enhanced life expectancies. A non-amortal might go through such a phase, throw his or her life into the air like a deck of cards, and then adjust according to the way the cards fall. Amortals are apt to play 52-pick-up throughout their lives.

One interviewee, in his late sixties and on his third marriage, confesses he has recently fallen in love again and is considering his options. I ask, given his record, whether this new love won't inevitably come to disappoint too. No, he insists, this one is his 'soul mate'. Surely he thought the same of previous loves? He scowls. Maybe so, but you have to 'work at life until you get it right. This is the lady I want to build my future with.'

'THERE'S NOT MUCH to be said about serial monogamy in an extended, in a post-aged world, because ultimately it's already happening,' says Aubrey de Grey. Even those who take the death-defying scientist's pronouncements with a pinch of saltpetre would have to agree with him on this point. A ruby anniversary used to signify a moment to look back with pleasure at 40 years of marriage. Now it may trigger forward-looking restlessness. In June 2010, only weeks after celebrating their ruby anniversary, America's former second couple, Al and Tipper Gore, announced their separation, 'a mutual and mutually supportive decision that we have made together following a process of long and careful consideration'.

The Gores are Democrats but to Americans they represented a conservative ideal of family life. Tipper played the attentive political wife to her ambitious husband. She campaigned successfully for warning labels to be affixed to rock and pop CDs containing explicit lyrics. Together with her husband she wrote the 2003 book *Joined at the Heart: The Transformation of the American Family*. 'For us, as for most Americans,' declared the Gores, 'family is our bedrock, and we believe the strength of the American family is the nation's bedrock.' Their split may represent a fissure in that bedrock but Al and Tipper, 62 at the time of the announcement, are bang on trend. Divorce among the over-50s is rising everywhere, even in countries that have seen a dip in divorce rates across other age ranges. In November 2009,

British couple Bertie and Jessie Woods, both 98, set a dubious world record, becoming the oldest couple to divorce, after 36 years together.

The increase in later-life divorce is accompanied by a rise in later-life coupling. An increase in sexually transmitted infections inspired a campaign by Britain's health authorities to persuade older lovers to use condoms.

Long-lived men who enjoyed limited success in the dating game in youth are able to reinvent themselves as Casanovas as their potential rivals predecease them. At the Sun City retirement community in California, Simha Skinner, 66, jokes with her friend Mary O'Brien, 70. Both women are widows and belong to the community's dating organisation, the Solo Club. Women outnumber men by a wide margin. 'We do have men in our Solo Club,' says Skinner. 'I call it the buffet for the men. They just go around. The ladies, they're happy because they get their turn.'

Older pairs sometimes prefer to keep their relationship unofficial, to avoid compromising their children's inheritance for example (a non-amortal consideration). Others opt for the amortal theatrics of the late-life wedding. The oldest recorded groom was Harry Stevens, aged 103 when he tied the knot with 84-year-old Thelma Lucas in Wisconsin in 1984. Minnie Munro, 102, took the record for the world's oldest bride. She married 83-year-old Dudley Reid in their native Australia in 1991.

Britain's oldest newlyweds posed for the cameras in July 2010. Henry Kerr, 97, and Valerie Berkowitz, 87, married in their north London residential home. 'By the time I was in my mid-nineties and found I was looking at this young lady and fancying her, I thought how ridiculous. How could she react to a silly old codger like me?' recalled the groom.

As it turned out, the object of his affections laughed until she cried, but eventually accepted Kerr's proposal after his protracted campaign of poetry-writing. 'Life is now a continuous honeymoon,' Kerr told the news teams that turned up to mark the marriage. He added that he was pleased fellow residents would no longer gossip about the pair sharing a bedroom.

THE ASSUMPTION THAT OLDER FOLK aren't interested in sex is in no small part a product of our youth-obsessed culture. We conflate desirability with youth, so we find the idea of sex with or between older people comical or perverted. It can be both. In 2009 at a sex industry trade fair in London called Erotica – the least erotic of experiences, believe me – a man strolled through the appropriately titled exhibition hall wearing only a posing pouch, socks and sandals. There was much to amuse in his jutting belly, his mode of undress and especially the footwear. But in a room teeming with exotica, what drew attention was his advanced age (he was, at a guess, pushing 90).

As the Swedish study shows, that shouldn't surprise us. The male libido – or at least the male focus on maintaining and feeding the libido – endures well into old age. What has changed is the variety of ways in which amortals of both sexes are stoking their libidos and the openness with which they pursue this goal.

Justine Roddick has noticed an upswing in older customers at her boutique. One customer in his eighties has become a regular at the Coco de Mer sex seminars. ('It's like cooking,' Roddick says of the seminars. 'Not everybody's born a great cook. Everybody's got that potential but you need some hints and tips and some tricks and ideas.')

'The first time that [the customer] came in I thought that he'd got the wrong place,' says Roddick. 'I was like "I'm not sure" and he was like "I've got my ticket". Oh, OK then. I was thinking, "Oh my gosh, please don't have a heart attack." We have live demonstrations and you couple up with people in some cases to practise your knot-tying or whatever. He's got a wealth of education now. He's done spanking, rope bondage, he's done role-playing.'

Everybody needs a hobby, and the older you are, the more truth to the phrase 'use it or lose it'. Mental stimulation and physical exercise are two key prerequisites of healthy ageing. Roddick's older clientele or members of the many web-based organisations hooking up 'silver swingers' or offering more conventional dating services for older people are doing nothing that their geriatricians wouldn't heartily recommend.

Some of these sites are not for the faint-hearted. I adopted the persona of 'Craig', 65, to tour a website aimed at over-50s swingers; within hours, my email inbox was groaning with badly spelled invitations to group sex. I also joined an online service connecting 'cougars', older women looking for younger men, or 'cubs'. Every username that came to mind had already been taken, so in desperation I finally signed up as Angela Merkel and uploaded a photograph of the German chancellor, adding the motto: 'I'm more fun than I look.' A potential suitor contacted me in less than a minute.

A 2009 study of online dating sites by the University of Wales Institute, Cardiff, questioned whether the cougar phenomenon is a media construct, and the following year a planned international cougar convention in a London nightclub was cancelled because of poor ticket sales.[115] Both cases may speak to the reluctance of older women to be stereotyped as predators – and of amortal women to think of themselves in age-defined terms.

Amortals sign up to dating websites that are not age-specific. Experts in displacement and distraction, they often derive as much enjoyment from virtual interaction as from real encounters. Says one amortal, who met her last two boyfriends online:

> My ex, the one I was with for two years, he dated 14 women before he met me, then we split up and he went and was with a woman for a year and now that's split up, so he's dating again …
>
> He said there are some women that are on the site now that were on when he first went on seven years ago. And he said, and it's true, a lot of these women don't really have the time anyway, they're all busy, they're running a business, they've got families, they've got kids, they don't really have the time. They have to look up their diaries to see if they've even got a free day.
>
> I'm a bit like that, I've got a full diary too. So it does become a hobby and it's addictive and you just play these games and just

see who's out there and if there's anybody that remotely seems attractive and it's funny.

The two website-based organisations she has joined are both open to all ages. If you're looking for amortal love, you're unlikely to find it among the silver swingers and cougars. Amortals, disconnected from chronological age, seldom identify with labels and movements that segment by age. Love is blind and amortal love is age-blind.

'I HAVE ENDLESS DREAMS and in all my dreams I'm young. I have a lot of erotic dreams, lots and lots of them,' says one interviewee. Now in her seventies, a veteran of many affairs and two marriages, she is flirtatious and outgoing. Her younger husband tells her that their neighbour, another 20 years younger still, fancies her. The husband is joking, mock-jealous. The interviewee suspects that their neighbour really is a little bit smitten.

She will never test that suspicion. Although amortal, and despite her dreams and her ageless lifestyle, she knows that society sees her as old. There are virtual worlds where such judgements are never made because they are impossible to make.

For about six weeks in 2005, I immersed myself before work and again before sleeping in the virtual world Second Life, persuading myself that journalists need to understand such cultural phenomena. To explore the strange and beautiful territories of Second Life – and they are strange and beautiful – one must first create an avatar, the digital emissary of the real self. My effort was unimaginative, a cartoon self-portrait, but Second Life is full of weird projections, half-human, half-beast. What all avatars have in common is that they are ageless and self-constructed, yet the relationships they form and their experiences seem disturbingly real. 'Studies have found that people actually do begin to really identify and feel that they are that avatar,' says futurist Ray Kurzweil. He predicts fully immersive experiences will become available in the near future.

At a 2001 conference, Kurzweil reversed the usual pattern of such technologies, bringing the avatar out of virtuality and on to the podium. The avatar was his female alter-ego, Ramona:

> I had these magnetic sensors that picked up all my movement that created in real time a semi-realistic image of Ramona, moving, as I did, in real time, and my voice drove her lips and my voice was turned into a woman's voice. As I looked into the cyber mirror, I saw Ramona and she was moving the way I was. It was realistic enough that I felt that the body I actually inhabit is not the only way to be. That's not really me.
>
> I mean, that's a body I happen to have, but you can have a different body. It felt very liberating.

You're only as old as the person you feel, as the old joke goes, and until Kurzweil's vision of immersive technology is realised, the only certain way to feel a younger person is to find a younger mate. But creating profiles – for dating sites or Facebook or Friends Reunited – entails some of the sense of liberation Kurzweil experienced as Ramona. We control our image and representation and, in theory, exert greater control over the way people react to us.

My experience with a dating website showed how easy it is to misjudge reactions. A friend considering dipping a toe into the world of online dating asked me to help her select possible mates on one particular members-only site. At her request, I went through the rigmarole of creating a profile and, keen not to attract interest from genuine members, devised a singularly repellent male persona, a heavy drinker with violent tendencies, inscribing, as a one-line description of this invented self, 'I am the darkness. Save me from the darkness.' The phrase proved catnip to otherwise sane and intelligent women in search of a soul to rescue. In this secular century, we rarely look to God, but trust in our own godlike powers to change reality.

3

faith in the future
NO LONGER BOTHERING GOD

'There will always be suffering
It flows through life like water.'
Nick Cave, 'Lime Tree Arbour'

'What I have learned is that I like all religions,
but only parts of them.'
Uma Thurman

'I need more church in my life.'
Kanye West, on Twitter

RICHARD FLINT NEVER looked to God for salvation, but he did put his faith in science. Until his thirties, when a hereditary condition began to strip him of movement, he hoped for a breakthrough that would enable physicians to rewrite his faulty genetic coding. Once dropped dishes and stumbles could no longer be explained as clumsiness, and as his body failed and speech slurred, the focus of his secular prayers for a scientific miracle shifted to his nephew and niece. Their mother, his older sister, died before him, so weakened by the nervous disorder cerebellar ataxia that a common cold took her. The same disorder had destroyed Richard's mother and aunt. It affected each family member differently – ataxia is cruelly capricious, speeding and slowing like a car with a sticky accelerator, and inflicting a changing palette of symptoms on every sufferer. By the time he finally began to let go, aged 47, he was emaciated, powerless and largely mute. The last time I saw Richard, in the spring of 2007, he lay against his pillows like dead Jesus leaning into Mary, a faint fluttering above his jutting collarbone the only indication that he was still resisting oblivion.

It had taken a long and merciless process to extinguish the fizzing energy that had been his defining characteristic. When we were students, that energy regularly propelled us into complex excursions involving borrowed vehicles and improbable destinations. In late 1979 or the first half of 1980 he chivvied me into a trip to London. There was probably a party somewhere – there was always a party somewhere – but our main goal was the Friends House near Euston Station, the headquarters of the Quakers in Britain, which on that evening was hosting the living founder of another belief system: Raelism. Richard was allergic to most religions, and he didn't expect to be won over by this juvenile creed – the movement had been founded just five years earlier – and he never did convert, despite a later habit of declaring himself Raelian on official forms. But he endorsed a central tenet of Raelism: that there is no such thing as divinity, only science.

Raelism's eponymous (and self-christened) leader, Rael, formerly known by his birth name of Claude Vorilhon, claimed a series of encounters with extraterrestrials. First contact was in December 1973, when a flying saucer disgorged a petite stranger, an emissary of the Elohim. 'His skin was white with a slightly greenish tinge, a bit like someone with liver trouble,' Vorilhon recounted in *The Message Given by Extraterrestrials*.[116] 'Why did you come here?' the future Rael asked his alien interlocutor:

'Today, to talk to you.'

'To me?'

'Yes, to you, Claud Vorilhon, editor of a small motor sport magazine, married and father of two children.'

Somewhat less plausibly, the aliens told Vorilhon they had chosen him because he was French and France was 'a country where new ideas are welcomed and where it is possible to talk about such ideas openly'. If we were sceptical about the motives of this recently anointed prophet – and I'm sure we were; this was only a year or so after Jonestown – Rael's seminar at the Friends House did little to allay suspicion. Money came up right away. Rael explained that he required funds to build a well-appointed embassy for the Elohim. (They feared violating planetary air space and needed a diplomatically neutral place to land.) But other aspects of Rael's pitch appealed to Richard: especially the strong libertarian message and subversion of long-established faiths. The Elohim had invented humanity in their laboratories, said Rael. Tales of the divine and the supernatural in all world religions could be understood as imperfect human explanations of encounters with this hyper-intelligent race. Their science was so advanced that their leaders had already lived for 25,000 years, and knew how to use cloning and other technologies, on earth still in their infancy or not yet discovered, to defeat illness and ageing.

By 19, Richard was intimately acquainted with illness, if not ageing. The life expectancy of ataxians varies, but in his family the condition had proved particularly aggressive. His mother reacted to her incapacity with rage, which she directed against her children. Richard had already resolved that if he carried the genetic mutation, and if science left him in the lurch, he would nevertheless manage to live, and die, with grace.

WHATEVER YOU THINK of the major world religions – and to attempt a balance sheet of their contributions and toxicities even over the past 24 hours would take up the rest of this book – they provide a framework and a narrative that might have helped Richard, and those close to him, to realise that ambition. The linkage of religion and comfort draws a snarl from Richard Dawkins, the high priest of atheism. 'Many people who concede that God probably doesn't exist, and that he is not necessary for morality, still come back with what they often regard as a trump card: the alleged psychological or emotional need for a god,' Dawkins writes in *The God Delusion*. 'If you take religion away, what are you going to put in its place? What have you to offer the dying patients, the weeping bereaved, the lonely Eleanor Rigbys for whom God is their only friend?'[117]

The answer, Dawkins argues, are two types of earthly consolation: the physical sort (brandy, a hug) and the 'discovery of a previously unappreciated fact, or a previously undiscovered way of looking at existing facts'. He ventures one such paradigm shift: 'A philosopher points out that there is nothing special about the moment when an old man dies. The child that he once was "died" long ago, not by suddenly ceasing to live, but by growing up. Each of Shakespeare's seven ages of man "dies" by slowly morphing into the next. From this point of view, the moment when the old man finally expires is no different from the slow "deaths" throughout his life.'[118]

Richard Flint was brave and elegant in life and death, but neither of these 'consolations' would have lived up to that billing. Drinking exacerbates the symptoms of ataxia and by the end of his life his nervous system was so ravaged that the lightest touch hurt him or intensified his feeling – unfortunately real, not imagined – that he was suffocating.

And he was amortal. His consistency was remarkable; his core of principle and personality remained unchanged by the terrible changes happening to him, which combined into a facsimile of the worst kind of ageing. He developed over the three decades I was privileged to know him, in the sense that his understanding of the world and of the human heart increased, but the 19-year-old Richard never 'died', in Dawkins's terms.

As for his actual death, a thing as unlike a gentle transition from one phase of life to another as it's possible to imagine, Richard knew it was coming but never *accepted* that it was coming, and did his best to ignore its shadow. When he was well – and even when he wasn't but could still hoick himself around on crutches or, later, power up a succession of electric wheelchairs that proved only slightly more reliable than his body – he kept busy. He campaigned for his vision of social justice in his job for the International Transport Workers' Federation and devoted much of his leisure time to lobbying for disability rights.

An early – and enthusiastic – adopter of new technologies, in 1986 he connected the Apple Macintosh Plus he'd persuaded me to buy to the embryonic Web, using my landline to dial a number in America and accidentally leaving it connected for the best part of a day. As his ataxia worsened he deployed technology to perform functions that were becoming too difficult for him. Kurzweil Voice, a software that allowed him to dictate emails to his computer, worked reasonably well for a while.

Eventually Richard's speech became too strangulated for Ray Kurzweil's invention to decipher. 'Like Christianity in the past, the modern cult of science lives on the hope of miracles,' says John Gray, but science continued to disappoint Richard.[119] Denied its salvation and deprived of any spiritual or earthly consolations, my friend latched on to another idea: assisted dying. If he could select the time and manner of his death, that might remove some of its sting.

AMORTALS SEEK TO DEFEAT DEATH by ignoring it or conquering it. When those options are removed, we attempt to control it instead. Assisted dying crops up frequently in the amortal ontology. The idea that it's possible to die painlessly and of our own volition consoles us. Acting on the idea is another matter. Richard often talked to me about the possibility that I might help him to die. He never asked me to do so.

That may simply have been out of consideration. I watched Richard silently suffer the pangs of an unrequited love he would never declare in case the object of his affections reciprocated and damned herself to sharing his difficult life. In the same way, he must have reflected on the legal and emotional repercussions that helping him to die would surely entail. But he was never *ready* to die, even when the concept of quality of life no longer retained a shred of meaning and his physical discomfort was intense. His horror of extinction was greater.

Amortality is underpinned by that horror, which appears to be most effectively mitigated by membership of the enveloping, prescriptive, proscriptive mainstream religions, not their cut-and-paste New Age incarnations. Congregations are shrinking, even in Middle America. Eighty-six per cent of Americans described themselves as Christian in 1990; by 2008 the figure had dropped to 76 per cent.[120] That's still quite a high proportion, but the same study found that less than 70 per cent of Americans believe in the traditional theological concept of a personal God.[121] 'Christian' has come to be an increasingly elastic term, its offer of post-mortem life supplemented with other reassuring myths, from astrology (our fate is written in the stars) to more esoteric notions of spirituality.

As the hold of mainstream religions weakened, so amortals multiplied. And many amortals are driven to try to address the absence of faith − or rather the consequences of that absence − that helped them into existence. As we shall see, amortals are often spiritual backpackers, thumbing lifts from one promising religious pitstop to the next. We are attracted to creeds that, like celestial resveratrol, promise us we can continue to indulge ourselves and still be delivered from the consequences. Unfortunately the ability of such creeds to deliver us from fear of death is limited.

For the demi-believer or the non-believer, immersive faith is a mysterious phenomenon that we observe but cannot ever viscerally comprehend. We can sometimes persuade ourselves into experiencing a semblance of such faith, much as Ray Kurzweil 'experienced' his transformation into Ramona, but we will never be free of a kernel of doubt, or self-consciousness, that dilutes the impact of such experiences. Unlike Dawkins, my atheism is neither a source of pride nor pleasure. I used to wish I had been brought up to believe, if only to have the chance to test and reject those beliefs, in the way that actor Richard Wilson describes:

My father was an elder of the Kirk; my mother was non-church-going and we were never really allowed to ask why that was. Why she didn't have to go to church. I used to go with my father, really mainly to keep him awake because he kept falling asleep. My father was a champion sleeper.

When I was still in my teens my two art school chums and I had a very serious attempt to find out about religion. We were losing our religion and we had meetings with a Catholic priest and we had meetings with a Presbyterian and a Wee Free, so we were very methodical about it.

I lost any faith I had when I was still in my teens.

My lack of religious education is still a source of regret. 'Scripture' lessons at an English secondary school involved an ineffectual attempt by a virginal teacher to prepare pubescent girls for conjugal relations. ('You'll find you use muscles you didn't know you had. Rather like a strenuous hike in the Peak District.') In an attempt to redress that educational lacuna (religion, not sex), and to understand how a disaffection with organised religion presaged the rise of amortality, I went to the experts: the Archbishop of Canterbury, the head of the worldwide Anglican communion; Rosa Sayer, a lifelong Christian; and ex-rabbinical student and comedian Josh Howie and his rabbi Thomas Salamon.

I did not investigate Islam, although perhaps I should have done so. Unlike other faiths, Islam is expanding its influence and reach in Europe and the US. But its adherents remain a small minority in these cultures and it also seemed to me that the faith in most of its expressions offers the following antibodies against amortality: a strong narrative and sense of community, the assignment of roles within the family and society, the promise of eternal life. Amortality and Islam, from an insider view of the former and outsider take on the the latter, wouldn't appear easily to commingle.

LAMBETH PALACE HAS HOUSED successive Archbishops of Canterbury since the 13th century. Its current incumbent Rowan Williams kindly hosted a discussion of amortality with his special adviser, Tim Livesey, and three external guests: the psychologist Oliver James; the Catholic priest and Dominican friar Timothy Radcliffe, author of *What Is the Point of Being Christian?*; and George Pitcher, an Anglican priest and journalist whose latest book declares its position on the cover: *A Time To Live: The Case Against Assisted Suicide and Euthanasia.*

As we talked, dying blossom drifted past the Archbishop's windows and, across the river in Westminster, an unfolding drama underscored the limits of temporal power and the haemorrhaging of faith in temporal institutions. Parliamentary elections held five days before, on 6 May 2010, had delivered Britain's first hung parliament for 36 years. Voters, it seemed, had lost faith in parties and politicians. The parties and politicians were struggling to come to terms with the result and the Labour government was in its death throes, its prime minister as reluctant to cede as my grandmother Jane on her death bed.

In Lambeth Palace, the discourse also centred on death – the church's role in preparing its followers for the end of life, the amortal fear of extinction, the reflexive desire for control. 'Our ancestors didn't control their death, but they laid hold of their death,' said Radcliffe. 'A death was something that you did; it didn't just happen to you. You prepared for it, it was ritualised and it was part of a drama in which the dying person had a central role.'

Williams nodded, mulled, replied. He is a tall man who speaks in a still, small voice. The rest of us leaned forward to hear his response. 'Assisted dying connects very clearly with people's fear of dependence,' the Archbishop said.

> Age normally has entailed dependence; a lot of our culture encourages us to think dependence is not the ideal state to be in. So whether it's control or carrying on as far as possible with all

the activities you've been used to, it's about fending off that awareness that at some point you're quite likely to be dependent.

I remember one of my teachers, a very complex, difficult man, talking to me in his old age about his first real experience of surgery and saying what a shock it had been to realise how much he was pushing back against being completely in somebody's hands.

And I'm also inclined to connect it with the litigious mood around some medical questions. It's as if the risk of putting yourself in somebody else's hands is something you have to bolster all round with protective measures because you can't cope with the idea that there just may be some circumstances you can't control.

The amortal instinct is to fend off exactly that awareness. As amortality takes hold, ever larger numbers of people reject or blot out the notion that we will be forced to rely on others. We flinch from considering the possibility that we may not remain physically or mentally able to go on doing the same things. We tell ourselves stories we don't entirely believe about being left to die on ice floes or taking trips to Switzerland. I hoped that this company – four leading representatives of organised religion and a psychologist – might be able to identify the exact points of rupture between the world as it was when organised religions held greater sway and the fractured, secular society we now inhabit, and to articulate how these ruptures are impacting our perceptions of age and ageing.

Interestingly none of the participants disputed the premise of the conversation: that the church had lost influence, both in terms of numbers of adherents and the strength of their adherence, and that this decline fed through into social change that the church would once have moderated, not only from the pulpit but through the mores of community life based around the church. Their views on the nature of this change and its other drivers did not diverge in most respects from secular analyses. 'What happens,' mused Williams, 'if you get to a cultural place where there's not really very much to enable you to hand over or pass on all the language of generations coming and going, yielding to a rising generation?'

Livesey concurred, describing what sociologist James Côté would recognise as the decoupling of the life course, the weakening forces of cultural transmission: 'The young right now are trying to make sense of the world that is incredibly different, even from the one that I grew up in,' he said. 'And I'm [only] 50. In traditional cultures, religions [and] societies, the story was about *assuming* your place. It was largely determined for you, socially or religiously, and so it was about learning how to be that kind of person at that stage in your life. Whereas now, in this individualistic society, it's all about *finding* your place. There is no conferment. I think a lot of us are finding it extraordinarily difficult to know what our place is.' Pitcher deplored the legacy of 'growing individualism and the markets of consumerism, the booming 1980s and the "me generation" that grew out of it.'

The key distinction between these observations and my own is one of interpretation. Surrounded by the austere beauty of Lambeth Palace amid the accumulated symbols and furnishings of centuries of tradition, all these men seemed bereft or anxious – or in James's case, angry – about the changes we were discussing, as if upstart phenomena such as amortality might sweep away all that beauty, rather than augmenting it, as I would suppose. On this we agreed: the culture that spawned amortality undervalues age and shies from death. There is a rising fear of dependency, not least because the family and social structures that used to soften dependency have eroded. We accept far fewer lessons from family, church and state. But to my mind, this last observation promises opportunity as well as torturous uncertainties: not least the chance to try new modes of ageing and to slough off outdated prejudices about age.

Williams linked our increasing 'dependency anxiety' to precisely the sorts of reductive views of older people that ignore 'a certain reciprocity;

the old person has reached that stage in life where they have something distinct to give as well as having to receive the dependence. The more we erode the sense that there is a narrative, there's a story to human life, there are stages of life, the more you homogenise your experience.'

The idea of amortal homogeneity – the shark moving unchanging through different environments, rather than the lobster growing and shedding its shells – seemed the locus of greatest concern for Williams and his guests. James suggested that amortals risked failing to make 'certain psychological maturational developments' necessary to be comfortable inside one's skin. That brought Radcliffe back to a meditation on religions' role in preparing their adherents to cope with frailty and death:

> I met one of my elderly brethren, 86, trying to climb into the fridge this morning. He's entirely blind, he's been blind since birth, and as he gets older he gets more and more disorientated and so you're always having to find him and say well you're actually in the refectory now, that's the fridge. He's extraordinarily content and part of his contentment is he knows that he's on the way to infinite happiness. That's fundamental for how he lives; becoming increasingly disabled, near death as well, he really has a belief that he is on his way to infinite happiness.
>
> There was a big shift in that narrative on this. In the first centuries of Christianity, the basic story was that God became human so we might become divine. So you lived a story of you're on your way to radical transformation, divinisation. That was lost, partly anyway, in the 16th and 17th century so that all you're promised, basically, is ordinary domestic bliss. Maybe forever, but you lose the great adventure of transformation. And once all you can imagine is more of the same forever, then this ceases to make sense of a lot of suffering along the way and dependency and sickness and facing death.

'The homogenisation extends beyond the grave?' I asked.

'That's right, homogenisation beyond death,' Pitcher replied.

'Unless you say,' added Oliver James, 'I don't fancy more of the same, for whatever reason, so you go over to Switzerland.'

The notion of assisted death as an act of selfishness permeated the discussion. This reinforced the participants' wider assumptions about amortality: that an elision of the stages of life implies that amortals are all caught in amber at similar stages of selfish immaturity. I trust that the depiction of amortal diversity and amortal achievement in this book helps to debunk that misconception. And to the notion that amortality is a synonym for solipsism I give a two-word riposte: Richard Flint.

Richard would have enjoyed taking on Williams and his guests in a debate. The amortal actor Richard Wilson would question the point of such a debate. 'I find it really difficult to understand why there are so many learned people, like the Archbishop of Canterbury, who spend their lives talking about a book that just has no basis for anything at all,' he says. I know what he means. But inside the palace, listening to the humanity and wisdom of Williams and his fellow participants, it occurs to me that my misconceptions of Christianity are at least as distorting as theirs of amortality. Moreover, all of us, amortal or not, believing or unbelieving, are involved in the same struggle, to make the most of life and the least of death.

HERBERT GRÖNEMEYER, a German rock star and actor, remembers his father as 'the happiest person on earth', not a description one expects of a Calvinist, never mind one whose life was shaped by loss. At four Grönemeyer Senior lost his own father in a mining accident and as a young conscript he lost an arm at Stalingrad. Despite these experiences and his physical disability, he remained a pillar of strength, intimidated by nothing, not even, it seemed, death. 'He said this nice thing to me once,' remembers Grönemeyer. 'My father said: "I'm growing like a tree and in the shadow of my being strong you can grow. I'll shelter you. And the moment you're tall, I'll fall and it's fine." Two or three years before he died, I was with him in Switzerland, in the pool, and suddenly he said, "When I die, will I see my mother and my father?" Out of the blue. I never spoke with him, ever, about death in that sense. And I was so surprised this 85-year-old man who was very strong was suddenly childlike.'

Even old soldiers are afraid of the dark. The closer we come to death, the more our nerves – and our faith, if we're lucky enough to have such – are tested. At 94, Rosa Sayer told me she had no qualms about dying. Indeed, she had planned her funeral to the last detail. Her son, Richard, shies away from the subject. 'My mother is a strong Christian and there-fore doesn't have a fear of mortality,' he says. 'I just like to pretend those things aren't going to happen.' Recently retired after a long career as a cardiothoracic surgeon, Richard Sayer has witnessed death more often than most, but as part of a storyline that casts mortality as an enemy he was trained to defeat and death, if it occurs, as failure: the patient hasn't fought hard enough; Richard and his team haven't succeeded in keeping the patient alive. His mother's narrative is more cheerful. 'Well, I do believe, I do believe in the afterlife, I do,' she says. 'I do believe that I shall meet my parents and my husband Charlie.'

At 88 and facing surgery, she experienced a moment of doubt. She asked the then rector of her local church if she could talk to him.

> 'Of course you can,' he said, 'I'll pick you up, and you come and have lunch with us.' Which I did.
>
> And I said to him, 'What if I don't come through?'
>
> 'Well,' he said, 'I'll put it like this. There's two ways about this,' he said. 'One is that you'll meet up with Charlie, or the other one is you'll still be with us. So,' he said, 'the choice is yours.'
>
> I thought that was lovely. So I'm still here.

A year after I first met Rosa, she invited me to her cottage outside Cambridge. By now 95, she was a handsome woman, as pin-neat as her front room, and on this occasion wearing a vibrant burnt-orange cashmere sweater. 'I love clothes. I've always loved clothes. And I've often been complimented on my clothes,' she said. She lives a stone's throw from the church she's attended since moving to the village 60 years ago. As we walked to lunch at a local pub – Rosa setting a vigorous pace – we peered over its flint walls and Rosa discussed, in turn, each of the rectors she has outstayed. ('He was absolutely lovely'; 'He was a man of God'; 'I loved him'.)

She was noticeably cooler about its current incumbent. 'He just came, he came in and changed everything on the first Sunday he was there. He changed everything, without telling anyone, he didn't hold a committee meeting or anything and when we arrived on that Sunday the whole service was different.'

The new rector has become more inclusive and she's come round to his way of doing God's business, she said; she praised him as a kind man. But she also admitted that the institution that has been, along with family, the centre of her life had lost some of its allure: 'I used to love going over there on a Sunday morning, absolutely; as I used to say, I'd go in with joy in my heart, but [after the new rector arrived] I could just as easily have not gone and that's not me.'

Regime change isn't the only cause of Rosa's disaffection. The church, which at every previous stage of her life helped to define that stage and her place in its community, has now given her the impression she is surplus to the community's requirements. 'I expect some people think I'm an old fuddy-duddy, I don't know, but I feel I move with the times. I really do,' she confided.

I get hurt at times, very much, with the Church in particular …
I feel left out a little bit, you know. Because I was so active, in anything and everything. And I can do it, that's the point.

The cooking is one thing. Any events or anything that we had, I was always up in the forefront really. With Harvest Supper, this is only a silly little simple thing, but we always finished up with apple pie and cream and I always used to make about 15 apple pies and now I don't do anything like that.

Lots of things, I don't get asked. I don't get asked to do things. And I wish I did. I could do them. I can do them.

Ageism rears its head even in institutions that purport to value age. Rosa is sharp and funny and fit and suffused with the values that Christianity supposedly represents: a sense of the common good, of doing unto others as one would be done by – pretty much the same impulses that burned so bright in atheist/Raelian Richard Flint and are easily discerned in Rosa's own Richard. To spend time with her is also to catch a last glimpse of disappearing worlds; her Norfolk girlhood, apprenticeship to a milliner at 17, her marriage to Charlie at the worryingly late age of 24, her first sight of a car and, wonder of wonders, an aeroplane. She remembers her mother complaining about the noise on their first radio, the music of the day. She still resists suggestions from her children that she get a computer. ('I don't go online. I could do. I don't want to.')

Running through these reminiscences, the words in her stick of rock, is 'the church', a benign presence and second home. Her daughter takes her back to Norfolk several times in the year 'and we go through the village, it's a very small village, and we circle the village and end up at the church just to see how things are. And it's open all day; although it stands a long way away from the village somebody opens it at nine o'clock in the morning and closes it at sunset. And so you can go in, which I find very nice.'

The church – whichever church, in Norfolk or in Cambridgeshire – reliably supplied Rosa with many of the commodities that prove hard to source in modern life: a sense of purpose and of history, a set of milestones and markers for development, community. The church gave her pastoral care when her husband died unexpectedly, aged 62, and a framework and focus to her life.

And barring a short wavering in confidence when she faced surgery, the church also gave her one of its greatest gifts: immunity to the mortal terrors that plague non-believers. Only once Rosa reached a biblical age, and the church responded by ceasing to value her, did that immunity fail. 'I went to a funeral, some time before Christmas,' she told me. 'And I've never experienced anything like it, I just had to come out. The coffin that stood there was mine. And I can't describe, standing there, at my own funeral, really, every time I looked at this coffin, it was my coffin. I had to apologise to several people but I just had to walk out and come home.'

TERROR MANAGEMENT THEORY explains religion as a defence against such visions. Rosa has developed doubts, but she spent some 90 years in enviable contentment. 'Religions are one way of managing terror, in fact a particularly good way, because it's a very strong system, generally with millions of followers, so you get a good consensus. And a very strong immortality formula, sometimes not just symbolic, but a literal promise of immortality,' says Professor Burke. Religious fundamentalism flourishes in communities that are most exposed to death, through poverty or conflict, he adds, echoing Renaissance thinker Michel de Montaigne's anguished question: 'With such frequent and ordinary examples passing before our eyes, how can we possibly rid ourselves of the thought of death and of the idea that at every moment it is gripping us by the throat?'[122]

Given its deadly history of persecution and conflict, Judaism might be expected to have developed a particularly concentrated immortality formula of the kind that proofs against amortality. Yet in researching this book it became apparent that Jews – at any rate the metropolitan Jews found in the ranks of my family, social and professional circles – are if anything slightly more prone to amortality than other groups.

There's one obvious reason: Jewishness is for many Jews a cultural identity and a genetic heritage as well as, and sometimes in place of, a belief system. Adriane Berg, the CEO of sales and marketing consultancy Generation Bold (motto: 'Youth: It Comes In All Ages'), tells me, 'I am spiritual. I do worship in my own faith of Judaism, but also meditate frequently and have been moved in both the Vatican and in Hindu

Temples.' Brooklyn-born Berg, 61, who also gives lectures and seminars, and runs a brace of websites, has written 13 books on personal finance including *How Not to Go Broke at 102*. I ask her about amortality: does it strike a chord? She tells me she is amortal. 'I rarely give up on old dreams,' she says. 'I just recast them.'

Charlie Ferber, a dentist with a special interest in 'non-surgical facial aesthetics' with a practice near Harley Street and a patient list entertainment publicists would kill for, is a believer but not a deeply observant one. He absorbed his relaxed attitudes from his father: 'We were having Yom Kippur, where you fast, so we went to synagogue, we did the Yom Kippur prayers, and then we came home and my father said, "It's lunchtime. But don't eat too much because we're fasting." And that's the way I am still now. I laugh about it, because I'm never strict. It's never 100 per cent with me, it's like OK, let's see what we can eat.'

Whatever it is that Ferber eats, it doesn't make him fat. He looks at least a decade younger than his chronological age. 'I'm 10 stone now, I was 10 stone [as a teenager],' he says. 'And I eat a lot. I don't smoke, I drink alcohol like everybody else, a few drinks here and there, I don't take drugs. I walk a lot, we walk miles and miles every week with the dog. I just keep fit. A lot of exercise. A huge amount of exercise. But I'm lucky I think, some people just put on weight. I'm too active to put on weight, so I was a skinny little kid. Now I'm still Charlie Boy at 58, still 10 stone.'

Ferber often refers to himself in the third person as 'Charlie Boy' and it's easy to see that boy, though harder to imagine how he's come through life so externally unmarked by his experiences. Born in Krakow in 1952 into the aftermath of horror (88 family members were exterminated in Auschwitz) Ferber's peripatetic childhood took him to Israel and Flatbush in Brooklyn and, after his mother succumbed to cancer, to Britain in February 1970.

'England was tough,' he says. 'I had been speaking English for five or six years, I had a strong Brooklyn accent, I come from an area where we had Barbra Streisand and Woody Allen, all these people were in my high school so it's very Brooklyn, you know, street. And that's what I spoke. So when I went to medical school and there were all these posh kids, I used to speak louder, I was more brash, I was a New Yorker. They didn't like me at all. Complete culture shock. If it wasn't for the fact that I was half-decent at what I did, decent pair of hands and decent brain, I would have struggled. But I'm a fighter so I made sure that I do better and I work harder.'

Work harder, play harder still: Ferber, rather like a vampire but with much better teeth, used to come alive at night; he was a self-described 'playboy, a hedonistic party animal'. The play ethic is still strong – patients shouldn't expect an appointment on Wednesday, always kept free to 'recover a little bit', often by spending the day at the kind of club he now likes to frequent, a tennis club near his north London home, playing intensely competitive games against an 80-year-old semi-professional. ('Two years ago I couldn't take a set off him. That's what I want to be when I'm 80. I think 80 is a good age to say, "Charlie took a set off me," don't you? So when I'm 80 and some younger guys take a set off me, I'll say, "Good on you." But at 75 I want to kick ass still.')

He might have continued to inhabit the flickering world of transient pleasures if salvation hadn't arrived in the shape of his future wife, Mandy. He was ready for a companion with 'family values', he says. 'A lot of the girls I was meeting in wine bars, nightclubs, they were good fun girls but they were just never giving me the impression they were going to settle down themselves; they never hinted at the idea of being serious. It was all fun, fun, fun ... Wild chicks can be great but they can also be a pain in the arse. Mandy was just steady, she was just a normal, sane, sensitive, great girl.'

It was, says Ferber, Mandy's idea to convert to Judaism. 'I actually had very few Jewish girlfriends. Mandy thought ahead. Guys think for today. If we were blessed with children, then she wanted identity for the child. [They would go on to have one daughter, Imogen.] Plus she actually quite liked the history. She didn't know anything about Judaism or the Holocaust or anything like that, she was a typical Middle England girl. There was no religious aspect of it at all.'

Jews often combine a strong sense of cultural identity with an apparent flexibility about the terms of membership of that identity. The realities are often rather different. When Monique Duffy committed to life with comedian Josh Howie, she also opted to convert to Judaism before they married. The process took two years and culminated at Westminster Synagogue in a ceremony led by Rabbi Thomas Salamon. At the end of the service, I was asked to put my signature to a certificate attesting to Monique's conversion. (Josh's mother Lynne Franks would have performed this role, but she was in Australia competing in the reality TV show *I'm A Celebrity ... Get Me Out Of Here.*)

The certificate, also signed by Monique, acknowledged that despite her conversion any children she had would not be considered Jewish by the more orthodox strands of Judaism. But her baby, who noisily contributed to Howie and Salamon's musings on amortality when we met at the north London flat secured thanks in part to Howie's grandmother's loan of the deposit money, is being raised as a Jew, culturally and religiously, and Reform Jews will happily accept the child and his mother as their own.

The contradictions in Jewish culture arise, at least in part, from a historical imperative that has seen Jews resisting the imposition of externally generated – and often toxic – images of themselves in favour of hastily constructed alternatives. A cohort accustomed to setting its own definitions is hardly likely to be cowed by societal prescriptions and proscriptions about age. And there's something else that makes Jews especially inclined to amortality: Judaism doesn't make big promises about what happens after death. 'The Hebrew Bible does not mention or speak about afterlife,' Salamon told us.

On the contrary, Job is saying, 'Why do you want to kill me? If you kill me there will be no one to praise you.' The Bible talks about Satan, talks about God, talks about angels, but it's another world; it's the world of God as opposed to the world into which you're going to go when you die.

And the concept of afterlife is very vague. It came about possibly of the Greek influence in the 2nd and 3rd century. In rabbinical literature the idea arises that every Jew has a place in the world to come, but it doesn't say what the world to come is.

There is, however, a concept – again it may have been of the Greek influence – that when one dies the soul hovers and is unsettled. And it takes 12 months after death for the soul to settle, but again, we don't know where. That's why we say Kaddish, we say a prayer for the dead which actually doesn't talk about death at all. The Kaddish exalts God and calls for peace. It is said over 11 months, although it takes 12 months for the soul to settle, because only for a totally wicked person would you say it for 12 months. But as none of us are totally wicked, you say it for 11 months.

That blurry vision isn't quite as reassuring as the prospect of heaven as a kind of celestial dinner party reuniting friends and family that so many Christians apparently share. Jewish teaching focuses more on life than on death, says Salamon. A member of the synagogue recently died. As he lay in his hospital bed, in some distress and physical discomfort, he summoned his daughter. Did he wish the medical intervention to cease so he could die in peace? Not at all. The dying man begged his daughter to urge the medical staff to do everything in their power to keep him alive. He was 105. 'There is a meditation in the funeral prayer book which says that when a person dies let it not be said that he was good, but that he was good to life,' Salamon explains.

Judaism very much believes in preservation of life, that's why he was clinging to it. He said, 'If God wants to take me, he can, but I'm still here.' He was right that in Judaism it's the preservation of life that is of the utmost importance. We have to be good to life, as opposed to life being good to us ...

The whole concept of 'love your neighbour as yourself' doesn't mean that I have to abandon everything to love my neighbour and do everything for my neighbour. What it means in Jewish thinking is that you have to be good to yourself, then you have to be good to your closest and dearest and the most loved ones, and then you have to be good to others. As the proverb says, 'Don't do to others what you wouldn't like to be done to you.' And as long as you can adhere to this, that's a great thing.

Religion has tended to shore up collectivist instincts but this reading of Judaism puts the individual firmly at the centre of his world. The idea that you have to be good to yourself to be able to be good to others isn't a million miles from Cenegenics patient Maria White's observation that 'if you're not at your very best, how can you possibly be your best to your spouse, to your family, to your profession'. The search for nirvana, at least in Westernised interpretations, carries similar overtones. So, too, do many of the secular therapies popular with amortals that are explored in the next chapter.

Lynne Franks has experimented with a range of different belief systems and philosophies. Of course, however many faiths she samples, she'll never not be Jewish.

Perhaps her longest flirtation has been with Buddhism, which might seem to go against her amortal instincts. Amortals may appear impervious to change and Buddhism is a religion that more than any other stresses impermanence, *anicca*. Yet the instruction to 'be here now', in the catchy formulation of Jewish Harvard-psychologist-turned-spiritual-guru Richard Alpert a.k.a. Ram Dass, actually melds neatly with amortalist impulses. To live agelessly is to live in the moment, which is why our actual age so often takes us by surprise. ('I'm *how* old? When did that happen?')

Western – and amortal – interpretations of Buddhism also tend to stress and simplify the idea of reincarnation until it resembles an afterlife or series of afterlives. And for amortals it is an attractively devolved faith, investing its adherents with the powers to change their own realities, in more and less profound ways. 'I believe in reincarnation,' Dr Robert Willix, the chief medical officer of Cenegenics tells me. 'I believe that I've been here before, that even if there's really no reincarnated state I still have the DNA that can lead to me, that is a compilation of all the DNAs before me. So I have some connection to somebody in my DNA, it's just inevitable that I would be connected, we're all connected to our lineage so whatever that lineage is for me I believe that I have memories of it. And I think that there's good evidence that you can recover those memories.'

Amortals are experts at filleting religions or recasting them to a shape that allows them to define themselves, rather than be defined, and to run at life, rather than walking in sedate step behind a processional. Willix, 'just slightly under 100' (69 at the time of the interview), 'minored in theology in college and studied Christianity, read the Bible every day from the age of 18 until I was probably 40', he says. 'I've studied with a shaman in Peru, I studied Kabbalah, so my spirituality is not religion. I believe that each of us finds a way to whatever we call the higher power, I choose to call it God, you can call it whatever you want, I don't care, I think that I believe that there's some creative force, it may be the big bang, but there's a creative force. Something started a spark.'

Such faith is often partial and conditional; this allows amortals to pick and choose the religion, or the part of the religion, that strikes a chord, but it diminishes their protection against mortality salience. Here's Franks again:

> Seventy-five per cent of me believes, if not 85 per cent, in reincarnation and the soul surviving and coming back. Fifteen to 20 per cent says, 'Don't talk nonsense.' And 100 per cent of me believes in some kind of cosmic energy, whether it's internal or external, some kind of strong powerful force. Well, 99 per cent of me believes that; 1 per cent says, 'Don't talk nonsense.'
>
> I have this real split because I'm a very pragmatic person, very logical, and I like to see what I believe. The other side of me

is very intuitive and spiritual and creative. You know, it's the left-brain-right-brain thing, and so my right brain says absolutely, open to all, Buddhism, Hinduism, everything has some wonderful parts to it.

I don't know what my true belief system is except that it's based on values and human beings living to their highest potential. We are all human beings and we all make mistakes and we're all the results of our influences and environments from a young age and so we have these patterns that are part of our personality and our psyche and our behaviour. I have this real science-versus-God internal dialogue, and I believe in all of it, really.

Reality television presented Franks with a rare opportunity to face down her deepest fear, which, like Rosa Sayer's, centres on a nightmare vision of confinement in a coffin. The producers of *I'm A Celebrity … Get Me Out Of Here*, a reality TV contest which devises different ways for the voting public to impose stress and humiliation on a circus of famous and not-so-famous participants, nagged Franks to reveal her phobias. 'I do get claustrophobic and it's part of my breathing problems, the thought of being locked up, in a coffin,' she says. 'And they did put me down a dark hole, and they did throw rats and eels and goodness knows what else at me, and I did survive. I survived it fine and so it was interesting, I was in the dark and I was having stuff thrown at me. That's all part of my fear of mortality, the fear of death, and I survived. So maybe I'll survive death too.'

Ray Kurzweil would likely reassure Franks that survival technology will soon be available. Wide strains of science pour cold water on that flickering hope, while reminding us brutally of our insignificance. Jean-Claude Carrière nicely illustrates that point in his description of fellow philosopher Emile Cioran reacting to the notion of multiple universes: '"In my bathroom this morning," said Cioran (or words to that effect), "I heard an astronomer on the radio talking about hundreds of millions of suns. I immediately stopped shaving: why bother to wash and get dressed any more?" Cioran is not alone: the sense of the infinite can be profoundly discouraging.'[123]

But science can also dispel that sense of the infinite and promises deliverance from the ultimate infinity: death. That's science, Jim, but not as we know it. By relocating science inside belief systems, some New Age religions tame and defang its terrors, resolving what Franks terms the 'science-versus-God internal dialogue', and harnessing 'science' to promises of immortality. L. Ron Hubbard's Church of Scientology, for example, rejects the mercilessly random Darwinian theory of evolution in favour of an alien space opera involving scientifically advanced superbeings.

Scientology emerged from a form of psychotherapy called Dianetics, also devised by Hubbard, and now has a celebrity sales force that includes Tom Cruise, Kirstie Alley, Juliette Lewis, John Travolta and his wife Kelly Preston. Preston recently contributed a fulsome tribute to Scientology on its special celebrity website: 'If you want your life to be richer and fuller, and you just want to be really happy, then there you go. You need Scientology. I have much more care and love and responsibility for groups and mankind. I had always been quite insular with myself, my family and friends before. But now, I really feel great responsibility for mankind and people. My interests are so much higher.'[124]

IT CAN BE TRICKY to distinguish newer religions from newer forms of therapy, as the next chapter explains. Both tend to assume personal contentment should be the primary goal. Both tend to assume an understanding of the world proceeds only from an understanding of oneself. In 1967, The Beatles sought enlightenment from the Maharishi Mahesh Yogi in India. Ringo's lack of enthusiasm for the project could be divined from his luggage – his suitcase was full of baked beans. He left the ashram once he'd consumed the last tin. His road to spirituality proved winding, taking him through a period of post-Beatles excess that eventually culminated in rehab. The 12-steps programme did for him what the Maharishi could not. 'I was on my knees,' he told me when I interviewed him in 2007.[125] Since leaving rehab he kneels to a greater power, punctuating conversations with 'peace' and 'love', and writing lyrics such as 'You've got to love every breath that you breathe/ Look at the sky and believe'.

It often takes several attempts before amortals find the thing that suits them – and the search itself can be as satisfying as the result, as we'll see. Ellen, a shiatsu practitioner, took herself off to a silent Zen Buddhist retreat in France for two weeks, where participants meditated for eight hours daily. Sitting for such protracted periods was 'unbelievably painful', she remembers. Was it a useful experience? 'No,' she says decisively. 'It was the end of my searching. I do still meditate, but not on long retreats. I became a whirling dervish. That makes me happy.'

A different set of repetitive movements are often central to Raelian happiness: those associated with love-making. Sex should be freed from guilt, says Marcus Wenner, who organised the meeting with Rael that Richard and I attended 30 years ago and now devises 'happiness academies' for Rael's followers. 'The whole point is to be happy,' says Wenner. 'That's the bottom line, really.'

Happiness, it turns out, is achieved by dispensing with externally imposed concepts of how to live. Wenner's summary of Raelian belief could sound like a manifesto for a particular kind of amortality:

[Raelism] encourages people to do anything at any stage in their life and live one's dream whether one's 80 years old or 20 years old. Members tend to not have too many children, and it challenges the whole family unit, the nuclear family unit, encouraging people to be free, to have a certain freedom in terms of who they want to be, what their sexuality is and whether it's gay, bi or hetero.

It's against the idea of marriage, because marriage is a form of ownership. The Raelian movement very much encourages love, but not any behaviour which harms us, so if you've got people who are just staying together because they're afraid to go elsewhere, well [Raelism] definitely encourages them to go elsewhere, in a mutually beneficial way, and meet other people and start new relationships.

Wenner, 50, childless and in the final stages of study to become a doctor, used to be the top Raelian in Britain. These days that position is occupied by Glenn Carter, who may have gained useful preparation for the role when he starred as the eponymous hero of *Jesus Christ Superstar* in London, on Broadway and in a celluloid version of the biblical musical. Wenner remains in the Raelian hierarchy as a 'level 5', one of the 50-odd members licensed to determine policy and to elect a new leader should the need arise.

His happiness academies include seminars that in another context might be described as instruction in healthy ageing. 'It's very neurological, neuro-biologically based, looking at how neurones function,' he says. 'Of course one's body grows old, but the mind need not grow old if one uses it.' An organisation called Clonaid, associated with Raelism, proposes a more radical antidote to humans' unfortunate habit of getting old and dying. A private company touting itself as 'the world's leading provider of reproductive human cloning services', Clonaid, run by another level-5 Raelian, claimed in 2002 to have cloned a human baby, Eve. Scientists have not been given access to Eve to verify the claims.[126]

Christianity prepares its flock for death; Judaism encourages its faithful to focus on life; but newer creeds and therapies, made in the image of the amortal, promise to negate the need for any such considerations. Amortals believe in science and rely on distraction. Therapy culture offers the perfect meld of science and distraction.

4

the amortal mind
TRAVELLING HOPEFULLY

'Onstage I'm the happiest person in the world.'
Britney Spears

'They tried to make me go to rehab
I said no, no, no.'
Amy Winehouse, 'Rehab'

'Most things may never happen: this one will,
And realisation of it rages out
In furnace-fear when we are caught without
People or drink.'
Philip Larkin, 'Aubade'

THE SALES ASSISTANT APOLOGISED. She'd like to be able to affix the watch-strap bought to replace one that had just snapped, but she couldn't do it. 'My boyfriend left me,' she explained. 'And he took my *self*.'

'He took your self?'

'He took my self. Since he left me I haven't been able to find my self. Without my self I can't use my hands.'

This exchange, in a Los Angeles department store in 1992, seemed like a piece of cultural exotica, typical of the therapy culture flourishing on

America's West Coast. How different things were back in England, where even close friends hesitated to confide relationship troubles to each other and therapy-speak, the distinctive vocabulary and cadences of the therapised, sounded as foreign as, well, French. This wasn't necessarily a sign that the typical Brit felt *bien dans sa peau*, to use a phrase that several times cropped up in the Lambeth Palace discussion. But Britons and a broad swathe of buttoned-up northern Europe tended to believe that admitting to pain – of body or soul – made it worse.

Their royal highnesses the Windsors were classic exponents of this bracing approach, which eschewed public displays of any kind (when a starter pistol was fired at Prince Charles, his only visible reaction was to fiddle with his cufflinks). If one fell off one's horse, one jolly well got back on one's horse. If one succumbed to postnatal depression and bulimia, one jolly well got back on one's horse. 'Maybe I was the first person ever to be in this family who ever had a depression or was ever openly tearful,' Princess Diana told Martin Bashir in November 1995. 'And obviously that was daunting, because if you've never seen it before, how do you support it?'[127]

This interview marked a turning point for the royal family – the institution's mystery had preserved its mastery, but after Diana's illuminating confessional it proved impossible to restore the conventions of privacy and respect that had protected the monarchy. Yet the bigger significance of the interview was signalled in Diana's casual use of therapy-speak and the assumption, underpinning the interview, that the act of giving the interview was of itself therapeutic. She had self-harmed and suffered the eating disorder bulimia, the People's Princess admitted: 'You inflict it upon yourself because your self-esteem is at a low ebb, and you don't think you're worthy or valuable.' In the following exchange, she envisaged a public role for herself as an avatar of restored self-esteem, leading others not yet so fortunate to redemption.

Diana: 'I've been in a privileged position for 15 years. I've got tremendous knowledge about people and how to communicate. I've learned that, I've got it, and I want to use it … I'm not a political animal but I think the biggest disease this world suffers from in this day and age is the disease of people feeling unloved, and I know that I can give love for a minute, for half an hour, for a day, for a month, but I can give – I'm very happy to do that and I want to do that.'

Bashir: 'Do you think that the British people are happy with you in your role?'

Diana: 'I think the British people need someone in public life to give affection, to make them feel important, to support them, to give them light in their dark tunnels. I see it as a possibly unique role, and yes, I've had difficulties, as everybody has witnessed over the years, but let's now use the knowledge I've gathered to help other people in distress.'

TV therapist and author Dr Drew Pinsky might well perceive in Diana's conviction that her embrace could extend so wide more than a hint of narcissistic personality disorder, as he describes the condition in his book *The Mirror Effect*. Her words also pointed to the pervasiveness of the culture that only three years before had struck me as uniquely Californian. 'Diana's confession resonated with the new common sense that perceives low self-esteem as the principal cause of not only individual unhappiness, but also of much larger social problems,' wrote Frank Furedi, Professor of Sociology at the University of Kent and author of the influential book, *Therapy Culture*.[128] In this culture, the quest for self-esteem is conflated with the idea of accepting oneself *as one is*, unchanged, unchanging, as Furedi explained:

The passive narrative of the self-promoted today acquires its apogee with the celebration of self-esteem. Its advocates continually remind people of the virtue of the unconditional acceptance of the self. This static, conservative view of the self represents a rejection of previous, more ambitious calls for 'changing yourself', 'improving yourself' or for 'transcending the self'. Instead, the call for self-acceptance is a round-about way of avoiding change. Such a conservative orientation towards the future is clearly reflected within the role of therapy itself.[129]

Therapy culture is not an amortal invention, but it sprang from some of the same roots as amortality – the decline of organised religion, the erosion of received ideas about place and behaviour triggering a search for new modes. And the newer incarnations of therapy that offer momentum without any estimated arrival times are an attractive proposition to amortals, who will always prefer to travel hopefully than to arrive at the inescapable destinations of mortality salience and mortality itself. A 'journey' in therapy-speak is a desirable end in itself. Every reality TV show, every celebrity magazine, is an exercise in this new form of travel journalism. (The word crops up on the cover of *Hello!* almost as often as Angelina Jolie and they frequently coincide, as in this 2008 headline: SUPER MUM! MEET ANGELINA JOLIE, THE ULTIMATE 21ST CENTURY MOTHER – INSIDE HER INCREDIBLE JOURNEY.[130])

Therapy and therapy culture purport to provide a set of techniques for uncovering truths and then dealing with them; they can just as effectively be deployed as distraction from those truths. And amortals' love of distraction keeps therapists in business. As a young amortal, Woody Allen embarked on a course of psychoanalysis. Quizzed by chatshow host Dick Cavett in 1971 about how he would recognise the point at which his analysis had reached its conclusion, Allen joked: 'I don't know if you're ever really done. I know that certain characteristics about me are different now than they were when I started analysis. I started when I was 22 and I'm now 35, so I have aged. That's something. When I have sexual relations with someone I can now think of that person, rather than someone else, which is an enormous step forward to me.'[131]

Arguably many of today's popular therapies are not geared to teaching us to focus on other people; they encourage us to be good to ourselves, however we understand that concept. Since amortals often see therapy as a way of being good to oneself as well as a way of learning to be good to oneself, the amortal appetite for trying new therapies can be prodigious. One amortal, a successful businesswoman in her forties and veteran of multiple therapies, defends her therapy habit. A therapeutic intervention can help her to feel well in the skin, she says. 'It doesn't change the world, it just moves the dial.'

She has spent eight days laughing, crying and punching pillows as a participant in the Hoffman Process ('the last day of the course was the happiest I've ever felt') and once even checked into rehab ('it was the best six weeks of my life'). She's done 'Landmark, Cottonwood, EST – I'm always searching for the truth'. She pays regular visits to a psychotherapist patronised by 'everyone in London' – to prove the point she reels off some of the most prominent names in British media and entertainment.

She shows no evidence of drug or alcohol dependency and never has done; she appears cheerful and energetic; she has strong relationships with her children and her friends; she is widely admired (for her professional achievements and her indefatigable humour and physical beauty) and deeply loved (for these and a luminous generosity of spirit that assigns others' needs a higher priority than her own). She works long hours but is also intensely sociable. Like many amortals, the only visible lacks in her life are peace and quiet.

Without sight of her case notes or clinical expertise, it's tough to imagine any underlying issue all this therapy is meant to address other than a possible addiction to therapy. That may sound like a variant on one of Josh Howie's jokes – 'My parents are workaholics. Which unlike alcoholics isn't helped by meetings' – but therapy culture has proved remarkably adept at medicalising and therapising just about any pattern of behaviour, however inconsequential. No sooner had text-messaging become popular than a therapy was devised to address compulsive text-messaging. The rise of social media inevitably signalled the advent of rehab for social media dependency ('My name is @catherine_mayer and I am a Twitter addict'). It can only be a matter of time until clinics offer in-house rehabilitation programmes to fight rehab addiction. Here's Furedi again: 'Addiction plays the role of a cultural fetish through which society makes sense of diverse forms of behaviour. In attributing so much of human behaviour to this fetish, therapeutic culture demeans the potential for human action.'[132]

After trauma or bereavement we are no longer expected to clamber back on the horse without the help of counsellors. Amortals will be the first to hold out their hands. 'Therapists,' writes Furedi, 'have assumed the role of relationship experts and have succeeded in establishing a demand for their services in virtually every institutional setting.'[133] Some 80 per cent of Americans have received psychological counselling and in Britain, too, 'it is now assumed that people facing an unusual event are likely to need or at least likely to benefit from counselling'.[134] We are rich in labels for our behaviours ('bipolar', 'neurotic', 'addictive', 'narcissistic', 'obsessive-compulsive', 'depressive') and rich in celebrity role models for these descriptors. Therapy culture decrees that it's therapeutic to share; celebrities, gifted a more prominent platform than the rest of us, eagerly splatter their issues about the place like Jackson Pollocks, acrylic on newsprint. 'Six or seven years, I hid the bottles ... When you're that depressed you can't even [stop] for your kids – that's the most disgusting thing,' confided Brigitte Nielsen, actress-cum-model-cum-Valkyrie, who gained some fame as the wife of Sylvester Stallone, in intimate conversation with *Hello!* magazine.[135] Her tale of love, alcohol and redemption filled five pages of the glossy, and opened with a landscape image of its 45-year-old subject beneath a huge sub-Warhol painting of her younger self. The current Brigitte leans coquettishly against fifth husband Mattia Dessi, 15 years her junior, whom she met, the article tells us, 'when Brigitte visited the restaurant where Mattia was a waiter. Two years later they married'. Mattia stayed true as she went through rehab and afterwards joined forces with his celebrity wife to work on 'projects including clothing and cosmetics lines'.

But in celebrityland – and, as it so happens, in therapy culture – happiness can only be validated by sharing. So Nielsen invited *Hello!* into her 'stunning home in the South of France' to reveal the secrets of her new glow:

The actress has not only undergone an emotional transformation, she has made a physical one, too. Weeks before our shoot, she had plastic surgery that included a breast lift, eyelift and liposuction. 'I'd cleaned up the inside and wanted to freshen up.'

Celebrities aren't always so honest about their plastic surgery, but Brigitte had hers filmed for a German reality TV show. 'My life is an open book,' she says.[136]

THE CELEBRITY-THERAPY COMPLEX encourages all of us to believe that opening the book of our lives provides a therapeutic release. In truth, it's not a comfortable sensation. For this study of amortality, I've badgered friends and family into baring their amortal souls; I'm grateful to my interviewees for tolerating these incursions, and I've attempted to reveal only those details that illuminate the subject. Their generosity placed on me a responsibility to be open to the same extent, to give readers enough information to understand, literally, where I'm coming from. When I mentioned my decision not to have children, for example, I did so because in setting my decision within the context of a broader trend, I might be seen to have an agenda.

Similarly, as I mull on therapy culture and attempt to unpick aspects of the intertwined celebrity culture that feeds it and feeds off it, it seems relevant to disclose personal experience that has shaped my views. I have some direct experience of therapy – a brief period in counselling after a series of deaths – and have also watched friends pass through therapy culture's enclosures. My own counselling was comforting, but the fly-on-the-wall views of rehab helped to inform my scepticism. Some friends were too broken to fix. Therapy culture deserves its brickbats; that doesn't mean therapy isn't necessary, and effective, at least in some cases, or that mental illness is a matter of self-indulgent choice. Many people can't climb back on the horse without professional help. Some people can't climb back on the horse at all.

Yet according to the twisted rules of the celebrity-therapy complex a spell in rehab can be seen as a desirable goal, a mark of true celebrity.

Amortals may not wish to reach journey's end, but if we land in the Priory (Kate Moss, Ronnie Wood) or the Betty Ford Clinic (Elizabeth Taylor, Drew Barrymore) or Charter Nightingale (Michael Jackson) or The Meadows in Arizona (Kate Moss, Ronnie Wood), at least we'll know we've arrived. Therapy culture provides a range of labels and behaviours that can gain us entry without the need to suffer any serious malfunctions. But amortals aren't short of real problems. There is a real danger of depression when the gap between our ageless sense of self and the reality of ageing yawns, and fear of mortality can push us into destructive behaviours. In conversation at Lambeth Palace, the psychologist Oliver James articulated his views on what it takes to feel well in the skin and in so doing hinted at a locus of amortal fragility.

JAMES IS A CLEVER, SPIKY MAN. In his 2007 treatise on the epidemic of unhappiness afflicting the wealthy world, he identified some of the drivers of 'affluenza', his word for the malaise. Globalisation and the Americanisation of global culture; rising affluence; loss of community; the decline in religious observance – these factors contributed to the spread of both affluenza and amortality, and it became evident during our Lambeth Palace discussion that he divined in both conditions a similar pathology.

To James the idea of ageless living signals a form of denial (agreement with the statement 'I would like to successfully hide the signs of ageing' is a symptom of affluenza[137]), and it's certainly true that amortal detachment from age can translate into a failure to anticipate later-life changes. During the discussion, James suggested that I interview one of his friends, a public figure, 'a very intelligent man, highly articulate' but also, said James, 'He's clinically mad in that he just does not believe in the idea that he's getting old.' The diagnosis of clinical madness suggests a person who is less than fully functional, perhaps openly unhappy. In fact, James's friend always looks as if he's enjoying life. He's a hedonist, if more hyperactive than the term suggests, internationally acclaimed and super-rich;

his younger girlfriend hovers protectively by his jeans-and-leather-clad side. Age-blindness has positive benefits, as Harvard professor Ellen Langer has demonstrated. Having money to burn most certainly helps too. In the later chapter on the science of ageing, we'll see the correlation between wealth and long health spans and the corresponding disadvantages in growing old on meagre incomes.

But James worries that the amortal tendency to shy away from the bigger questions of existence – and death – might stop us from being 'really alive'. When he was researching *Affluenza*, he encountered only a few people he felt were living life to the full:

> Whenever I met these people I would suddenly think 'hang on a second, we've got one here, this person is so balanced, they've got their own point of view and yet they're really open'. In every single case there were two common factors. The first was that they had all had some kind of life-threatening experience. They really had woken up and smelled the coffee. It made me aware of how much, if you go anywhere in the Third World and see people starving and dying, you realise how absurd your life is, how utterly absurd, how ridiculous our values are, how lucky we are. But the second thing, and I had no expectation of this at all, was that every single one of these people had some kind of spiritual observance.
>
> I use that term advisedly because [some of them] had a conventional religion but [others] just had some kind of practice; they stopped every day, or at least once a week, and sat down and thought 'what's it all about, who am I, why do I exist?' Of course it's not so extraordinary when you know the scientific evidence: that statistically, people who are religious do have much lower rates of mental illness.

Amortals rarely stop and sit down to address metaphysical questions. 'Searching for the truth' as described by the much therapised amortal businesswoman we encountered at the start of this chapter is an all-consuming, fast-moving activity.

Moreover, amortals are unlikely to enjoy the mental health benefits of religious observance. Researchers at Sheffield Hallam University produced one of the reports that have seemed to correlate religiosity and mental health. Their study also showed that people who questioned their faith or attended church for social reasons were not afforded the same protection against mental illness as their more devout counterparts.[138] That chimes with James's assertion that the protection offered by religion is diminished in the case of belief systems that have been retooled to appeal to a modern congregation; the sort, he said, 'where you go along on the first day and they say, "Think of something you'd like to happen next week" and you say, "I want a promotion" or "I want a pay rise" and they say, "OK, come back in a week's time and see what's happened."'

The Archbishop of Canterbury put it a slightly different way. 'Religion is only good for your mental health if you stop thinking how good it is for your mental health.'

His gentle witticism is especially apposite for amortals. As already noted, amortality is fundamentally linked with the decline in unquestioning religious observance. 'Maybe as we lost God, we lost faith in ourselves,' suggests Vivienne Curtis, a consultant psychiatrist at the Maudsley Hospital. 'And now we want someone to give it back to us.' That someone might be a therapist or a cleric or even a buff doctor at Cenegenics. Amortals are attracted to forms of faith that are plastic and mould to amortal concerns and ostensible needs, often blending the spiritual with the therapeutic. Mainstream religion itself 'has been forced to internalise important elements of therapeutic culture', says Furedi, quoting the complaint by Rowan Williams's predecessor, George Carey, that 'Christ the Saviour' was becoming 'Christ the Counsellor'.[139] With some Western renditions of Eastern theologies, it's hard to tell where religion ends and therapeutic regimens begin. Amortals such as Woody Allen yield to a higher power in the shape of a pen-sucking psychoanalyst. And just as some religions co-opt therapies into their practices so some therapies co-opt faith. At the heart of every 12 steps programme, you'll find God.

Alcoholics Anonymous first published the 12 steps in 1939 and subsequently allowed other addiction organisations such as Narcotics Anonymous to base their treatment on the model. This is the AA path to redemption:

1. We admitted we were powerless over alcohol – that our lives had become unmanageable.
2. Came to believe that a Power greater than ourselves could restore us to sanity.
3. Made a decision to turn our will and our lives over to the care of God as we understood Him.
4. Made a searching and fearless moral inventory of ourselves.
5. Admitted to God, to ourselves and to another human being the exact nature of our wrongs.
6. Were entirely ready to have God remove all these defects of character.
7. Humbly asked Him to remove our shortcomings.
8. Made a list of all persons we had harmed, and became willing to make amends to them all.
9. Made direct amends to such people wherever possible, except when to do so would injure them or others.
10. Continued to take personal inventory and when we were wrong promptly admitted it.
11. Sought through prayer and meditation to improve our conscious contact with God as we understood Him, praying only for knowledge of His will for us and the power to carry that out.
12. Having had a spiritual awakening as the result of these steps, we tried to carry this message to alcoholics and to practise these principles in all our affairs.

A cynic might say that 12 steps programmes succeed only by replacing one dependency with another. That dependency isn't necessarily religion.

'Nobody I know believes in God,' says the businesswoman and therapy veteran. 'The 12 steps are just about surrendering responsibility, saying "I can't do it alone."' Studies show that rehabilitation programmes are most effective in preventing recidivism when patients continue to attend meetings long after the initial treatment.[140] Of course, if going to church for social reasons is less effective as a shield against intimations of mortality than genuine devotion, so 12 steps programmes are less likely to cut it if attendees use meetings for reasons other than recovery. That doesn't stop some of them from doing just that, for example to meet partners or even partners in crime with whom they can indulge in the excesses they've pledged to abjure. It's also an open secret that AA and NA groups have provided fertile opportunities for actors to build relationships with powerful directors; certain Los Angeles branches are heavily oversubscribed. There's another pull, besides scoring and networking. For amortals, such therapies provide exactly the same benefit as the dependencies they're designed to break: diversionary activity.

WHEN ARRANGING TO MEET Paul Wilkes in the lobby of a Las Vegas hotel-casino, the question arises of how to spot him. 'I will be wearing a Superman outfit and a red cape with a giant "S" on it. I wear it everywhere,' he emails back. In the event, it's easy to pick out this superman from the glazed throngs around the slot machines, despite a disappointing absence of cape. The 43-year-old is a Cenegenics-assisted paragon of muscular good looks. He also proves to be amortal, intensely so, and in conversation illuminates the mechanism of the perpetual motion, the hopeful travelling, that is such a distinctive amortal hallmark. The mechanism has propelled him to the edge of disaster and peaks of achievement, as he reveals:

> If I find something that I like, I will wring it out until it's no longer fun. And it doesn't matter what it is. And so I have to be very cognisant of enjoying an experience to the fullest, but not

abusing that experience. And I'm not only talking about things like sex, drugs and rock and roll. I'm talking about working out, eating out, focusing on nutrition. Whatever it may be, I have the propensity to think 'if one's good, a thousand is better'. And so I have to put the clutch on every now and then and look around and say, well this is a great moment, and stay in the moment.

But I'm as guilty as anyone of having this kind of manic pursuit of something else. Of anything different to take me out of how I'm feeling.

For our amortal businesswoman, that 'anything different' would often be a new form of therapy. But for Wilkes, a gynaecologist, or 'high-risk OB-GYN' as he describes himself, any absorbing activity feels therapeutic. His doctors at Cenegenics, by setting Wilkes tough targets that set him competing against himself, have created one such activity. We dine at a restaurant called T-Bones on slabs of steak and salad. Wilkes declines the bread and potatoes and strongly recommends I do the same.

The Cenegenics buzzword is 'optimal'. Wilkes's default setting is 'optimal', starting with the physical regimen that has kept all signs of ageing at bay. It takes sweat and discipline and attention to detail to look this good. He keeps a regular Monday morning appointment for a 90-minute facial. His best friend joked that he wasn't sure whether to take a shower or make a salad in Wilkes's bathroom. Self-maintenance pitstops provide the only interludes of calm in the high-octane, risk-filled blur that is Wilkes's existence.

He wouldn't trade an action-packed second for a promise of serenity. 'I am terrified of living a mediocre existence. Terrified,' he says:

I can live my life one of two ways: I can live my life sprinting full speed ahead and just gulping in the air and getting every minute out of every hour out of every day and eventually I'm going to fall off a cliff. Or I can meander through life and eventually trip and just roll down this hill banging my head on rocks along the way and slowly die.

I have no interest in living an OK life. I have no interest in being an OK father. I have no interest in being an OK physician or an OK friend or an OK husband. I want to be the best at what I do. My idea of hell is when I look around and I see people coasting through life, nine-to-five, never taking any risks. There are plenty of people who are happy with that existence; it's just not for me.

I want to shoot for the stars. I've been a millionaire and I've been bankrupt. And, I have to say, I've been happy in both situations. And I've been miserable in both situations, but no misery compares to that nine-to-five life for me, where I do my eight hours, I take a half-hour at lunch and eat my cheese sandwich and drink my iced tea and then punch back in.

The former Mrs Wilkes jokingly asks when he'll emerge from his midlife crisis, he says. Some of Wilkes's leisure pursuits could easily be caricatured as the signs of a man clinging to his ebbing youth: he mentions pool parties and an annual trip to Hugh Hefner's Playboy Mansion for a golf tournament. ('When people hear about a 43-year-old physician going to the Playboy Mansion they roll their eyes so hard I can almost hear it.') Wilkes dismisses the notion that such activities are markers of crisis; his impulses simply haven't changed, he says, rejecting 'this preconceived notion that there's this blueprint for the way one ought to be in these different decades of life ... One of the greatest compliments I get is when I will spend time with someone and they'll say, "What do you do for a living?" and I say, "I'm a physician," and they say, "Come on, you don't strike me as a doctor." I take that as a huge compliment because I don't want to be like a doctor. My idea of a doctor is a guy in a white coat with a grey moustache who's very serious and goes home and smokes a pipe and sits in a recliner in front of a fire and reads journals. I'm not interested in that.'

Later in the evening, Wilkes shows me a photograph on his mobile phone of two hyper-glamorous women in bikinis. One is his girlfriend. 'She has an 18-year-old daughter. I can guarantee you there is not a picture ever taken of my mother that even remotely resembles this one. In 2010, in my world, that's a mom.' Hefner's world is also full of such yummy mummies, but Wilkes is surprisingly dismissive of the *Playboy* chief. 'The more you see behind the curtain over there in Oz the less impressive it is,' says Wilkes. But Hefner 'does have this aura about him of invincibility'.

That's important to Wilkes, who volunteers that his yen to live hard is strengthened by his regular exposure to death through his medical specialism in high-risk pregnancies. Although he identifies strongly with the concept of amortality, he's not sure how that squares with his fascination with death. Indeed he's so interested in death, he says, 'I almost went into pathology. I almost did,' adding, 'In moments of honesty, I can readily say I am not afraid of dying.'

Terror management theory offers a slightly different slant on the amortal relationship with death. Awareness – and fear – of mortality can provoke behaviours that could easily be mistaken for the absence of fear or even a death wish, according to TMT expert Burke: 'Men tend to take more risks [than women] to defend their mortality. So they'll do riskier behaviours when they're under mortality salience than women will; they might drive really fast, for example. That's a way to show that you're immune to death. Or they'll go for higher attractiveness in partners, or they'll join the military.'

In other words, the more Wilkes encounters death in his job, the more distraction from mortality he seeks, whether by taking risks or by boosting his pride in himself and his achievements. It's archetypal amortal behaviour.

THE 'FURNACE-FEAR' OF DEATH Philip Larkin describes in *Aubade* flares when amortals are caught without distraction, in the depth of night or without people or drink. Timothy Radcliffe, the Dominican friar, believes we need to learn to face death, not to flinch from it. He paraphrases the American writer Saul Bellow. 'He said ignorance of death is destroying us. He said death is like the backing on the mirror than enables you to see everything,' says Radcliffe. But the poem he hands me, 'Break the Mirror' by the 20th century Japanese poet Nanao Sakaki, uses the image of the mirror to describe a kind of blindness: the amortal capacity to overlook age.

> In the morning
> After taking cold shower – what a mistake – I look at the mirror.
> There, a funny guy,
> Grey hair, white beard, wrinkled skin – what a pity –
> Poor, dirty, old man!
> He is not me, absolutely not.
> Land and life
> Fishing in the ocean
> Sleeping in the desert with stars
> Building a shelter in the mountains
> Farming the ancient way
> Singing with coyotes
> Singing against nuclear war – I'll never be tired of life.
> Now I'm seventeen years old,
> Very charming young man.
> I sit down quietly in lotus position,
> Meditating, meditating for nothing.
> Suddenly a voice comes to me:
> 'To stay young,
> To save the world,
> Break the mirror'.[141]

Ellen Langer's work has demonstrated the benefits of breaking the mirror. You can think yourself old. To at least some extent, as the rejuvenated participants in her New England hotel experiment demonstrated, you can think yourself young. Amortals don't anticipate being old and so we avoid thinking ourselves into premature ageing. But there's a flip side to our age-blindness. We can be unprepared for the discovery that the capacity of the amortal mind to overcome age and death is limited.

At Lambeth Palace, we strayed into a discussion of a phenomenon Tim Livesey dubbed 'the illusion industry'; our enveloping, celebrity-studded, therapised popular culture. The hunt for authenticity in a world of synthetics has created the ultimate synthetics: reality television that is scripted and confected, a wider celebrity culture that confuses overexposure with honesty, and a consumer culture that commodifies fantasies and sells them back at a mark-up. 'The deliberate attempt to put before people possibilities which you can only achieve usually through monetary exchange and in return you get happiness or you feel better about yourself, those are the sort of industries that I'm concerned about,' said Livesey. 'The thing that most people struggle with is the gap between the illusion and reality. Those striking people, few in number, who are "right in their skin" – in French the phrase is literally *bien dans sa peau* – the people that I've met who've been like that, what sets them apart is that they have somehow been able to face reality and they are no longer afraid of it. In other words there is no gap any more. One of the reasons that we are probably seeing a greater gap is the amount of imagination and energy and money that goes into the illusion industry in its various manifestations.'

The idea of joyful ageing, of apple-cheeked old age, also seems illusory. Ask around the truly old and they will tell you that the physical aspects of ageing are at best unpleasant. But some people as they grow old achieve a kind of contented accommodation with reality, become well inside their unashamedly old skins. This is a consolation amortals may never enjoy. Oliver James notes that successive studies of Britons' mental health by the Office of National Statistics show higher rates of mental illness among younger people and the lowest rates among the elderly.[142] An ONS report on non-fatal suicidal behaviour reflects this pattern, with 17 per cent of 16–44-year-olds admitting to suicidal thoughts compared to 6 per cent of 65–74-year-olds.[143] That's particularly surprising, says James, when you consider 'the material pain, the difficulties confronted [by older people]'. He adds: 'It's quite possible as people get older, as they divorce, as awful things start to happen, people around them die, people go mad, my hypothesis would be that the illusion industry stops working on that population. I don't think it's very easy to con older people into believing that [the products of the illusion industry] are really going to make all the difference to their life.'

James's mother illustrated this counter-intuitive trend, becoming happier in her old age than she had ever been during a lifetime marked by depression and phobias. She 'moved into the zone or became alive' in the last years of her life, says James. 'I'll never forget sitting outside with her. There was a bird on a tree. Throughout her life she had been terrified of birds, if a bird got in the house she would run screaming out of the room – I remember as a child we all used to think it was hilariously funny – and she sat there and she said, "Look at that bird, isn't it beautiful, look at the colours." She was not depressed any more, she was certainly mentally healthy.'

Therapy can help amortals move into the zone – James is a supporter of the Hoffman Process, for example – but therapy culture is an offshoot of the illusion industry. The trick for amortals is to harness ageless living to healthy ageing in all of its aspects, including mental health. Though evidently sceptical that amortals can be well 'in their skin', James constructs his own possible refrain of the happy older amortal: 'I remember what it was like when I had small children, I remember what it was like when I had to earn a living, I remember the pressure. Thank goodness none of that's a problem for me any more. I know where I am, I know what I'm trying to do. I just want to go scuba diving.'

5

amortals at work
NEITHER SHY NOR RETIRING

'If you give up what you most care about, you start dying. It
doesn't matter what age.'
Baroness Shirley Williams

'I've got two crushed discs too. Never stop moving or you'll stop
moving.'
Liza Minnelli

'Is that all there is, is that all there is?
If that's all there is my friends, then let's keep dancing.'
Peggy Lee, 'Is That All There Is?'

IF ANY LIVING PERSON has a reasonable prospect of staying that way for all
eternity, Meryl Streep must be in the running. She already defies another
seemingly immutable law of nature: that no actress over natural reproductive age can carry a Hollywood movie. Many of the characters Streep
plays are equally untrammelled by the rules that generally apply to life.
In 1992's *Death Becomes Her* she drinks an elixir of youth and becomes
immortal. The plots of two recent Streep vehicles, 2008's *Mamma Mia* and
2009's *It's Complicated*, are marginally less probable. Released when she was

59 and 60 respectively, both films cast her as a mature woman besieged by eligible suitors.

That may stretch credulity, but where the movies cross the line into wildest fantasy is in their depiction of the lead character's finances. *Mamma Mia's* single parent Donna is supposedly struggling to run her Greek hotel in straitened circumstances, but the backdrop of azure sea and sun-bleached paintwork conveys a contradictory message of blissed-out simplicity. Jane, the merry divorcée of *It's Complicated*, makes plans to extend her already spacious house. Her luxuriant lifestyle is apparently sustained by a single bakery shop that requires little managerial input from its proprietress, but in a scene as sugary as a cupcake tolerates her midnight incursion into its kitchens to bake up treats for her smitten architect.

Off screen, financial turbulence, eroding pensions and uncertain property prices are hitting Streep's generation hard, as the prospect of being able to afford to retire recedes like a riptide amid tightening job markets. Baby-boomers may be more affluent than younger cohorts, but finding work has never been easy for fifty- and sixty-somethings; the task is becoming tougher and more urgent as they realise their savings cannot sustain them for the additional decades many will live. Barring underlying health issues, there's no reason most of us shouldn't go about our business agelessly – and age healthily – as the last section of this book explains. But financial hardship and its attendant stress are profoundly ageing. Without decently paid employment, the real-life Donnas, female single parents, have always struggled, and real-life Janes, divorced women, are particularly at risk of falling into poverty. Whereas men tend to become richer after separating from their spouses, researchers have found that ex-wives' income most commonly drops and remains depressed.[144]

There is one tiny nugget of realism in Donna and Jane's charmed lives. Both are self-employed entrepreneurs – or 'olderpreneurs' as Alec Howe, director of the London-based global trend analysts Breaking Trends™, calls the swelling ranks of people in wealthy countries who respond to the lack of decent jobs for older workers by developing their own businesses. Many of these entrepreneurial independents are amortals.

This chapter looks at the significant impact of amortals on the workplace, as employers, employees, freelancers and entrepreneurs at the helm of start-ups – and the importance of working to amortals. Geoff Dornan has experience as an employee and of unemployment, and now aims to start a business. When he was in his sixties, he lost his job as a youth worker after a dispute with his employers, a borough council. He took the council to an industrial tribunal and prepared his own detailed and, he says, ultimately successful, defence. Belfast-born Dornan is not one to be intimidated by the prospect of a time-consuming legal battle. Eight years later, aged 71, Dornan found a new crusade, when Sefton Council in Lancashire prosecuted him for breaching the following by-law: 'No person shall skate, slide or ride on rollers, skateboards or other self-propelled vehicles in such a manner as to cause danger or annoyance.'

Found guilty in February 2009, fined £300 and ordered to pay costs of £1,800 for ignoring several cautions and continuing to frequent a bustling shopping precinct in Southport on his roller blades – CCTV footage shown to the court revealed Dornan weaving at high velocity and with significant brio through lunchtime crowds – he mutated into something of a folk hero, topping the *Daily Mail*'s list of 'pensioners ... criminalised for trivial offences by target-driven police'.[145] Dornan was drawn to the precinct by buskers – he likes to skate to music – but rejected suggestions that he buy an iPod. That, he told me, would be dangerous because it would blot out the sounds of traffic and pedestrians. The court judgement depleted Dornan's savings but gave him a new purpose and, as he puts it, a career 'to try to spread this amazing idea that roller blades are an extremely effective way of getting around instead of riding in a car'.

He originally took up roller-blading after his 'very health-conscious daughter started nagging' that he not let retirement damage his health. Roller-blading enabled him to cut car use and maintain his fitness while doing his errands, he says. Indeed, when he attended hospital for a minor operation, his physical condition so impressed the staff that his surgeon asked him 'in a hospital gown, with flowers printed all over it, [to] skate round the three wards that he was in charge of. To be a lesson to all these poor, half-dead people propped up in their beds.'

Dornan now aims to spread that lesson, and its accompanying green message, more widely by giving lessons in a roller rink of his own conception:

I thought, naively, that I would only have to [roller-blade] for a short period of time, and people would begin to follow my lead. Everybody was telling me what a wonderful thing it was, but nobody was doing it. And I thought, 'Why is this?' And I thought, 'Hang on a minute, you've been able to skate all your life, and you haven't done it. Why didn't you do it?'

And the answer is, we do exactly what everybody else does and we never think about doing anything that's unusual. So I hadn't skated as a means of getting around, because nobody does in Britain. And then I realised that that was why no one was doing it now, because there's still only one guy in the whole of Britain who does it, and he's been hauled into court and publicly humiliated and made a criminal on the basis of it.

So I finally decided that the thing to do would be to get a roller rink and use that as a base and you could have a course in street skating. You would explain exactly the etiquette and the requirements and all the snags and pitfalls and you could just train people to do what I now have taught myself to do in a very efficient way. And you would get them qualified and then you would get a group of people together who would then be in a position to negotiate with the police and the local authority to, for example, have a pilot study. So you would have 20 people agreed by the council and the police and registered as competent to skate and you would just simply see how many dead bodies there were at the end of nine months. And if there weren't any, and everybody had reduced their [car] mileage by 85 per cent you'd get a university to do a little study of this.

At the time of our conversation, in March 2010, he had made little progress with his scheme beyond finding a potential location for the rink and negotiating a £1 million price for it with the current owners. 'All I've got to do is raise £1 million to buy it and then another £1 million to develop it,' said the irrepressible Dornan. 'I'm setting up a charitable company, I'm looking for trustees right now, and I'm finding that people are nervous. I've got this amazing scheme, and I'll go back to Brussels and I'll try to get money out of the European Social Fund and the Lottery funds and all the rest of it and we'll get this skating rink going.' He rang 11 months later to update me on his progress. The charity now had a name – Get Your Skates On – and a board made up of prominent local supporters. He had learned to use Skype, not least to talk to web designers in London working on the charity's website and to discuss arrangements with prospective hosts in China about attending a skating festival there as a guest of honour. 'I'm having a ball, let me tell you,' he said. One suspects that even if he fails to get Britain skating, the attempt to do so is far more congenial to him than the notion of retirement.

MUSIC, LOCOMOTION AND CRIMINAL ACTIVITY all feature prominently in the corporate history of one of Britain's best-known business empires, the Virgin Group, according to its website a 'leading branded venture capital organisation and one of the world's most recognised and respected brands' with 'very successful businesses in sectors ranging from mobile telephony to transportation, travel, financial services, media, music and fitness'. Virgin consists of 'more than 300 branded companies worldwide, employing approximately 50,000 people, in 30 countries', and aims to expand beyond mere terrestrial activities with 'space tourism flights'.

Virgin may be looking at the stars, but the first Virgin-branded business only narrowly avoided being washed down the gutter. Virgin Mail Order, a record distribution business founded by a 20-year-old Richard Branson in 1970, amassed debts of £15,000 by the following spring. The original business model hadn't taken into account the cost of administering the orders or the financial toll of customers claiming not to have received the records dispatched to them and demanding additional copies. In his autobiography *Losing My Virginity* Branson recounts that as the business struggled, he legitimately purchased a large number of discs direct from record companies without paying the purchase tax levied on goods destined for the UK market in order to fill an order from Belgium. He planned to drive the consignment to its destination, but was turned back by French officials at Calais because of a missing document.

'As I drove back to London, it dawned on me that I was now carrying a vanload of records that had apparently been exported,' wrote Branson. 'I even had the customs stamp to prove it. The fact that the French customs had not allowed me through France was unknown. I had paid no purchase tax on these records, so I could sell them either by mail order or at the Virgin shop and make about £5,000 more profit than I could have done by the legal route. Two or three more trips like this and we would be out of debt.'[146]

The scam was duly repeated. Branson says he later discovered that his larger competitors were also evading duty, but more cleverly concealing their dodges. Despite a tip-off to Branson that a raid by Customs and Excise was imminent, Virgin was caught selling records marked for export (under ultraviolet light, each disc proved to be stamped with a fluorescent 'E') and Branson spent a night under arrest. 'That night was one of the best things that has ever happened to me,' he declared.

> As I lay in the cell and stared at the ceiling, I felt complete claustrophobia. I have never enjoyed being accountable to anyone else or not being in control of my own destiny. I have always enjoyed

breaking the rules, whether they were school rules or accepted conventions, such as that no 17-year-old can edit a national magazine. As a 20-year-old I had lived life entirely on my own terms, following my own instincts. But to be in prison meant that all that freedom was taken away.

His mother posted bail, he reached a settlement with the authorities and avoided a criminal record. But for Branson this was a life-changing experience – he resolved never to do anything that might jeopardise his freedom. Anyone who has encountered Branson in the four decades since that night in the cells will know there are lessons he did *not* draw from his brief confinement. The serial entrepreneur still ignores conventions about age and has repeatedly sought to prove his control over his own destiny by taking significant risks, in business and with his own mortality. Branson is the very model of the amortal businessman.

His amortal appetite for diversion spurred him to develop a form of serial entrepreneurship that is now widely imitated, not least by easyJet founder Stelios Haji-Ioannou, who once told me that he had decided to start an airline because Branson seemed to be having so much fun running his. Fun or, better expressed, the irresistible lure of the new and different, has shaped the Virgin empire. The group's website rebuts anticipated criticism of this approach:

> Contrary to what some people may think, our constantly expanding and eclectic empire is neither random nor reckless. Each successive venture demonstrates our devotion to picking the right market and the right opportunity.
>
> Once a Virgin company is up and running, several factors contribute to making it a success. The power of the Virgin name; Richard Branson's personal reputation; our unrivalled network of friends, contacts and partners; the Virgin management style; the way talent is empowered to flourish within the group. To some traditionalists, these may not seem hard-headed enough.

To them, the fact that Virgin has minimal management layers, no bureaucracy, a tiny board and no massive global HQ is an anathema. But it works for us!

Well, yes, apparently so. At various stages, Virgin has overstretched and overreached. Virgin Music Group had to be sold in 1992 to ensure the survival of the airline Virgin Atlantic; financial reporters have repeatedly questioned Virgin's solidity and a 2000 biography by the investigative journalist Tom Bower was damning. 'Bower's premise was that the Virgin empire was built on sand and it was going to go bust. So as long as we don't go bust, that premise goes away,' Branson told an interviewer in 2002; as Virgin continues to expand its brand, that point gains force.[147]

Moreover, he's indisputably been embraced by the establishment, *is* the establishment, and regularly tops national popularity polls in his native Britain. ('Richard Branson Beats Jesus in Role Model Poll', Reuters reported in 2008.[148]) If the UK abolished its monarchy tomorrow, he'd doubtless be a frontrunner to head the new republic. It may have felt like a long haul from upstart to potential president, but his progress was speeded by a jet stream: amortality.

In this era of CEOs in shirtsleeves and chinos, it's hard to remember how startling Branson's informality once seemed in business circles: the long hair and beard, the trailing sentences, the compulsive blokey jokiness. Less than an hour after I first met him, at a starchy awards lunch organised by *Business Traveller* magazine in October 1991, he scooped up his fellow guest of honour, Ivana Trump, and literally upended her. Though Branson was known for such antics, often precontrived to garner publicity for his companies including his airline, the manoeuvre drew gasps, not least from Trump, whose immaculate beehive miraculously defied gravity. Back then Branson's David-sized airline and its Goliath-like competitor, the privatised former national carrier British Airways, were locked in increasingly ugly and open competition. BA's fusty chairman Lord King sat louring at the top table. Both airlines were due to receive awards for rival services at that time almost as different in style as the carriers' bosses.

For BA, a humiliating capitulation in court would follow less than two years later, with the larger airline forced into a public apology to Branson and Virgin for a campaign of smears and 'disreputable business practices' orchestrated to undermine its competitor. BA also paid damages and hefty legal costs. King stood down as chairman soon afterwards, and BA continued a process of modernisation that King had started but would never have been able to see through.

His clash with Branson had been almost as much about business culture as about business. Although King had transformed BA from an inefficient nationalised company into a service-oriented private enterprise, his strategy and understanding were rooted in a dying era of deference, one in which younger generations could be expected to listen and learn from their elders and betters. He was affronted by Branson and out of sorts in a world that not only tolerated his shaggy, show-offy rival, but seemed actually to appreciate Branson's age-blind irreverence. The order to 'do something about Branson', the starting signal for the dirty tricks deployed against Virgin, was widely reported to have come straight from King.

Branson, by contrast (and what a contrast it was), never considered himself too young for any challenge. He now shows no sign of considering himself too old for any challenge, and in 2010, despite an overfilled schedule that saw him training in 23 different cities, he completed the London marathon just ahead of his 60th birthday – the same goal lawyer David Battiscombe has set himself.

A marathon is but a gentle stroll in the park compared to the entrepreneur's repeated efforts to smash world records for sailing and ballooning, some successful, others culminating in dramatic rescues and all involving significant risk to himself and his co-adventurers. A 1991 attempt to cross the Pacific by balloon came close to disaster after a mechanism intended to jettison empty propane tanks dumped the craft's full tanks too. The loss of weight sent the balloon soaring dangerously high; by the time its ascent had slowed Branson feared the balloon would run out of fuel before reaching the coast of America. Then the balloon caught a jet stream. 'I do not believe in God but, as I sat there in the damaged capsule, hopelessly vulnerable to the slightest shift in the weather or mechanical fault, I could not believe my eyes,' recalled Branson. 'It was as if a spirit had entered the capsule and was helping us along.'[149] He added: 'During the rest of my life, I am – to a greater or lesser extent – in control of my destiny. Up in a balloon we are at the mercy of the elements, the technology, the teams of engineers who have built it, and we are 30,000 feet up. The odds are not the best but I have always been unable to resist taking on odds that look formidable and then proving them wrong.'[150]

MOVEMENT AND RISK: these amortal addictions can be powerful drivers of business – and of bankruptcies. Amortals have transformed corporate cultures and sectors and pioneered new models and areas of activity. Amortal energies, properly directed, build empires and boost productivity. But a benign spirit can't always be relied on to enter the capsule to steer a craft to safety. Amortality isn't responsible for the failure of banks and businesses, but amortals like to gamble, testing and denying their mortality; amortals create structures that encourage risk-taking and they take risks themselves.

Unsurprisingly, the financial services industry proves attractive to amortals. 'Risk management, the buzz word of the financial markets since the collapse of Barings Bank in 1995, is clearly an oxymoron.' So said Nick Leeson, the rogue trader jailed for toppling Barings, as he contemplated the fall of institutions such as Lehman Brothers and Northern Rock 13 years later.[151] Rehabilitated since his release as a critic of the system he once sought to play, Leeson has penned an autobiography and consulted on a film version of his story starring Ewan McGregor, written a guide to coping with stress, served as CEO of an Irish football club, and taken to competing in internet poker tournaments after being introduced to the online action by footballer-turned-actor Vinnie Jones. 'The returns on the money can be phenomenal but I am well aware that I can lose too, so I won't be repeating the mistakes I made in the past,' said Leeson.[152]

In 2008, as the fate of Lehman Brothers and Northern Rock sent shudders through the global banking system, politicians on both sides of the Atlantic tried to figure out how to stabilise the international financial markets and guard against the mistakes made in the past that caused the crisis. And in both America and Britain, political veterans sought to turn their long years of service to electoral advantage. The US presidential campaign pitted 72-year-old John McCain against 47-year-old first-time Senator Barack Obama. 'I am fully prepared to be commander in chief ... I don't need on-the-job training,' said McCain. In Britain, 57-year-old Gordon Brown took a similar swipe at his unlined opponent, the Conservative David Cameron, then just shy of his 42nd birthday. 'I am all in favour of apprenticeships,' Brown told delegates to the autumn Labour Party conference, 'but this is no time for a novice.'

Brown's sentiment briefly resonated with the British public — Cameron's poll ratings dipped — but Obama trounced McCain and in 2010 Brown would lose to Cameron, suggesting that voters were less moved by songs of experience than by the idea, summed up by the great 19th-century politician Benjamin Disraeli, that 'almost everything that is great has been done by youth'.[153]

These words, often taken to represent Disraeli's views, are actually uttered by a character in one of the politician's satirical novels — Disraeli completed his second stint as Britain's prime minister at the age of 75 — and politics still values maturity. Too much so, says Sion Simon, who served as a minister in Gordon Brown's government and talks of the demeanour of 'relentlessly po-faced solemnity' that his forty-something colleagues feel impelled to adopt in order to seem old enough for power. 'Not to mention their clothes,' says Simon. 'On second thoughts, let's mention the clothes. It's good shorthand for what you're talking about. Why don't politicians look like normal people? Even when you see them interviewed in their back garden on a Sunday afternoon, why have they just taken their tie off and are still wearing a suit? Nobody wears a suit in their back garden on a Sunday afternoon, and all the people watching it know that.'

At 37, Simon was introduced to the President of Italy. 'He was shocked, plainly appalled. He said, "It's ridiculous that you're an MP at your age."' When Simon disagreed, the Italian politician responded 'with a quotation about standing on the shoulders of giants … It was almost straightforwardly insulting and patronising, it was very striking, the utter contempt for youth,' says Simon. Some professional cultures, even whole countries (Italy, by strange coincidence), are effectively gerontocracies, run by the old for the old.[154]

In the legal world too, grey hair can still be an asset. 'The fundamental thing you're selling is judgement and experience. And typically clients get a bit anxious if they're faced with a 25-year-old lawyer,' says David Battiscombe. But the lawyer admits his profession looks increasingly like an exception rather than the rule. 'A 25-year-old IT worker will be exactly what clients want, and a 50-year-old IT worker, they'll probably think, well, they'll be out of touch.'

In fact, age prejudice at either end of the spectrum is baseless and damaging; in many cases the opposition between experience and youth is a false one. Age gives no reliable indication of ability or even experience as serial careers become increasingly common. Jean Pralong, a professor at Rouen Business School in France, carried out an inter-generational study on 400 people of similar educational backgrounds and ranging in age from twenties to sixties. He found that the assumed differences between the generations – the ease with which younger workers use technology compared to the greater dedication of older employees, for example – didn't hold up to closer scrutiny.[155] And research by Lancaster University's Management School suggests that the most productive workforces are age-diverse.

A team led by Professor Paul Sparrow established that recruiting a familial spread of generations in the workplace can lead to happier employees, which in turn feeds through to improved profits. His findings were based on analysis of detailed performance data from 635 outlets of the fast-food chain McDonald's, which revealed substantially elevated footfall and sales at sites where staff expressed themselves contented with their jobs. Drilling down into these results, Sparrow found that branches with one or more employees aged 60 or over scored 20 per cent higher on customer satisfaction than stores where nobody older than 50 was employed.[156]

A PERSISTENT FALLACY distorts the political debate on employment. It's the idea that there's a block of jobs to be shared out, for example, between nationals of a country and immigrants, or between young workers and older jobseekers. To be precise, says David Cameron, it's the 'lump of labour fallacy'.

Cameron might be said to have succumbed to this fallacy — 'this idea that somehow in an economy there's a fixed number of jobs and you just have to work out how to carve them up', as he defined it for me — in arguing for tighter immigration controls. But one of his government's first significant moves after coming to power was to launch a consultation process looking at scrapping Britain's default retirement age from the autumn of 2011. Under existing arrangements, employers have been able to force workers into retirement, without compensation, at 65. Sitting in the VIP lounge of Newquay Airport in July 2010, Cameron explained why the proposed change would not disadvantage younger jobseekers:

> [This fallacy] is what led some countries towards the 35-hour working week or compulsory job shares. You should be thinking about it in a dynamic sense of 'how do we make the economy bigger, how do we create more jobs?' It's defeatist to think that actually raising retirement ages will cut the number of jobs available to young people. It's not a zero-sum game.
>
> If you think of an economy like a zero-sum game you're on the road to ruin actually, because what will happen is the lump of labour will just get smaller each year as your economy gets more and more uncompetitive. In Europe we sit around discussing the

ills of the Eurozone and the problems of Europe's economy and all
the rest of it, and the fact is unless we get to grips with the cost of
doing business, with the cost of ageing, the cost of welfare, the
burden of our pensions, the unfunded liabilities of the public
sector, unless you come to terms with these we will be uncompetitive with the rest of the world.

Cameron's position isn't ideological – very little that Cameron does is
ideological – and is surely not based on narrow self-interest. The youngest
prime minister since 1812, Cameron would have to hang on in Downing
Street for 32 years to reach Disraeli's age at retirement. The mooted change
is simply a pragmatic response to Britain's greying population. The ratio
of British workers to pensioners (based on the current retirement age) is
projected to decline from four to one in 2010 to two to one by 2060. By
the middle of the same decade, the proportion of centenarians among the
UK populace is expected to have swelled to 17 per cent.

Christchurch, a Dorset resort town, has deposed another resort,
Eastbourne, known as 'God's waiting room', to claim the oldest population profile in Britain. For every five workers, Christchurch is home to
three retirees, and one in six of those retirees is 85 or over. A recent report
identified several such aged enclaves which 'present significant funding
issues as there will be far fewer young people entering the working population to fund the retired population through direct taxation' according
to Chris Horlick, managing director of the financial consultancy Partnership that conducted the research.[157] 'The impact of our ageing population
on the oldest councils will be extreme.' Unless something changes, Britain
won't just be uncompetitive, as Cameron fears. Swathes of the country
will cease to function in significant ways as younger workers stagger under
the insupportable burden of taxation to fund care of the elderly that
threatens to be sorely inadequate.

How big that burden is, how large the resourcing shortfall, how
unbearable the realities for the resentful young and the poorly provisioned

old, depends on how many people actually retire, at what age and in what condition. 'Work spares us from three evils – boredom, vice and need,' as the wise Turk told Candide. Some gerontologists and psychologists would add a fourth and potentially greater evil: decline. Research suggests a linkage between retirement and physical and mental deterioration. A 2006 study, for example, reported that:

> ... complete retirement leads to a 5–16% increase in difficulties associated with mobility and daily activities, a 5–6% increase in illness conditions, and a 6–9% decline in mental health, over an average post-retirement period of six years. Models indicate that the effects tend to operate through lifestyle changes including declines in physical activity and social interactions. The adverse health effects are mitigated if the individual is married and has social support, continues to engage in physical activity post-retirement, or continues to work part-time upon retirement.[158]

There are arguments about whether these phenomena can be blamed on the transition to a post-working life. David Ekerdt, now a professor of sociology at Kansas University, argued in a 1987 paper that 'the cultural celebration of work' helped foster misplaced and exaggerated assumptions about the toxic effect of retirement.[159] A longitudinal study in the Netherlands suggested that retirement per se was not a problem. The results, published in 2007, attributed declining health after stopping work to 'employees' failure to control retirement according to their wishes ... Older workers who perceived retirement as involuntary showed decreases in perceived health.' Moreover, 'psychological factors play a role: Fear of retirement and self-efficacy are associated with health change in retirement.'[160]

My mother reluctantly left her job as head of press at the Royal Court Theatre after her employers discovered her real age. She had been hired at 57; she was assumed to be significantly younger. She was rumbled just before her 65th birthday when the authorities wrote pointing out that she shouldn't be subject to national insurance contributions at pensionable age. 'I got married, far too young, and had children, far too young,' she says. 'And having been a very young mother and a very young wife and really failing to have a firm enough identity of my own, when I began to have a career, work became such an important part of my life. I went to work [for London Contemporary Dance Theatre] in 1969, left the Royal Court in 1999, so that's 30 years. I had to learn to be Anne Mayer of no fixed abode as it were, and I really didn't think at all about what would happen to me when I left the Royal Court, I didn't give that any considered thought, I didn't think about whether I would continue to work. I didn't realise I would become so depressed.'

Setting up her own consultancy rescued her from that depression. The decisive factor in healthy ageing – and especially in amortals' healthy ageing – isn't whether we keep working, but whether we keep moving. For the residents of Sun City in California that movement may take the form of long bicycle rides and a perpetual social merry-go-round. But for those still interested in work – or who simply can't afford the alternative, and that's going to be a seriously large number of us – delaying retirement will do us more good than any elixirs of youth currently available via the internet. Lawyer David Battiscombe has no intention of giving up the law he came to late, but says if its fascination ever waned, retirement would be out of the question and he'd develop a new career: 'It might be something more manual, it might be something involving more travel. It would involve challenge and it would involve some requirement to keep the brain working. If it wasn't intellectually challenging then I'd just get very bored.' 'I'm going to keep working until the day they carry me away,' declares Lynne Franks.

'I'm always saying to older people, "Don't stop",' says actor Richard Wilson. 'If you do stop work, find some interest. The reason I work is because I enjoy it still. But I also realise how much happier I am when I'm working. I used to say, when I'm not working I get very indolent, but I don't think it's indolence, I think it's actually depression, in a way. It's taken me years to decide that, for example, if I've got time off I'm going to get this room organised.'

Now in his seventies, Wilson is a whirlwind of activity, directing and acting and also politically engaged (he's a long-time Labour Party supporter). I ask him if he has any other secrets to staying vibrant. 'There's no Botox going into this face,' he says. 'Some days it would be very helpful. I should think about it.'

IF HE WERE BASED in Hollywood rather than Hampstead, Wilson might long ago have been urged by his agent to get the needle or do something more radical to boost his career longevity. In the epicentre of amortality, growing old has never really been an attractive option, and it's career death for leading ladies. Hollywood's studio system is as inherently conservative as its assets are not, and has remained shackled to wider societal conventions that find the sexuality of older women troubling.

Ironically, the industry's discomfort with ageing women used to generate some fine roles for its veteran actresses. Bette Davis was only 42 when she played Margo Channing, a hard-boiled Broadway diva supplanted by the eponymous young schemer of *All About Eve*. By 54, Davis had graduated to the raddled horror of deranged former child star Jane Hudson in *Whatever Happened to Baby Jane?* At 51, Gloria Swanson took on the role of the deluded and ultimately murderous Norma Desmond in *Sunset Boulevard*.

If you're tempted to see in Streep's box office ascendancy signals that Hollywood is learning to love, or at least not flinch from, female maturity, consider how few seriously meaty roles have been written for actresses in their fifties and sixties in recent years. Streep and a handful of her exceptionally well-preserved colleagues apparently get first refusal on the trickle of opportunities that do arise. Fortyish actresses compete to mine the *Sex in the City/Cougar Town* seam, in which plotlines – and comedy – revolve around the idea of women over 30 remaining sexually active. The actresses who succeed in snaffling parts as cougars are uniformly glamorous. 'I thought I was washed-up at 40. There were not a lot of interesting scripts. I could find one a year, maybe,' Streep told an interviewer in 2008.[161] Many actors rely on cosmetic surgery, she added. 'It's not just women. You'd be amazed at how many men in this industry have gone down that road. I just don't get it. You have to embrace getting older.'

The actress may feel ready for her close-up; a glance at the patrons of the private club Soho House in West Hollywood suggests that many of her industry colleagues, even those in behind-the-scenes jobs, spend quite a bit of time and money to ensure they're prepared to face the world. Before Los Angeles-based entertainment writer Rebecca Keegan arrives for our meeting, I while away a contented half-hour observing executives discussing deals in hyperbolic terms that help to compensate for their Botoxed inability to facially emote. ('We just love your work. Love it. Love it.')

Streep 'is exempt from all the rules about females; she gets away with a movie like *It's Complicated*, which is really a fantasy for a 55-year-old woman. The gorgeous house, the cool job, two attractive and age-appropriate men interested in you,' enthuses Keegan. A fresh-faced native of upstate New York, Keegan observes California with an amused outsider's eye. 'Grooming is a competitive sport here,' she says.

> Women wake up, they go to their Pilates class, they go for their facial, it's an exhausting regimen of maintenance. There are people who professionally have to be beautiful and then there's people who have to be beautiful to hang on to the person who pays the mortgage.
>
> This woman came and sat down next to me, a very elegant woman, I would say in her mid-forties, beautiful bag, lovely hair, everything, and she sat down in the chair and she just sighed, 'I am so exhausted.' And her cellphone rang and it was obviously her husband or partner asking her to get dinner and she said, 'Honey, I've had such a day, I had tennis with the girls, I had to

take Barney to the vet, I had to go to the bank.' The things that she is describing for any normal woman would be like what you would accomplish on your lunch hour in between the 4,000 things that you really have to do.

We might visit all sorts of common-or-garden professional environments to observe the impact of amortality – and the roadblock to ageless living that ageism represents – but we'll stick with the entertainment business. We'll do so not least because the business is full of amortals. But what makes the business especially interesting is that it both reflects and shapes our attitudes to age and ageing. Hollywood disseminates amortal attitudes yet also enforces age prejudice in its worship of youth.

These conflicted views colour its wider environs. Los Angeles, remarks Keegan, 'is ground zero for denying ageing exists'; America is a divided country, split between 'ageless, super-thin' celebrities and the vast fleshier majority: 'I think [the entertainment business] is influential in the sense that most people aspire to it, but not in the sense that most people actually look like that and pull it off,' Keegan ventures. Our gaze pans to the neighbouring table. Two women are lunching together, if that is the appropriate verb for rearranging quinoa salad on a plate; they could be sisters, or mother and daughter, or share a surgeon. 'It's hard to tell in this town,' says Keegan. 'There is a weird thing you see here where there's competition between mothers and daughters about staying hot and sexy. Because women in California tend to stay young-looking and available-looking longer, they and their daughters can be attractive to the same men and the same men can be attractive to them.'

At a popular brunch spot in the Valley, I find myself again surrounded by people focused on staying hot and sexy: actors, agents, producers, directors and the LA interpretation of 'waiters' – actors waiting for a big break and beautifully delivering skinny caffe lattes and low-fat muffins until it comes. Surveying the scene, screenwriter and actor D.V. DeVincentis (his writing credits include the movies *Grosse Pointe Blank* and *High Fidelity* and he's working with *High Fidelity* director Stephen Frears on a new project) remarks that cosmetic surgery has become a complicating factor in casting decisions. 'Because of plastic surgery a lot of women can't express themselves with their face like they used to,' he says. 'Because they're frozen. Botox, or their lips have been enhanced or their faces have been pulled. And then there's also the ideal that all the plastic surgeons seem to move towards. And their clients all start to look the same. I first started to see that face on Park Avenue and in Beverly Hills where older wealthy women are trying to look younger, and so when I see younger women with that face, unconsciously they seem older to me.'

Streep has proved that a mature woman can be box office, but films featuring mature women and aimed at mature women are few and far between. Yet the film industry is often age-blind when it comes to its male stars, pairing 60-pluses with onscreen love interests young enough to be Hugh Hefner's fiancée or dispatching their heroes creaking into action. So why its continuing failure to serve the swelling populations of older women? Well: it's complicated. With big-budget films 'it's absolutely just about money. Anything can happen if it's financially supportable,' says DeVincentis.

> And Hollywood is wish fulfilment. They talk about it all the time in creating movies and creating stories: wish fulfilment. When we talk about movie concepts, a guy puts on a magic hat and every woman is in love with him, that's wish fulfilment.
>
> Hollywood is not cynical in that they're not so much telling people what to think, they're trying to understand what people think and please them. In the process they end up affirming ideas that are out there, healthy or unhealthy, but they're certainly not ideological …
>
> There is lots of wish fulfilment in living forever. There's lots of wish fulfilment in being a 65-year-old man who still somehow gets to date 30-year-old women without it being weird. To be a

middle-aged woman fought over by men, to have affluence without even thinking about it, that's wish fulfilment.

It's more than 200 years since Mary Wollstonecraft – the mother of
Frankenstein authoress Mary Shelley – criticised the socialisation of women
('Taught from infancy that beauty is woman's sceptre, the mind shapes
itself to the body, and roaming round its gilt cage, only seeks to adorn its
prison'[162]). Nevertheless, few of us grow up untainted by the idea that
our attractiveness determines our worth. The thing is, that's still not so
far from the truth, and not just in Hollywood's worldview. As teenagers,
we watch attractive friends receive more and better dating offers. If we
hope to reproduce, we should aim to snare a mate by our thirties, at least
until reproductive technologies improve. And in the workplace, our
qualifications, achievements and professionalism may not be the only
determinants of success. One 1991 study ascertained that for each additional 'unit of attractiveness' a female MBA graduate could expect to
earn an extra $2,150.[163]

Good looks also boost male earning power, but definitions of male
good looks are as elastic as young skin, not least thanks to Hollywood's
weathered and leathery male stars (and some of the cosmetic surgery
displayed by male leads could further extend those definitions). A movie
that cast an actress women considered plain as a romantic lead wouldn't
seem like wish fulfilment to a female audience without a transformative
plotline revealing hidden beauty. The problem with age is that it narrows
the scope for such transformations. When a sixty-something Miss Jones
loosens her severe topknot and takes off her glasses, she's still a sixty-
something Miss Jones, destined only to get saggier.

Unless, of course, she's Meryl Streep. The actress represents an ideal:
a mature woman well in her smooth skin, not obviously fighting age but
largely untouched by its processes, timeless. The problem with youth is
that it reminds us of the alternative. Streep allows us to dream. She is a
conspicuous example and beneficiary of female amortality.

THERE'S ALWAYS SOMEONE struggling to break the mould, says DeVincentis, someone trying to make a meaningful film or piece of art. 'Once you have leisure time, culture is created; once man has got all the food he needs he starts to think about other things and he paints a picture on the cave wall.' Hard economic times mean studios are on the hunt for easy prey. In times of plenty, 'those people who run the studio would really love an Oscar. So then they look out for serious filmmakers and actors who want that same thing and they start looking at prestige possibilities.'

Art-house movies, made on smaller budgets in anticipation of smaller returns from more discerning audiences, are granted greater latitude to depart from the box-office-friendly, wish-fulfilment model, and they're a good place to prospect for nuggets of amortal philosophy. Woody Allen's latest movie, *You Will Meet a Tall Dark Stranger*, premiered in May 2010 at the Cannes Film Festival (and by sheer coincidence was partly and distractingly filmed in the atrium of *TIME*'s London offices on a Friday evening and over a weekend in August 2009 as I toiled to meet a deadline). The film reprises Allen's enduring amortal obsessions: with mortality and the mercifully distracting pain of fractured love. The tall dark stranger, the hackneyed promise of a fortune teller, represents both the possibility of love and the inevitability of death, 'the tall dark stranger we all eventually meet', according to one character.[164] 'My relationship with death remains the same: I'm strongly against it,' Allen told reporters at the festival.[165]

That puts him in good company, to judge by the determined longevity of his fellow directors showing at Cannes. My colleague Richard Corliss observed that the festival never seems to disinvite directors, 'no matter how old [they] get, how pensive or creaky [their] new work'.[166] Corliss kicked off an enthusiastic review of *Tamara Drewe*, a film by DeVincentis's collaborator Frears, at the time just shy of his 69th birthday, with the following lament:

This year, especially, Cannes is the country for old men. The senior member is Manoel de Oliveira, who at 101 presented *The*

Strange Case of Angelica; he is accompanied, just in the first six days of films, by the directors of *Robin Hood* (Ridley Scott, 72), *Another Year* (Mike Leigh, 67), *You Will Meet a Tall Dark Stranger* (Woody Allen, 74), *The Princess of Montpensier* (Bertrand Tavernier, 69), *Film Socialism* (Jean-Luc Godard, 80 in December) and *Certified Copy* (Abbas Kiarostami, 70 in June).

We've got nothing against a Golden Boys senior circuit – we could name a dozen film critics here who'd qualify for member-ship, at least in terms of age – but it does mean that this gorgeous Riviera resort, full of young people with movie-star good looks, will play host to a slate of films about death and decay.[167]

BY CANNES STANDARDS, Anton Corbijn was a mere stripling when his film *Control* opened there in May 2007, three days short of his 52nd birthday. Then again, the movie, about the life and suicide of Joy Division singer Ian Curtis, marked Corbijn's directorial debut; he came late to directing and continues as one of the world's best-known portrait photographers with sidelines in video-making and stage design and a significant body of non-commercial art photography that has been widely exhibited. Corbijn's work ethic is merciless; he has scarcely paused since he got his first job as a small boy in Holland:

I've worked since I was 10, actually. I worked for a milkman on Saturdays. I lived in this village and the milkman came with the horse still. On Saturdays I would work there for five guilders. And even when we moved from that island when I was 11, I would come back in the holidays and I would work the whole holiday. So I saved money for my first bicycle and I was very aware of buying something nice because I worked. Because I wanted to buy my own things, I was very proud of my first bicycle, of my first bought bicycle.

I still think I should take some time off at some point, just take a year off, but I haven't got round to doing that, and especially now that I've discovered film, it just seems time is at a premium. I'm busier than ever.

I've never had a proper break. The longest break I've had was six weeks. I went to India and I woke sometimes dreaming about pictures and saying, 'It's too grey, it's too grey.' So I couldn't let go.

Work is Corbijn's life; he makes strenuous efforts to maintain his many friendships, but admits a peripatetic schedule renders routine contact difficult. An early marriage ended years ago, and he has no children. 'I never wanted kids when I was young because I was sure the world would come to an end, and I don't think I was ready for it ever, anyway,' he says. 'Of course if you're a man you can become a father in old age, you know it's an advantage. I have six godchildren so that's my connection to youth and my sister has a boy who lives in the same town as me who is now 11. That's the closest I think I've come to observing a child growing up.'

You might think someone who frequently seems too busy to breathe might also be too busy to contemplate mortality, but meditations on death suffuse Corbijn's work. The disbelieving son of a Protestant minister, he acknowledges the influence of the church in his instinct to create stark, iconic images, but found no comfort in its doctrine. As a young photographer, he was drawn to subjects who 'were not the happiest people, some of them were suicidal', including the Nirvana frontman Kurt Cobain and the Dutch musician and painter Herman Brood. 'Even [in] my first two films, the main person dies at the end,' says Corbijn. When we met to discuss amortality, he was considering a third film project in which the main protagonist also dies before the final credits roll.

The introspective Dutchman appears to have little in common with the amortal butterflies that flutter through his intersecting worlds of movies, rock and fashion. Yet he is attracted to those environments because they promise a lightness of spirit, a release from dull inevitabilities.

For amortal artists there are several ways of responding to mortality salience. You can crowd it out with work or party furiously in the company of less complicated amortals, the kind who are happily unaware of the passage of time. Or you can combine these avoidance techniques with an intensive focus on death, fetishising it, turning it into a work of art. That's the creative equivalent of driving too fast or abseiling off skyscrapers or indulging in any of the daredevil behaviour recognised by terror management theorists as a symptom of, and response to, underlying anguish.

In an echo of Oliver James's observation about the transfiguring power of life-threatening events, Corbijn reveals that a brush with death diminished some of that anguish and taught him to better appreciate life.

> Part of that change happened when I was 29. I got ill in England, and I had a really bad experience with the NHS. So I managed to get to Holland although I could hardly walk; my lungs were full of water …
>
> It was a slow recovery and while I was in hospital I thought if I die, I should have possibly enjoyed life a bit more. I remember on my 29th birthday night I went to the Scala for an all-night [showing of the movies of Andrei] Tarkovsky. But you know, to illustrate the change, on my 30th I was with the guys from [synth-pop group] Yello in a night club in Havana. So I did change a bit, I did start to enjoy experiences more. And I try to live a bit more in the now.

IN 2000, THE GRONINGER MUSEUM in the northern Dutch town of Groningen staged a 25-year retrospective of Corbijn's photographic work. Bono, transformed in Corbijn's early shoots with U2 from ordinary mortal to rock immortal, opened the exhibition. 'Having your picture taken is an intimacy,' said the singer. 'It's like having sex. I've been having sex with Anton Corbijn for nearly 20 years now.' Corbijn's elderly father, his knowledge of English sufficient to understand only the last sentence, conspicuously failed to join in the laughter.

What resembles tender love-making in youth may feel more like violation in later life, especially since digital technology has replaced the flattering softness of analogue imagery. That's helping to push down the average age of models, says Corbijn, and to increase the trend to airbrushing as stars of Bono's vintage find themselves cheek-to-cheek in glossy magazines with models less than half their ages. During the making of *Control*, Corbijn's lens forced his friend Herbert Grönemeyer into an unwilling recognition of physical change. 'Anton put a wig on me and glasses,' says Grönemeyer. 'I thought, "Oh God." You're really shocked, you think, "God, no, that's not true, the double chin." That's hard. I imagine if [film acting] were my only profession and I had five-year steps of getting older and older and older and you always see it, that would be pretty nasty.'

Grönemeyer isn't without ego – rock star-actors without ego are as noteworthy a phenomenon as Hagrid's bat – but unlike many of his counterparts in Europe and America Grönemeyer ruefully acknowledges the advancing years. That may be easier to do in his native Germany, especially in its chilled capital, Berlin, now Grönemeyer's primary residence. 'The air is very good,' he says. 'You have a lot of lakes and forests and the town is very used to old people, it's made for old people in some ways. Even before the Wall came down [Berlin] was famous for great retirement homes and nice [retirement] communities … Germany is not so much about a beauty contest, especially not Berlin. Berlin is not about being flashy, being richer, or trying to look more beautiful. Old people are respected and integrated.'

Some wealthy Germans prefer not to test the depth of that respect and integration. My first encounter with a uniface dates back to a private view at London's Royal Academy, a few days before the invasion of Iraq and attended by Tony Blair and German Chancellor Gerhard Schröder. The exhibition of magnificent old masters that had survived Dresden's experience of shock and awe more than six decades before drew throngs of German industrialists and their wives. I was introduced to one of these wives, her visage as stretched and painted as a canvas. She showed no sign of recognition when our paths crossed a few minutes later. At the third such encounter, realisation dawned: these were different women, but shared a uniface – and, presumably, a surgeon.

People with money tend to live longer, but they may also fall into the trap of thinking they can buy cures and fixes. Grönemeyer's lesson in the limitations of medical science was especially cruel: in 1998 his 44-year-old brother and his 45-year-old wife died of different cancers within two days of each other.

If personal loss forced Grönemeyer to confront mortality and begin to cope with it, his one-armed, Calvinist father had already furnished him with some of the philosophical tools to do so. Grönemeyer tries to emulate his father's parenting, letting his own children flourish under his protective canopy just as his father sheltered him:

> I try to grow strong. A tree always grows and gets more beautiful, it doesn't get old in that sense, it gets bigger. And when the younger trees [have grown], then you just fall. And then you can make a little bench out of me.
>
> My father was like that, he was really upright, had no problems with his looks, never ever. He always felt extremely beautiful with his one arm, he had an amazing confidence, not arrogant, but he felt very well in his own skin.
>
> And I think the only thing you can do is not to keep yourself young, [but] to keep yourself happy in your skin. The skin is a bit more wobbly and you don't have muscles but you still have joy in your brain and you meet funny people and you have a great life and you grow big.

For Grönemeyer there is no question of stopping work. Making music, he insists, is as much a part of his routine as 'taking a shower'. 'Artists don't retire,' he says. For performers the issue is how to grow old in public and on stage. Mick Jagger and Iggy Pop choose an overtly amortal route, flinging themselves around with much the same conviction as they have always done. Grönemeyer plans instead 'to get old in a very decent way, rather than running around like an idiot on stage pretending that I am still very funky'. But he is not lacking in ambition: 'My father said, "I'll get to 87", and he got to 87. So I've decided I'll get to 96. And the last concert I do will be at 89, I decided that. Yes, that's the last concert I'm doing.'

AS I STUDIED MY AMORTAL FAMILY in preparation for this book, it dawned on me that among seven first cousins in my family, I am the only long-term employee. That's partly because my sisters and two cousins work in entertainment, a field where salaried positions are rare. But they may also have been attracted to work in entertainment because they didn't like the idea of salaried positions. The cousins who are not in show business have gravitated into self-employment, either as freelancers or heading their own start-ups.

My first cousin Adam Bezark set up the Bezark Company 18 years ago, but his entrepreneurial spirit showed long before that, when he invented his own degree course in order to gain the skills to become an 'imagineer', a vocation which in the 1970s barely formally existed. He persuaded the University of Southern California to let him combine classes in everything from film studies and architecture to management and accounting, and went on to work first with the Disney Corporation, directing his first Disneyland show at 24, and then Universal Studios (Adam designed Universal's *Ghostbusters* and *Jurassic Park* attractions, put more bite into the *Jaws* ride, and worked with James Cameron and Arnold Schwarzenegger to create the huge 3-D *Terminator 2* virtual experience). He's been back to Disney, worked on museums and theme parks across the world, collaborated with Cirque du Soleil on their Las Vegas shows and his one-off projects have included writing and directing the *son et lumière* for the 50th anniversary of the Golden Gate Bridge in San Francisco and the $13 million spectacular of fireworks, lasers and illuminated boats that marked the return of Hong Kong to Chinese sovereignty.

Despite the weighty curriculum vitae and more than half a century on the planet, Adam is still recognisably the child who was once my favourite playmate: wildly imaginative, funny and ridiculously enthusiastic. In May 2010, he drove me from his home in Pasadena to my appointment at Sun City and the two-hour journey was punctuated, as journeys with Adam always are, by his delighted exclamations: 'Would you look at that!' 'That's neat!' 'Isn't that cool?!' 'Woweee!' A verge of charred trees along the freeway, testament to a recent wildfire, morphed in his designer's eye into gothic loveliness. 'I like most things and life is there to be enthusiastic about,' he responded, when I teased him.

I can't remember if anybody told me that you should do what you love but I just did it. I remember there was a point back when I was in high school when I was trying to decide what I should do for a living and my dad said, 'Put down engineer,' which was hilarious, because that was the last thing I was ever going to be, but it's what he was. Then later on I seem to remember sitting around the dinner table and we were talking about my ongoing obsession with Disneyland and Dad said, 'Well, if you like that so much why don't you do that for a living?'

It was like a boulder hit me: you mean I could do that? So then I got completely doubly obsessed not just with Disneyland, but with how to get into that place and how to be part of it. There was no mechanism to guide me at all; there was no path to that career as there is today. You can study environmental design, museum design, and people like me go out and teach classes to [aspiring theme park designers], but there was nothing like that then.

He demurs at my suggestion that his childlike enthusiasms are suited to his specialism in children's entertainment, and he's right to do so. Theme parks were not devised just for kids but to entertain the whole family – in the days when a family still might be expected to consist of small children, teens, parents and grandparents – as seamlessly as possible. The genius of the Disney parks lay in their ability to capture the interest of all those different age groups for hours or even days, and by charging for entry rather than per attraction, lulling the purse-holders into spending freely on food and merchandise. There were rides for the smallest tots and the biggest adrenalin junkies, and the Mickey Mouse T-shirts came in all sizes, but the experience was primarily one of ageless, unified appeal.

That's still the case but the twinkling magic of theme parks has dimmed as immersive, virtual experiences become widely available as home entertainment. 'If I was starting my career again today I would still be looking for the thing that I would get obsessed with, but it might be something very different,' says Adam. 'It might be computer graphics or virtual reality games. And if I am labouring over anything in this stage of my career, it's to reinvigorate this industry so that it's as cool as it was when I got into it. To find what's the next really cool thing to do … It seems if you want fantasy, artificial entertainment, you do that at home, and if you want to go out of the house, then what you want is real entertainment: you want to go to a real restaurant or you want to really go scuba diving.'

The next chapter looks at amortal consumers and highlights two qualities likely to grab our attention in a crowded marketplace: authenticity and atemporality, timelessness. The first does what it says on the tin: in an age of copies and fakes and virtuality, the appeal of the real, and the inimitable, is strong. And in the age of transience – fast food, fast fashion, fast turnover – atemporality has a special cachet. Most goods and services are marked like records for export by unseen codes locating them in a specific period. But there are designs that transcend time to become timeless classics. Some of the oldest Disney attractions achieve a degree of atemporality, despite their clunky audio-animatronics. The dark rides Pirates of the Caribbean and the Haunted Mansion are set in a past that never was.

Tomorrowland, by contrast, depicted a future that never would be. When Disneyland opened in 1955, 'Americans couldn't wait to get to the future,' says Adam. 'Everybody was drawing robots in every house and a flying car in every garage and I was growing up on TV shows like *The Jetsons*, and popular science was doing all these amazing things. It was the great flowering of science fiction writing, too, optimistic science fiction. There was always dystopia, but a lot of it was Buck Rogers stuff. The future was unarguably sunny. You couldn't imagine anything ever going wrong in the world, so of course the future had to be fantastic.'

A 1962 guide to Disneyland brims over with optimism about the coming 'wonderful age', describing Tomorrowland as 'a living blueprint of our future'. That future boasted luscious curves recalling a 1950s Oldsmobile and included 'Monsanto's all plastic House of the Future' and 'rocket ship rides into outer space' exactly 50 years before Virgin Galactic took its first deposit. 'In Tomorrowland you will actually experience what many of America's foremost men of science and industry predict for the world of tomorrow,' promised the guide.

For its creator, Walt Disney, tomorrow couldn't – and didn't – come soon enough. Like Ray Kurzweil and Aubrey de Grey, Disney believed passionately in the power of science to liberate individuals from their inbuilt obsolescence. Tomorrowland was just a school science project by comparison to the vast ambition of his plans for a stretch of Floridian swampland.

Visitors to EPCOT – the acronym stands for Experimental Prototype Community of Tomorrow – an annex to the Disney World complex outside Orlando, find an odd jumble of futuristic visions and national caricatures bordering a lake. If the attraction lacks the coherence of the main Disney theme parks, that's because it was never intended to be a theme park. Walt, amortal to his core, sought authenticity and atemporality. EPCOT, he told a 1966 press conference, would be a real city, 'like the city of tomorrow ought to be'. He continued: 'It will be a planned, controlled community; a showcase for American industry and research, schools, cultural and educational opportunities. In EPCOT there will be no slum areas because we won't let them develop. There will be no landowners and therefore no voting control. People will rent houses instead of buying them, and at modest rentals. There will be no retirees because everyone will be employed according to their ability. One of our requirements is that the people who live in EPCOT must help keep it alive.'[168]

In Disney's world, there would be no retirement and no death. Unfortunately, in the world he had not imagineered, he was suffering from lung cancer and feverishly investigating cryonics and other life-extension technologies in case his determination to attend the opening of EPCOT proved insufficient to sustain life. One of the many stories about the dying Disney sees him lying in his hospital bed and using the squares in the ceiling above him to allocate EPCOT land use.

In November 1966, one of his lungs was removed and cryonically frozen. He died less than a month later. The official notice stated that he had been cremated and his ashes interred at Forest Lawn Memorial Park in Glendale, California. Rumours persisted that Disney's body had in fact been frozen. 'He's going to be good and mad at what they have done to his City of Tomorrow,' one former associate told Disney's biographer. 'When he comes back, a lot of heads at Disney are going to roll. That's for sure.'[169]

6

amortal consumers
BECAUSE WE'RE WORTH IT

'Diving adds purpose to your travel and can bring new wonder
and adventure to a holiday which other, less fortunate people
may spend just lying on a beach.'
Sport Diving: the British Sub-Aqua Club Diving Manual

'I always say shopping is cheaper than a psychiatrist.'
Tammy Faye Bakker

'The problem of leisure
What to do for pleasure.'
Gang of Four, 'Natural's Not In It'

EPCOT TAMED A STRETCH of swampland. Sun City Shadow Hills, like
Vegas, overlaid desert with verdant life. The 771-acre compound south-
east of Palm Springs encloses the smooth, green contours of a golf
course, the arterial blood reds and pulsating pinks of oleander,
bougainvillea and tea roses, and a flourishing plantation of 'active adults
aged 55 and better', as the sales brochure describes those fortunate souls
old enough to qualify for the right to buy into the Sun City dream.
When a construction magnate called Del Webb opened the first Sun City

retirement community in 1960, only a few years before Disney began plotting his City of Tomorrow, few would have guessed that Del's legacy would turn out much closer to Walt's original conception of EPCOT than EPCOT itself. People don't move to Sun City – to any of the more than 50 Sun Cities now dotted across America – to wait out their final years. They arrive at Sun City in expectation of a new lease of life.

'When I see what we've built, it's the most satisfying thing that's ever happened to me,' enthused Webb, interviewed for a 1962 *TIME* cover story about his brainchild. 'An old fellow came up to me once with tears in his eyes and thanked me for building Sun City. He said he was planning to spend the happiest 40 years of his life there.'[170]

Webb died in 1974 and his company was swallowed by housebuilder Pulte Homes in 2001, but the Del Webb brand lives on. Sun City Shadow Hills in the Coachella Valley, California, is among the newest of the Del Webb communities, opened in 2004 and expected to reach a final tally of 3,400 homes by 2015. Driving along its flawless red macadam streets in yellow sunshine beneath unrealistically blue skies, you start to wonder if you've strayed on to a backlot at a Hollywood studio. The technicolour township is eerily still. Distant figures shimmer in the heat haze on the fairway and a golf buggy hums along a perimeter road, but the sidewalks are empty. Then you ring the doorbell at Patti and Phil Wolff's house and discover one reason for the unnatural calm. The Wolffs, 62, and their friends Larry Johnson (62) and Bruce Atkinson (65), and Mary O'Brien ('70 and a half') – a fair chunk of Sun City's boisterous population – are already ensconced in the Wolffs' large open-plan kitchen and living area. They're joined by Simha Skinner, 66, who lives in an older Sun City gated community just up the road. At the back of the house, through big sliding patio doors, there's a lush garden their next-door neighbour describes as 'bitchin'' and a barbecue sending aromatic smoke signals to the rest of the community that one of Patti's famous meals will shortly be served.

The Wolffs haven't yet been two years in Sun City, but they're already pillars of its thriving social life. 'One of the interesting things about Sun City is that this is a made-up community,' explains Johnson: 'Everyone comes in here, they're not second generation. They don't have kids who live in this community – they may live in Palm Desert or Palm Springs but that's pretty few and far between – so the playing field is sort of levelled. Everyone comes in and so I think there's this desire to participate, to interact.'

Some residents maintain a foothold in their old lives, typically spending winters at Sun City and returning to their family homes in the summer. These are the 'snowbirds' and another reason Sun City seems quiet. The May 2010 edition of the community's magazine, *The View*, reminds snowbirds to return library books prior to departure; it also carries reports of residents' more strenuous pursuits, including a fitness challenge that pitted five different Sun Cities against each other in categories including running, cycling, swimming and pet-walking (Shadow Hills came second overall). Four full pages list the coming month's scheduled activities from Pilates to ukulele classes and the fitness sessions that Patti used to attend until her 'gym buddy' O'Brien left her in the lurch (pleading work commitments) and she 'kind of went off the trail' too.

That's not to say she's been putting her feet up. In January 2010, Patti completed her most ambitious catering challenge to date, a dinner-dance that drew 81 guests, organised by the Rainbow Club, the community's gay and lesbian social club (Atkinson, Johnson's partner, is its founder and president). Patti bats away praise for the production, which involved chicken parmesan, vegetarian pasta, salads, desserts and cakes. 'When I found out they were going to have a caterer and they told me what it was going to cost per person just for the food I said, "Oh, come on, I can do that for half. And give you choices." So that's how that started,' she says.

Her husband Phil is a different kind of dynamo. Connected to the mains, he could power his whole street with its air-conditioned residences and 24-hour sprinkler systems. He plays softball, patronises the state-of-the-art gym at Sun City's 35,000-square-foot Montecito Clubhouse and indulges a passion for cycling, racking up as many as 175 miles per week. 'Basically he does so many things that I hardly see him,' says Patti.

Patti: 'It's like if he was back at work again. When he worked he'd
 leave at five in the morning and wouldn't get home again
 until like six-thirty, seven at night. I mean I see him more
 now but it's like gee ...'
[Skinner nods her head furiously.]
Skinner: 'He's always on his way to something.'
Patti: 'Is he playing softball today, is he riding his bike? There's so
 many activities that he does that it's like he's gone. He's gone,
 I don't know where he is, he's just gone. He'll be back.'

Phil's action-packed, work-free lifestyle comes thanks to his erstwhile
employer, telecoms company Pacific Bell, which feather-bedded him into
early retirement, along with Patti and Skinner. They were all in their forties
when they gave up wage slavery. None of them had ever been wealthy. It
took the move to Sun City to make them realise they were now rich – in
leisure. 'It is a dream,' says Skinner. Phil agrees: 'To us, this is a very luxurious lifestyle. You know, it's like country club living. And we were not ever
in a position to have a country club membership. Far from it. Now there
are people here in this community who have lived this more luxurious
lifestyle forever but most of the people that we seem to be friends with are
more in line with our experience. We're like, "How did we get this lucky?"'

O'Brien still devotes some four months a year to paid employment,
doing 'accounting, taxes mostly. And I absolutely love it.' Johnson, once
the manager of a funeral home in Oregon, these days offers a similar service for pets, assisted by Atkinson, for 32 years a probation officer in New
York and Phoenix, Arizona. 'The pet crematorium is Larry's business,' says
Atkinson. 'I just work there, I'm an unpaid lackey assistant so I take the
grunt work and I tell Larry not to spend so much time doing grief counselling. At the Pet Expo [organised by the Sun City pet club] we have a
booth and all the literature and urns on display. Hundreds of people show
up who have old dogs and cats, and eventually those dogs and cats will
die so Larry gets a lot of business.'

'IT IS EVERYTHING YOU DREAMED OF. It is nothing you'd expect.' The slogan, a perfect fit for Sun City, was coined not in the Del Webb marketing department but in Hollywood, as the tagline for a 1985 science fiction movie, *Cocoon*. The film centres on three old men from a retirement home, who trespass to use a private swimming pool and find its waters mysteriously rejuvenating. It transpires that aliens – masters of immortality technology, like the Raelians' Elohim – have infused the water with a life force to sustain their cocooned and hibernating brethren. Looking at the spry and sociable Sun City residents, one wonders if the two pools at the Montecito Clubhouse are really filled only with saltwater. But no technology has yet been able to stop the biological clocks that keep Johnson's business ticking over and will eventually disrupt the idyll that he and his friends have built.

O'Brien and Skinner are widows. Their husbands died after the move to Sun City. 'I always wondered why was I destined to move to a place like this, and then you lose your husband and then you know why. Because if I was in my old community, as nice as it was and I had family around, it would never be the same. I would never have this fulfilled life,' says Skinner.

> O'Brien: 'And that's why my kids are so happy for me. Here you have everything. You can meet somebody, there's something going on at the clubhouse at the drop of a hat.'
>
> Skinner: 'And we get together for no reason, you don't have to drive far, you know if someone calls, "Come over, let's have a drink," before you know it Patti has made a meal for 50. I think about it a lot and if you live in a mixed community where you have younger married people, they're busy with their kids, they're not going to ask you to dinner, they're not going to be your friend. They're your neighbours. But it's different here and it really helps to make a life. Am I right, Mary?'
>
> O'Brien: 'Definitely, yes. You don't ever feel like you're alone.'

For the moment, Sun City Shadow Hills offers the ideal support network for widows and widowers. But as their numbers inevitably swell, the support network will contract. On a recent night out at the Boulevards restaurant at Sun City Palm Desert, Johnson and Atkinson caught an uncomfortable glimpse of the future. 'We were standing there and we both made the comment, "God, these are really old people." I made the comment, "That's me, in 15 years, I'm going to be hobbling in,"' says Atkinson. 'Things will change in 15 years because you age in place.' Sun City Palm Desert opened 12 years before Sun City Shadow Hills; the average age of its residents is proportionately higher.

And because ownership of properties in these developments is restricted to those 55 and over, estate agents, like fertility clinics, offer one of few and increasingly important options for community renewal. Sun City typifies the kind of contradiction often found at the heart of amortal behaviours. Only someone with amortal tendencies would fail to notice the inherent flaw in the Sun City model: the communities are formed at the same time, grow old together and risk dying off together. Conversely, its sales pitch has at best limited traction for amortals, who seldom identify with the notion that they are old enough to belong in such a place (remember my 76-year-old mother's complete disassociation with 'grey elderly people' and actor Richard Wilson's reflexive 'look at that poor old man', though the object of his pity may be younger than he is). Amortals like my mother and Wilson don't recognise themselves in the images of smiling, silver-haired folk routinely deployed to advertise retirement communities. In her memoir *Crazy Age*, 77-year-old Jane Miller neatly summarises the attitude that makes the selling of age-related products and services to amortals a Sisyphean task: 'I avoid all articles and programmes advising me to insure myself now for dementia and other debilities, book a place in a home or negotiate a granny flat, let alone join EXIT or look into the fees, legality and conditions of death-delivering doctors in Switzerland. I should come clean. I'm not sure that I really believe that I will be dead one day, any more than I entirely believe that I'm as old as I am.'[171]

As the property market has cooled, some retirement communities have opted to lower or loosen age restrictions to widen the pool of prospective buyers and to enable children who inherit properties in retirement communities to enjoy full use of them.[172] Sun City Shadow Hills as yet maintains its 55-plus age bar. 'My daughter wants to buy in here so badly. I told her, I'm sorry, dear, you're only 40, it's not happening,' jokes O'Brien.

It's hard to imagine that these jovial sixty- and seventy-somethings would seriously begrudge younger generations a slice of their paradise, but admitting all comers might threaten it anyway. Towards the end of *Cocoon*, too many humans jump into the alien water, draining its life-giving force. An influx of younger residents at Sun City could destroy its magic. The absence of youth permits a powerful illusion of agelessness in which many of the phases associated with the whole life span – the excitement of discovering new passions, forming friendships, falling in love or at least joining the 'buffet' – are re-enacted in Sun City's charmed environment. Like Professor Langer's test subjects secluded in a retro-fitted New England hotel and shielded from reminders of their chronological age, Sun City's residents feel – and therefore become – less old. A dip in one of the Montecito Clubhouse pools may not make a person younger, but it works a different and potent alchemy. At Sun City, everyone becomes amortal.

THE BILLOWING NUMBERS of amortals, not just at Sun City but in the wider world, represent challenges and opportunities for business. 'The old ways of labelling are increasingly functionally outdated,' says Breaking Trends™ director Alec Howe. Marketers can't segment by age because people are doing and buying the same things throughout life and 'growing old is so last millennium'. In that one observation he identifies the biggest challenge and the biggest opportunity.

This chapter looks at what amortals buy, why we buy it and how we buy it. Some of the forces that combined to fuel amortality have also transformed consumer behaviour. In *Ageless Marketing*, a strategic guide to these changes, authors David B. Wolfe and Robert E. Snyder observe that television 'initially changed how people came to be informed about products, but did not initially generate big changes in leading marketplace behaviours'.[173] The internet, by contrast, swiftly revolutionised both marketing and buying. We have moved 'beyond the era of centralised, top-down, command-and-control communications', writes Greg Verdino in his 2010 book *microMARKETING*, adding: 'Big media and advertising aren't dead, but it would be naive to ignore the fact that the rules have changed … Simply put: mass isn't as mass *as it once was*, the things we've long taken for granted no longer work as well *as they once did*, and in a variety of ways the real action seems to have shifted from the centre to the edges.'[174] Verdino is the vice president of Powered Inc, one of the many specialist online agencies seeking to stay ahead of these fast-paced trends and keep in touch with today's mercurial consumers.

Older consumers – that is to say cognitively older consumers, who consider themselves old – have not disappeared. Indeed, as populations age, their numbers are swelling too. These are the old folk marketers know how to recognise; typically more conservative, stick-in-the-mud and frugal than their cognitively younger counterparts.

'Cognitively old adults would probably favour [marketing] appeals that emphasised playing it safe with brands that are known and accepted, since they tended to score high on cautiousness,' wrote Nancy Stephens, an associate professor of marketing at the W.P. Carey School of Business at Arizona State University in a 1991 analysis of the interrelationship between effective advertising and the cognitive, rather than chronological, age of its targets.[175]

Trying something new for comparison or for variety is not likely to appeal to the cognitively old. They appear to be risk averse …

The cognitively old appear to be harder to reach. They apparently do not seek information for its own sake and probably stick to media vehicles that are known and familiar to them.

For example, they are more likely to throw away direct mail advertising, and they do not like to window shop.

The patterns of consumption, and accessibility, of cognitively older adults are completely different from those of their chronologically equivalent but cognitively younger amortal counterparts. 'Older adults who are cognitively young are not very different from middle-aged and younger consumers. They lead active lives and enjoy many of the same goods and services. They may be good prospects for travel services, automobiles and recreational products. In general, the cognitively young may necessitate no special targeting.'[176]

You need only to look at customers of all ages browsing side-by-side at one of Apple's superstores to spot how the cognitively, but not chronologically, young broaden and deepen the consumer pool for products previously considered age-limited. In August 2010, the market research company Nielsen released a piece of analysis by its senior vice president and telecoms specialist Roger Entner entitled 'Who is buying the iPad, and will they also buy an iPhone?'[177] The research, based on a survey of more than 64,000 mobile subscribers in the US, noted that only about 15 per cent of iPad users were 56 and over but added: 'Over time, we believe the over-56 age segment could represent a significant growth opportunity for Apple.'

Moreover, Nielsen research showed that half of iPhone users were aged 37 and over, with the proportion of younger users only slightly greater for the more recently introduced iPad. What is striking is not how many older consumers buy Apple gadgets but that customers of all ages – and all types – are attracted to the products. (When David Cameron tired of explaining economic theory to me in Newquay Airport, he broke out his iPad, first demonstrating an app called Toast that his children enjoy and then accessing iTunes to listen to a track by my husband's band.)

Apple's example seems to promise great things about the universal appeal of products in the age of agelessness. Yet amortality's enlargement of the potential customer pool comes, like Winston Churchill's view of the Russians, as a riddle wrapped in a mystery inside an enigma. That's partly because marketing strategies are often based on fixed ideas that have for years gone unchallenged, despite the fact they're no longer valid or in some cases have never been valid. In *Ageless Marketing*, Wolfe and Snyder attempt to take an axe to one such shibboleth, asserting that 'the idea that companies should spend money to get younger people into their brands so they will "have them for a lifetime" is specious'.[178]

That idea would seem to be in incontrovertible action in Apple stores and in Downing Street and beneath my fingers as I type this sentence. (I bought my first Apple in 1986 and have composed most of this book on a temperamental MacBook Pro that overheats as often as my prose. I've owned at least six Apple computers and an iPod and if *TIME* didn't provide me with a company mobile, would almost certainly have succumbed to the iPhone by now.) The get-'em-young-keep-'em-forever philosophy that worked for Apple in my case and could turn the prime minister's kids into lifelong devotees underpins the continuing trend to throw advertising dollars at younger consumers and ignore the swelling demographic of the older market. But, Wolfe and Snyder counter with a study commissioned by the AARP – formerly known as the American Association of Retired Persons and later restyled to reflect the trend that sees many of its aged 50-plus members still working – to assess brand loyalty by age. The study found that 'product category correlates better with brand loyalty than age does. Within some product categories – for example, athletic footwear, leisure wear, car rentals, hotels and airlines – people aged 65 and older were less tied to specific brands than 19- to 44-year-olds were.'[179]

In other words, Apple falls into a product category capable of inspiring, or losing, our lifetime brand loyalty, whereas even if we're won over in our youth by Nike or Juicy Couture or Avis or Hilton or, God help us, Ryanair, we're just as likely to choose competing brands and services in later life.

This highlights the folly for many companies of focusing on recruiting young consumers if they do so at the expense of older, often richer, cohorts

– 'the New Customer Majority' of adults 40 and older, as Wolfe and Snyder call the biggest and growing mass of consumers.[180] The duo sees demographic change as the key driver of changing consumer patterns. But that is to identify the enigma while ignoring the mystery and leaving the riddle unsolved. Shifting demographics alone aren't tearing up the rules of advertising and marketing, neither are they single-handedly responsible for the radical reconfiguring of our shopping habits.

As our demographic bulge moves up the age range, distorting the population outline to the point that it closely resembles Antoine de Saint-Exupéry's drawing of a snake that swallowed an elephant, amortals are redefining the meanings of age, and new technologies are shredding the sales and marketing rulebook. No wonder the corporate world is confused.

THE RISE AND FALL OF SCION, a US car model, illustrates that confusion. Launched in 2003 exclusively in America and aiming to ensnare young car buyers who previously would have opted for second-hand motors (and whom its parent company, Toyota, assumed could subsequently be groomed to stay loyal to Toyota and move to upscale models in later life), the Scion soared, a boxy creation to fly so high, rising from first-year sales of 10,898 units to 173,034 in 2006. But the following year sales declined and that trend has continued, with a 49 per cent drop in 2009 and a further 20 per cent slippage in 2010, despite bullish predictions of a rebound by Scion vice president Jack Hollis at the New York International Auto Show in March of that year.[181] Two new Scion products were launched at the show to assist in that aim. 'I don't think Scion needs to be reinvented, but we need to find the next dimension,' Hollis told *Automotive News*, confirming that Scion was considering extending its range still further.[182]

These conventional responses to a downturn in sales ignore the reasons for Scion's initial success. At the outset, the Toyota subsidiary positioned itself as a different kind of brand, almost a guerilla outfit. The company eschewed a traditional launch campaign centred on television and print advertising in favour of generating online and word-of-mouth buzz. 'Keeping things low key made sense,' observed Dan Lienert in *Forbes*.

> After all, [Scion] was designed to attract younger buyers, who are notoriously inscrutable and tend to resist overt marketing efforts …
>
> The initial marketing may have been comparatively quiet, but it hit hard by using unconventional targets. Befuddled Toyota PR people spoke at the time of hosting press conferences in which a majority of reporters in attendance would sport body piercings and/or tattoos and work for publications with names such as *Yellow Rat Bastard* and *Art Prostitute*.[183]

But Scion's marketing approach couldn't have worked if the product itself didn't offer something that's increasingly sought after and increasingly hard to find: exclusivity. That may seem an unlikely attribute for a range of budget-conscious vehicles. Standard business thinking sees exclusivity, and its soul mate authenticity, as commodities that can only be guaranteed by high prices. The rich buy one-off exclusivity; the rest of us make do with cheap fakes and copies from the high street.

That is to ignore the possibility for consumers to customise, personalise, to create exclusivity and authenticity. Content creation is the hallmark of Generation C, a phenomenon originally named and defined by the consumer trends firm Trendwatching.com and described by Verdino in *microMARKETING* as a 'new creative class … in a highly distributed micro-content environment that empowers everyone to be a media outlet and gives anyone the ability to be a not-so-hidden persuader.'[184]

Scion appealed to Generation C because the cars were pitched to these micro-creatives not as finished items but as products waiting to be customised, in much the same way one might personalise a Facebook profile or add apps to an iPhone, but using accessories and peripherals supplied by Scion. The buyer demographic was and remains younger than the industry average. Nevertheless, as sales have declined, the median age of purchasers, especially of some Scion models, is ascending, provoking hand-wringing among Toyota executives forced to watch their cool youth brand co-opted by oldies who refuse to recognise Scion isn't meant for them.

There is an uncool explanation for Scion's burgeoning ageless appeal: in an era of high petrol prices and financial squeeze, good mileage and a reasonable price tag look just as good through bifocals as through RayBans. But that's not the only reason the cars have collected a passionate band of devotees who bear little resemblance to the hipsters Toyota wants to see associated with its brand. With social media and technology use rising rapidly across the age spectrum – an AARP survey in June 2010 found 40 per cent of 50-pluses 'extremely' or 'very comfortable' using the internet and women over 55 are the fastest blossoming segment among US users of Facebook – Scion's marketing campaign and its appeal to content creators resonated beyond its intended targets.[185] [186]

Verdino pointed me to an online Scion users' forum, where owners of the xB model debate the pros and cons of their cars. 'I'm 60 years old and love my new xB,' posts BPG.

It's a great little car and not just for the younger folks. I'll bet that there are more of us old farts out there driving xBs than people believe ...

Why did I jump ship and buy my first Japanese car? 1) I love the look of the xB. 2) Can't beat the price. Being on a budget, where are you going to find such a cool vehicle from a proven high-quality manufacturer for $15,000+. Having fixed pricing and making the selling price attractive to the younger buyer is a bonus for us older folks. 3) Getting in and out. Having the mind of a kid and the bones of a 60-year-old it's great being able to plant my butt on the seat and get out of my xB without having to use the door frame as a hoist. 4) Everyone that rides with me can't believe how roomy the interior really is. Fold the back seats down and you've got tons of room to cart stuff around. 5) I love all of the great web sites, including this one, and the sellers of interesting products available for the xB. I've already added cruise control, fog lights, alloy wheels and my new Boomerang armrest is on its way. No, most of us old farts will not be adding iPod radios, high-power amps and speakers, radical exterior mods or LED lighting. It's fun to see all of the mods that have been done. 6) The ride is great! I love the handling.

But, come on, you Scion Marketing guys. Let's have some accessories/options for the over-40 set. How about factory cruise control, a dome light over the dash (just try and read a map in the dark), bright incandescent lights in the front footwells, heated front seats or maybe better/more instrumentation?

A forum user calling himself Easyoboe2 responds:

You are telling it like it is young man (I'm 75). You can easily have cruise control installed, search around and you can find dome lights for the front … If you do any driving of an hour or more you should put in an armrest. You can't wish for a lot more standard equipment or the initial price will exceed what some people are willing to pay. And adding things is fun. My xB is my serious transportation, but it is also my hobby.

It's never too late to have a happy childhood.

BPG is unlikely to find the 'Scion Marketing guys' responsive to his requests. Like a dancing dad at a teenage party, Toyota is instead redoubling its efforts to go after younger buyers, not least by attempting to keep up with young folks' changing tastes in music. 'Scion is gently shifting away from its hip-hop music connection. A hip-hop offshoot known as electro is now commanding more attention from teens and college students – and, therefore, from Scion. The brand's link to street art and student film will continue,' reported *Automotive News* in 2008.[187] Scion Vice President Hollis struck a defiant note at the 2011 Detroit Auto Show, telling reporters that the car had 'lost numbers, not youth', and adding, 'Scion has to find new ways to attract youth … I think Scion will take the lead.'[188]

Scion's efforts to grab the youth market seem unlikely to impress Angus MacKenzie, editor-in-chief of *Motor Trend* magazine. Blogging on the 2007 launch of an updated Scion xB model, MacKenzie offered this critique of Toyota's strategy:

> Here's the thing: If you've built up a brand on the basis it's hip to be outside the automotive mainstream (Sample tagline from a Scion xB ad: 'So wrong for so many'), what happens when you start behaving too much like any other automaker, launching carefully contrived updates of your hit products?
>
> If Toyota had simply discontinued the Scion xB at the end of the original's model life, all those who had bought one would own a cool pop-culture icon, like a limited edition Casio G-Shock watch, a one-off Paul Frank handbag, or vintage loom Evisu jeans. Now when the new one launches they'll just own an old Scion xB. Which is about as cool as being the schmuck who owns an old Toyota Echo.

WILLIAM GIBSON ISN'T SURE he qualifies as a futurist. The author means this in all modesty, but his record of anticipating future trends and developments places him in a league above most self-proclaimed futurists and trend spotters. 'Some of the things I wrote about happen to be similar to some things that have subsequently come to be,' he says. 'I'm using the tool kit I was issued by a genre of science fiction at age 14 to examine the stuff outside the window or on my laptop screen.'

When Gibson first started publishing novels in the 1980s, the world outside his window was overwhelmingly analogue, yet he glimpsed the World Wide Web a decade before it came into being and coined the word 'cyberspace' to describe the interconnected virtual universe that the web created. He sensed that the web would not only offer fresh ways to work and entertain and communicate, but would create new forms of work and entertainment and communication; that cyberspace might stir, and begin to fulfil, a desire to create parallel realities. He described societies in which cosmetic surgery was routine, and multinational (or 'post-geographic') corporations were more powerful than governments. He didn't get everything right, as journalist Mark Sullivan pointed out in a piece marking the 25th anniversary of Gibson's 1984 book *Neuromancer*. The plot sees a dying hacker's brain downloaded and digitised. 'Very good reading, for sure, but very future-tense technology,' opined Sullivan.[189] Tell that to Ray Kurzweil, who at the time Sullivan handed down this judgement was already attempting to digitise his dead father.

Given Gibson's track record, he seemed a good person to ask about the changing meanings and realities of age and ageing. Yet we kept getting sidetracked from amortality into discussions about fashion and something cooler than fashion, which Gibson felt might be connected to amortality: atemporality and the lure of products that, like amortals themselves, are divorced from external markers of age and era.

Over the past decade Gibson has again spotted something outside his window not readily visible to the human eye: the swirl of stealth marketing and other sophisticated ways of pushing product as corporate interests seek to capture the atomised attention of the online masses. The original Scion xB had the potential to become an atemporal classic if only Toyota had resisted the idea of updating it; the original Scion launch might have been something dreamed up by one of the central characters in recent Gibson novels, Hubertus Bigend, the Belgian boss of Blue Ant, an agency that seeks to take ownership of trends and promote them virally.

In *Zero History*, published in 2010, Bigend has become involved in the clothing industry, with a stake in the designer label Tanky & Tojo (Gibson once tweeted that he imagines virtual hyperlinks hovering over his novels. It's worth Googling 'Tanky & Tojo'). The Belgian is not beyond industrial espionage in his hunt for the next big thing. That might be combat gear interpreted so cleverly for the high street that its wearers feel they are part of an elite police or military unit; Bigend speaks of a 'Mitty demographic' of 'young men who dress to feel they'll be mistaken for having special capability'. 'Sounds like fashion,' responds his interlocutor. 'Exactly,' replies Bigend. 'Pants, but only just the right ones. We could never have engineered so powerful a locus of consumer desire.'[190]

Bigend's greatest obsession, however, is to track down, presumably to buy up and exploit, a secret brand, Gabriel Hounds. The label is so exclusive that it has no physical or virtual shopfront, no marketing team, no sales people, no public identity. Nobody knows who makes the clothes – all one-off pieces, utilitarian yet indefinably elegant, in gorgeously textured denims – or how to track them down. 'The idea is that you buy this very expensive, beautifully made clothing and keep it and wear it for years, it's designed to be as atemporal as possible,' says Gibson.

To understand the appeal of the atemporal for the amortal – and the difficulties of successfully retailing atemporally – take a stroll through your local outpost of the US giant Gap. The brand lost ground in the 1990s after a flirtation with fast fashion; sales recovered after the chain rediscovered an atemporal aesthetic that makes it hard to distinguish one year's collection from the next. That aesthetic has also enabled the retailer to draw customers from across the age ranges – an irony in light of its history. Its founder Donald Fisher chose the name Gap to highlight the yawning generation gap between the stuffy retailing establishment and the rebellious youth of 1969 he hoped to lure to his records and jeans store.

Despite its ageless positioning, Gap hit hard times again in the new millennium, buffeted by economic downturn and squeezed by competition from fast-fashion outlets, notably in the case of another US company, Forever 21, targeting amortal shoppers with the premise that dressing young keeps you young. But Gap was also hurt by competitors selling atemporal designs at lower prices, or seemingly better made, than the American behemoth's versions. Atemporality is only appealing when well executed. Gap's recent return to healthier profits has been helped by clever initiatives to polish its image as an ethical brand – consumers don't just buy a pair of jeans, they buy a lifestyle and a set of values, and Gap in common with other major retailers was damaged by revelations of sweatshop conditions among some of its suppliers. But the 1969 Premium Jeans line, launched in 2009, is the biggest contributor to what some observers believe may mark more than just a brief uptick in Gap's fortunes.

Unveiled, like a collection of Gabriel Hounds clothing, at a pop-up shop in West Hollywood, the 1969 Premium Jeans sold like hot cakes. The company responded by extending the line to its babyGap infant and toddler range, putting 'customers in its jeans from birth until, well, the final fade-out', as retailing expert Mike Duff joked.[191] Quality and atemporality are the jeans' selling points, as a People.com report on the celebrity-studded launch made clear: 'Gap creative director Patrick Robinson is to thank for the new recessionista obsession: Robinson spent a year and a half fine-tuning the line, from shopping around for fabrics, and teaching factories how to make those perfect hand-made finishes, to working with several body types to master that perfect fit. "For me, honestly, these are the best fitting jeans in the world. We'll go up against any brand of any jean, and these fit better," says Robinson.'[192]

The creative director seems to have locked on to a mass-market vision of timelessness. But there are some qualities that simply cannot be mass-produced. As fast fashion gets ever quicker on its nimble feet and demi-celebrities dress their pocket pooches in Burberry, the value of authenticity and exclusivity is spiralling. Secret brands offering concentrated essence of both these rare fragrances may already exist outside the pages of Gibson's novels. Gibson says he's heard of 'a clothing line, no one's ever seen the clothing, but occasionally in the shop in Harajuku they will sell a few Rolex watches that have the dials customised to refer to this thing that may be a clothing brand. And someone goes in and pays thousands of dollars for this watch, which derives all of its extra status from the logo of something that you can't get.'

Here's where Gibson, a seer if not a futurist, predicts our desire for authenticity and exclusivity will lead us:

> If it's just about the price, you can buy it in Kansas City; anybody anywhere can have anything they want if they can afford to pay for it – unless they can't find it. Unless part of the price is whatever labour of knowledge you have to spend to find it.
>
> My hunch would be that that's where that stuff will go in future. It'll be about knowledge.

THE ONLY THING MORE SEDUCTIVE to the amortal consumer than the perfect purchase is the hunt for the perfect purchase. Amortals, as we know, are highly skilled at finding diversionary activities. Little could be more absorbing than the quest for a Gabriel Hounds jacket; the tactical challenge of a bidding war on eBay; or the immersive entertainment of exploring a giant mall (like Vegas casinos, such malls are atemporal, shielded from natural light and other external reminders of passing time). If it's hard to get, we want it more. We queue overnight for iPhones and become embroiled in near-riots for 'limited edition' clothing lines (limited to those aggressive enough to survive the melee).

Amortals are not conscience-free. Indeed, we're particularly susceptible to sales pitches that link the act of purchasing, or owning, to collective acts of virtue. Our pizza tastes better if it persuades us we have the power to stop Venice from drowning; we feel good about our (PRODUCT)[RED] branded phones and sneakers and cups of coffee because they promise to pass on to HIV/AIDS sufferers the gift of (EXTENDED)[LIFE] we desire for ourselves. Green consumerism may be an oxymoron but we buy eco-goods with abandon. In the London Regent's Street branch of Anthropologie, a clothing and furnishings retailer singled out in *Ageless Marketing* as 'a catalyst of delightful experiences' and temple of ageless retailing, my gaze is caught by an artwork, a collage of scrap metal on canvas bearing an unlikely legend. [193] Maybe it's for sale, just like the chandeliers fashioned from waste materials that overhang the staircase. Or perhaps it's one of Anthropologie's carefully conceived decorative features that also include a wall of living plants and a lumber yard's worth of rough-hewn wood. The message on the canvas: 'Use it up/Wear it out/ Make do without.'

As shoppers happily pick through racks of flouncy dresses beneath this austere anti-consumerist message, I remember my conversation with terror management theorist Burke about the complexity of the things we do to protect ourselves against the metaphysical anguish of mortality salience. He believes we find a comforting sense of immortality in building up our self-esteem within the context of the values of our culture, which we must also fiercely defend for the anxiety buffering to be effective. Amortals not only shop as a distraction from uncomfortable thoughts but as a way to bolster self-image. Those 1969 Premium Jeans improve us cosmetically, without the involvement of needle or knife, and place us firmly in the cultural flow. A garment from Gabriel Hounds would have that effect to the power of 100. But exclusivity isn't an option for the majority. Buying a tangible symbol of our commitment to saving Venice or African lives or the planet is an alternative manifestation of ego-enhancing shopping, and here's the cool thing: it may even help to save Venice, African lives or the planet.

Of course, to paraphrase Cenegenics patient Maria White, if you're not at your best, how can you save Venice, Africa or the planet? We've already touched on the ways in which the huge, multifaceted global immortality industry thrives on amortals' desire to buy self-esteem – and eternal life. Amortals are dedicated followers of fads and fables, high-end cosmetics and low-end snake oil: products and services, in short, that promise to give their customers control over their life course.

Few experiences more reliably illuminate the limits of that control than commercial travel. A trip on Virgin Galactic might make us feel like superheroes, but could also bring us uncomfortably close to Emile Cioran's hundreds of millions of suns and the scary sense of infinity they arouse. A flight with Ryanair – delayed or just crammed with sharp-elbowed humanity – is more likely to provide rude reminders of our temporal impotence. But some forms of leisure travel and packaged experience represent the apotheosis of amortal desires. For amortals, the true holiday in paradise is one that makes us godlike.

ON THE THIRD DAY, the prison regime at the Complete Retreat began to work its rough magic. Rousted from bed for a pre-dawn yoga session, my husband Andy and I discovered that the savage migraine of caffeine withdrawal that had blighted the previous 24 hours had eased. Since arrival, participants had eaten nothing but raw foods, submitted to twice-daily high-speed route marches up and down steep Spanish hills and endured massages so painfully deep they'd have cracked the resolve of the bravest resistance fighter. Light of heart and head, yoga, and especially its soundtrack of tinkling bells and chanting monks, seemed irresistibly funny. Later, after another punishing yomp and a leafy lunch, the retreat's director, naturopath Lisa Jeans, gathered everyone into a semicircle on the living room floor for instruction in meditational methods of combating anxiety. She needed a volunteer, she said; somebody with a deep-seated phobia.

Nobody owned up to the greatest of these. When you're dying of exhaustion, you seldom worry about dying. We couldn't even summon up the energy to speak and the silence lengthened. Years before, a magazine had sent Andy to the cookery school at the doubly Michelin-starred Manoir aux Quat' Saisons, tickled by the idea of a post-punk musiscian learning to bone quails. As he sat slumped with fellow students after a long day at a hot stove, the establishment's famous chef-patron Raymond Blanc paid an unscheduled visit and, mistaking the students' slack-jawed fatigue for awe, issued this reassurance: 'You can talk to me. I am not a god.'

The cool, blonde Jeans, by contrast, is most definitely a deity, and as such drafts her own natural laws. (My green eyes, she told us, would be blue, if reckless living hadn't polluted the irises with tawny waste products. Still, there was good news: the close-knit fibres of the irises indicated robust good health and unusual longevity.) She's not a goddess one cares to disappoint, and as she looked around for volunteers, Andy rediscovered the strength to speak. 'Spiders,' he confessed. 'I'm scared of spiders.'

He might more accurately have said that he feels towards arachnids only slightly more warmly than Richard Dawkins does towards Pope Benedict. When Jeans asked that Andy imagine himself covered in a blanket of tarantulas, his face contorted with disgust and fear. Jeans set out to banish that fear, instructing Andy to tap two pressure points in his hand, then to roll his eyes in a figure of eight and, maintaining these actions, to hum. Had he chosen another melody, there's a chance I'd have suppressed my laughter but his strangulated version of 'March of the Toreadors' destroyed any last vestiges of control. He convulsed too, though still humming, tapping, eye-rolling and ultimately shedding tears in his efforts to regain composure. Jeans stood over us, impassive as Athena, as the rest of the flock caught our contagion and rolled and rocked at her feet.

That's pretty much the posture everyone adopts at the end of the Complete Retreat: prostrate at Jeans's feet. You may question the alternative therapies such as iridology and kinesiology that underpin her regimen (and most participants happily cherry-picked the parts they found plausible), but the results were unimpeachable. Everyone emerges healthier; those who need to, shed kilos. Andy lost a degree of arachnophobia, not least because memory of the cure still makes him guffaw, and we departed with renewed self-confidence in our power to make ourselves sleeker, stronger, to achieve what Cenegenics would call 'optimal' fitness. Jeans had infused all of us with a little bit of her divinity.

How long the halo can last under fluorescent office lights is not really the issue. 'Holidays' such as the Complete Retreat, if that's the appropriate word for a week's hard labour on slim rations, suit amortals not because they are life-changing but rather the opposite. Amortals seek movement, not change; we want to be restored to the condition we assume is our natural state but the age-aware might call the prime of life.

And busy, structured breaks, even if they bear more than a passing resemblance to incarceration in Colditz, suit us admirably. Heaven for non-amortals – an empty beach, an empty diary – is the amortal hell. Some of my kith reading this passage will disagree or declare this means they don't fit the amortal profile after all. 'We want nothing more than to relax,' they insist, 'if only we didn't have so much to do,' and they mean it. But they are the architects of their own, frazzling busyness, constructed precisely because time free from external imperatives can be frightening. On that empty beach, dark thoughts may cast darker shadows. Activity holidays offer a break from quotidian stress without opening the door to the spectres stress excludes.

The Ageless Traveler, a website founded by Generation Bold's Adriane Berg, offers tips and recommendations to suit amortals, from 'lifelong learning vacations' to 'voluntourism' ('life fulfilment and lots of fun'). The market for activity holidays grew continuously for five years until the economic downturn reined in discretionary spending; travel experts expect the sector to boom again. Research published by the research organisation Mintel in February 2010 noted that in Britain 'activity holidays are no longer just the preserve of young adrenalin junkies but are becoming more "mainstream", attracting more women, more over-50s and more families'.[194] One study estimated the global spend on such holidays at $89 billion in 2009, with an additional $53 billion outlay for related gear and accessories.[195]

The report distinguished between 'hard' and 'soft' adventuring. The latter category includes everything from the exacting cookery courses at

Manoir aux Quat' Saisons and other forms of learning-cum-leisure to cruises. To the first category belong activities that insurers categorise as higher risk and TMT might see as 'another way to show you're immune to death'.

Divers like to pretend the sport isn't about taking risks; on the contrary, they'll tell you it's about minimising the risks that exploring the blue entails. Training, especially the British Sub-Aqua Club system, geared to prepare stout-hearted enthusiasts for the cold, murk, deep wrecks and rough seas around Britain, emphasises caution. The BSAC manual carries a 16-chapter section headed 'Medical' and a seven-chapter section called 'Safety' before it even gets round to the main course of 'Diving Techniques'. 'In sport diving, risk must be reduced to the minimum and this is achieved by staying within your capabilities,' warns the author.[196]

Some of the loveliest dives are the most tranquil: lazy meanderings through corals and eel gardens in the kinds of warm, still, clear waters you won't find off the coast of Cornwall. But ask a pod of experienced divers to nominate favourite dives and most of us will choose faster, deeper, more dramatic diving experiences: drift dives that sweep you along underwater cliff faces, descents into fathomless canyons, the strange lure of the open hatch on the listing deck of a tanker.

Nothing beats the excitement of diving a giant wreck in the restricted visibility typical of British waters. There's nothing to see, just the shot line and a profound darkness swirling with tiny particles of seaweed and sediment, until your torch picks up an edge of a hulking structure too close to comprehend, and suddenly you're reduced to a speck, Cioran confronted by millions of suns, except that there's no light but for circling torch beams. Ahead of you looms the darker darkness of the ship and another dimension of darkness to explore: through the hatch. Swimming into a ship brings fresh risks: morays with heads as big as Shetland ponies, and lost bearings. You don't want to suck air needed for decompression stops as you hunt for an exit.

A fundamental pleasure of diving is the exercise of control. Cioran was forced to recognise his impotence. Diving of this nature, like Branson's ballooning, proposes the idea of powerlessness in the face of natural forces only to disprove the idea as we deploy our skills and our state-of-the-art technology to survive. There are cheaper, easier ways of subduing mortal fears that lurk like morays. You can tap pressure points, roll your eyes, hum 'Toreador'. Or you can try spending your way to peace of mind. That impulse, writ small, fuels amortal consumerism. On a larger scale, it funds every research project and biotech start-up dedicated to extending human life.

part three

the appliance of science
HOW TO LIVE AMORTALLY

'I want longer telomeres!'
Oprah Winfrey

'Life and death appeared to me ideal bounds, which I should
first break through, and pour a torrent of light into our dark
world. A new species would bless me as its creator and source;
many happy and excellent natures would owe their being to me.'
Mary Shelley, *Frankenstein*

'Time is a great teacher, but unfortunately it kills all its pupils.'
Hector Berlioz

MIRACLES DO HAPPEN. Babies are immaculately conceived in Petri dishes.
Craig Venter created a man-made life form by building a synthetic genome
and inserting it into a cell. Humans have stolen fire, harnessed the wind
and the water, learned to survive beneath the sea and on the pockmarked
face of the moon, and, perhaps most remarkably, to accept and adjust to
each extraordinary development. 'We went out when a car came – there

were only two in the village, the rector's and someone else's – and to see the car go past was, well, we just went to see it. And an aeroplane: that was the most wonderful thing of all,' reminisces Rosa Sayer as she sits in her cottage, a former almshouse, erected in 1665 and equipped over the centuries that followed with conveniences its previous inhabitants might have mistaken for magic and future tenants will deplore as outdated.

In the same decade the almshouse was built, an eminent British physicist and chemist called Robert Boyle drew up a list of future scientific achievements. His predictions included 'the art of flying' that enchanted the young Rosa, 'the making of armour light and extremely hard' that could describe the Kevlar jackets I've sported in war zones, and 'the art of continuing long under water, and exercising functions freely there' that gives my father so much pleasure.[197] Few challenges appear invulnerable to the inexorable advances of science and technology. Ray Kurzweil, a man personally responsible for a parade of technological marvels and a fervent exponent of the transhumanist near future, believes progress is exponential. 'Take mobile phones,' he says.

Fifteen years ago if someone took out a mobile phone in a movie this was a signal that this person was a member of the power elite because you had to be very wealthy to have a mobile phone. They didn't work very well and they were the size and weight of a brick. Then over the next ten years we put out a billion cell phones and in the next three years we put out the second billion and over the next 14 months the third billion and over the next eight months the fourth billion. Two years from now, everyone on the planet will have not just a phone but a smart phone. You've got half the farmers in China now with these devices in their pocket. They can access all of human knowledge in a few key strokes. It's actually remarkable what they can do, but just accessing Wikipedia alone is pretty powerful.

Kurzweil chooses an interesting example. Mobile telephony connects areas of China previously too remote, and too poor, to merit the laying of fixed lines. In a single decade from 1997, the number of Chinese mobile phone subscribers surged from 10 million to 500 million, and continues to balloon.[198] As communications technology has become more widely available, so the government devised fresh ways to control information flows and turn technology against technology. China has more than once erected a Great Firewall around Wikipedia and regularly blocks access to the websites of humanitarian agencies and other organisations its rulers perceive as dissident.

No scientific discovery comes with meaning and impact predetermined; every technological breakthrough carries the potential for good and ill. 'When you see something that is technically sweet, you go ahead and do it and you argue about what to do about it only after you have had your technical success,' explained Robert Oppenheimer, the leader of the Manhattan Project, the US-led programme to develop the atom bomb. In 1945, at the test site he christened Trinity, in the glare of the nuclear explosion that he had facilitated, Oppenheimer recalled a verse from the Hindu scripture, the *Bhagavad Gita*: 'If the radiance of a thousand suns were to burst at once into the sky, that would be like the splendour of the Mighty One.'

Mankind stands on the brink of another achievement of blinding magnitude, at least according to Kurzweil: the defeat of death. 'We're going to go from people thinking that they're going to live a little bit longer than their parents to hearing from experts that they're actually going to live indefinitely,' says Kurzweil's fellow immortalist Aubrey de Grey. 'This is going to be a serious *Wizard of Oz* moment.'

Yet if the quest for immortality really is 'doing God's work' as de Grey argues, its fruition might signal that God was enjoying a sly laugh at our expense. Endless life might very well bore us to death. 'There is no desirable or significant property which life would have more of, or have more unqualifiedly, if we lasted forever,' observed philosopher Bernard Williams in his meditation on the jaded fictional character Elina Makropulos and her decision to die after enduring more than three centuries of life.[199] 'Why do you want to live to 220, honestly, why?' asks Bob Geldof. 'The repetition, the heartache of all those relationships breaking up, the endless children that you'd lose track of, you know, great-grandchildren, the disappointments. And you know, there wouldn't be endless children, because you'd be trying to keep the world for yourself.'

Sociology professor James Côté argues that many of us are already trying to do just that, but even if the birth rate slowed further in response to radically increased longevity, a population given universal access to life-extension technologies would inexorably expand, adding to the pressures on earth's resources and ecosystems.

Immortalists insist that scientists clever enough to deliver eternal life would also find fixes for any problems eternal life threw up. But it's hard to see how science would tackle the inequities of entrenched gerontocracies that might be expected to reserve the benefits of life extension, and the spoils amassed over eternity, for their own class. It's a dystopian vision William Gibson's occasional collaborator, the science fiction writer Bruce Sterling, explores in his 1996 novel *Holy Fire*, set in a society dedicated to preserving – quite literally – its ruling elite. 'The medical-industrial complex dominated the planet's economy,' writes Sterling. 'Biomedicine had the highest investment rates and highest rates of technical innovation of any industry in the world.'[200] Gibson himself applies a 'street Marxist pragmatism' when he tackles transhumanism in his books; he assumes the beneficiaries of life-extension technologies would be 'people who have homes in Monaco, dictators of African countries, Colombian cocaine lords. They can afford it and in a way they have nothing better to do. It won't be the girl next door or the guy in the corner office; that's not going to happen unless the singularity comes and we all experience the rapture and start turning hamburgers into gold.'

Power tends to corrupt, but perpetual power could corrupt in perpetuity. When Gulliver arrives in Luggnagg on his travels, he encounters the struldbrugs, an immortal race whose mortal compatriots keep them in check by declaring them legally dead at 80 and stripping them of their assets.[201] A similarly robust approach might be indicated in Europe if research into life-extension technologies, funded by Silvio Berlusconi, proves successful. At a recent summit, the veteran Italian premier told Vladimir Putin of his investment. The Russian leader perked up. 'So we're going to live to 120?' Putin asked. 'It seems so, yes,' replied Berlusconi. 'But that would be an average age. I'm told leaders will have an even longer life.'[202]

THAT WAS THE BAD NEWS. And there's more. The problem of immortal life isn't likely to trouble us any time in the near future. In researching this book I've come to the conclusion we're probably not on the verge of turning hamburgers into gold or reanimating the frozen dead or keeping ourselves alive significantly beyond the record 122 years notched up by Jeanne Calment.

Robert Boyle made two predictions about age and ageing. He was right to anticipate 'the recovery of youth, or at least some of the marks of it, as new teeth, new hair colour'd as in youth'. He wasn't wrong to forecast 'the prolongation of life'.

Huge strides in reducing infant mortality, improving sanitation and controlling and combating communicable diseases have lengthened our life spans. Advances in medical science have added more years still. Kurzweil and de Grey argue that further inventions are set to slow and then stop the clocks. But at the time of writing, there is only one documented way to lengthen the life of some animals and organisms – caloric restriction, the severe reduction of nutrition that resveratrol's proponents hope it mimics – and that hasn't been conclusively demonstrated to work for humans.[203] There are no proven easy fixes, no proven ways to lengthen life and only one proven path to extending our health spans: to eat well and exercise regularly and maintain positive involvement with the world.

Later in this chapter, we'll look at how strict the diet and exercise regimen have to be to make a difference (a short and welcome answer: not too strict at all).

Many scientists are sceptical of claims that nanotechnology or regenerative medicine are set to change that reality in the near future by providing a real antidote to ageing. 'These guys would be great writers for *Star Trek*,' says Dr Thomas Perls, an associate professor of medicine at Boston University and the director of two key studies into longevity, the New England Centenarian Study and the National Institute on Ageing's Long Life Family Study. 'I see absolutely nothing in what they talk about grounded in good science. We're experiencing a point of diminishing return now in terms of longevity. We saw huge growth in average life expectancies, but as time goes on we really start to see a point of diminishing returns, to hit a wall where any further big improvement isn't going to happen, where we are really starting to experience the potential of the human body.'

Perls, in his own work, hopes to figure out why some people live to be robust centenarians, semi-supercentenarians (105 to 109) and even supercentenarians (110 and older), while most humans fail significantly earlier, often after suffering years of illness. The ultimate aim of such research is to see if something can be done to give us all the chance of not just living longer but living healthily longer. Scientists believe that lifestyle and environmental factors play the biggest role in determining both health and life spans, and psychological outlook is also considered highly significant. People who stay active and involved – whether working or enjoying the good life Sun City-style – tend to live not just longer, but better. But genes are decisive too, and not only in making some of us vulnerable to illnesses that will shorten our lives. Centenarian studies suggest that the exceptionally long-lived seem to be genetically predisposed to longevity. In other words – and it's one of those findings that really comes as no surprise – very long life runs in families. In July 2010 the journal *Science* published a paper by Perls and colleagues based on a genetic analysis of 801 centenarians and a slightly larger – and of necessity, younger – control group. They said they had found 150 unique genetic markers that could predict with 77 per cent accuracy whether their subject was a centenarian or a member of the control group.[204]

That doesn't mean there's genetic screening for longevity coming to a chemist near you any time soon, much less are there any gene therapies to reprogram the less genetically advantaged on offer even in the most exclusive of clinics. (It's doubtless only a matter of time until someone *claims* to offer such treatment.) The more scientists discover, the more they realise they don't know. Indeed, the validity of Perls's recent study has been questioned by critics who say different scanning systems used for the centenarians and the control group may have skewed results. At time of going to print, Perls's team had set out to review all of its findings and *Science* planned to re-evaluate the paper before deciding what further action to take.[205]

In 2002, Perls endorsed a position statement on ageing formulated by Jay Olshansky, a sociologist and professor of public health, Bruce Carnes, a geriatrician, and Leonard Hayflick, the microbiologist and professor of anatomy who observed that human cells in vitro stop dividing. The statement provides the clearest summary of current mainstream scientific thinking on the science of ageing. Other signatories included the International Longevity Center founder Robert Butler and 46 other prominent gerontologists from a range of different disciplines. 'The prospect of humans living forever is as unlikely today as it always has been,' the authors declared, 'and discussions of such an impossible scenario have no place in a scientific discourse.'[206]

After reading that sentence, it's startling to find de Grey snuggled cosily alongside the statement's other endorsers. 'I viewed (and still view) the "endorser" status as implying support for the general thrust of the document, but not necessarily for every sentence,' he emails when I query his support. 'I – and, I can tell you, a number of the other endorsers – fought pretty hard for a change to the wording of that sentence and others (many of which we succeeded in getting altered). However, we felt that the refusal of the three authors to adopt more cautious language in every area was insufficient reason to outweigh the argument for supporting the core message of the article, which of course was that ageing is (a) bad for you and (b) amenable in principle to significant delay by medical intervention, hence (c) deserving of far higher priority in public funding decisions.'

The statement argues that gains in longevity have been achieved by neutralising many threats to our lives, but that the main threat – ageing – remains untamed. This analysis is based on the idea that there's a kind of biological hourglass inside cells that eventually runs out when it reaches the eponymous Hayflick limit. When too many cells become senescent, we die. Thus, say the authors, 'even eliminating all ageing-related causes of death currently written on the death certificates of the elderly will not increase human life expectancy by more than 15 years. To exceed this limit, the underlying processes of ageing that increase vulnerability to all the common causes of death will have to be modified.'[207]

And that is exactly what a growing number of research teams are attempting to do. Scientists are looking at ways to limit cellular deterioration, for example, by protecting mitochondria, the cells' power plants. Damaged by free radicals – unstable atoms or groups of atoms that wreak havoc by bonding wildly with other molecules – mitochondria generate more free radicals. But the power of antioxidants, assumed to neutralise free radicals, has been queried by recent research, in turn calling into question the basis of a large and growing industry that pushes antioxidants as supplements, nutraceuticals (food products that claim to offer a health benefit and are less tightly regulated than drugs) and additives to cosmetics.[208] 'Lots of people thought the reason fruit and veg seem to be good for your health is because of antioxidants, so they did huge trials of giving people vitamin E and vitamin C. They were not protective,' says Professor Sir Michael Marmot, an eminent British expert in epidemiology and public health. 'If you do observational studies you can show that the level of vitamins in the plasma seem to be protective at higher levels but when you give them as supplements they do not prolong life.' He has 'giant reservations' about supplementation because it is 'too mechanical'. 'It may well be that the antioxidant chemicals in plasma are a good measure of the kind of diet that you have,' in other words, a marker, rather than a cause of, better health, he says.

ONE AREA OF RESEARCH does seem to hold out more hope – at least, if you think the risk of giving fresh lease to despots is outweighed by the benefits of extended longevity. In 2009, three scientists, Elizabeth Blackburn, Carol Greider and Jack Szostak, collected a Nobel Prize for their work on telomeres, the repetitive sequences of DNA at the end of each chromosome, which shorten when cells divide in the normal DNA replication process. Blackburn and Szostak first identified telomeres, and then with Greider showed that shortened telomeres indicated approaching cellular failure – in other words, telomeres might just be the biological hourglass setting Hayflick's limit. Blackburn and Greider went on to discover an enzyme they named telomerase, which builds up telomeres, and is found in greater concentrations in the few types of cells that never hit the Hayflick limit: immune, egg and sperm cells – and cancers. (Stupendously aggressive cancer cells harvested from a terminally ill cancer patient called Henrietta Lacks in 1951 are still dividing and, as a result, ruling lab research today, as the cell line most commonly used in experiments requiring human tissue.) The Nobel committee explained its decision to choose the telomere researchers as recipients of the prestigious prize not least because 'cancer might be treated by eradicating telomerase'.[209]

De Grey calls his vision for telomerase eradication the Whole Body Interdiction of Lengthening of Telomeres, WILT. This envisages banishing every trace of telomerase from the human body and using stem-cell therapies to perform the repair functions the body could no longer manage without the enzyme. 'In the WILT procedure, patients would undergo periodic bouts of chemotherapy to kill all the cells in the bone marrow.

Then they would receive injections of bone marrow in which the cells had no telomerase,' explains Jonathan Weiner in *Long for this World*, his treatise on the science of immortality and its compelling prophet, de Grey.[210]

Yet even if WILT proved workable, the process is viewed as unfeasibly harsh by many gerontologists, echoing Bruce Sterling's bleak imagining of regenerative technologies in his novel *Holy Fire*. ('They shaved her, all over. They stripped her. They stuffed her with paste. Then they started on the lung work, and they narcotised her utterly. All the rest of it went into the place where experiences that cannot be experienced must go.'[211]) Our desire to cheat death might be tempered by the prospect of life – or living death – reliant on constant medical intervention. That, after all, describes the difficult final years suffered by those unfortunate beneficiaries of the affluent world's already extended life spans who have gained extra decades without a corresponding gain in health span.

For many scientists the real motherlode of telomere research would be a youth elixir. That prospect received a boost in November 2010 with the publication in *Nature* of a study showing that mice with suppressed telomerase production aged swiftly but could be rejuvenated if the telomerase supply was restored.[212]

Bill Andrews, the founder of a Nevada-based biotech company called Sierra Sciences (its website is cure-aging-or-die-trying.com), is looking for ways to suffuse the body with the enzyme so that our telomeres regenerate. That means finding telomerase inducers that are able to activate the telomerase enzyme gene without killing the cells. It's an arduous task. 'On a scale from 0 to 100, where 0 means "has no effect on ageing" and 100 means "likely to completely immortalise cells", the best compounds we've found are about a 15,' says Jon Cornell of Sierra Sciences. 'This is based on comparing the level of telomerase activation the compounds induce against the level of telomerase produced by the immortal HeLa cell line [Henrietta Lacks's earthly remains]. Unfortunately, our compounds at "15" are believed to be too toxic for human use; we need to do a lot of medicinal chemistry before we can get them to preclinical trials.'

Sierra Sciences hopes to win sufficient funding – some $130 million – to steer at least one of these compounds through the FDA approval processes and on to the market in 15 years.[213] In the meantime, Andrews endorses a telomerase activator called TA-65, a nutraceutical marketed by a company called T.A. Sciences. The nutraceutical 'does have a telomerase-activating effect', Cornell tells me. 'But, TA-65 is very weak compared to some of the other chemicals we've discussed ... TA-65 is less than a 1.' So why does Andrews promote it? 'It's better than nothing,' says Cornell.

Andrews concurs. He not only takes TA-65 but gave his father supplies of the supplement for his 80th birthday. 'Until there is something better I will take my TA-65 every day,' he says. 'The fact that it is produced by my competition is irrelevant in my opinion. It is the only legitimate telomerase inducer on the market – so far.'

THAT 'BETTER THAN NOTHING' is the logic that drives many of us into the arms of the immortality industry. 'While it is still too early to know if supplemental resveratrol will translate to significant life extension in humans, both Ray and Terry take 50 milligrams of resveratrol twice daily,' declare Ray Kurzweil and his business partner Terry Grossman in *Transcend*, their guide to living long enough to live forever.[214] Similarly TA-65 *may* lengthen telomeres; longer telomeres *may* mean longer life. To quote from the supplier's promotional literature, TA-65 'is not a drug and we make no claims that it prevents or treats any disease'. One outcome alone has been conclusively proven: TA-65 will cost you a fair whack. As Arlene Weintraub recounts in *Selling the Fountain of Youth*, a scathing account of the anti-ageing industry, the compound is only one element of the price tag. T.A. Sciences founder Noel Patton opted not to sell TA-65 'in individual bottles or even on the internet by subscription', she explains. 'Instead he required that everyone who wanted to try it enrol in his 'Patton Protocol' at a cost of $25,000 for the first year. Customers who signed on agreed to take TA-65 along with 55 vitamins and minerals and to have more than 90 blood tests every six months.'[215]

Andrews became the first paying TA-65 customer in 2006, shelling out the full annual $25,000 for a protocol that delivered a daily 5 mg of the active ingredient, derived from the astragalus plant; he's now on 100 mg a day. 'As soon as my present supply runs out I plan on going on the new price plan that they have of $200 per month. The price has sure come down!!' he emails.

If the regime of blood tests and expensive supplements seems familiar, so does T.A. Sciences' newest medical consultant, Dr Jeffry Life, the public face – and muscle-bound body – of the Cenegenics Medical Institute. T.A. Sciences and Cenegenics have similar business models, licensing doctors to sell complete programmes and deriving a fair chunk of income from laboratory and pharmacy services.

Concerns about the Patton Protocol and the Cenegenics programme also run in parallel. The key question relates to antagonistic pleiotropy (the theory that the characteristics that are positives at one stage of life might prove negatives at a later stage): is it safe to restore a simulacrum of youth to an ageing body, or might the elevation of telomerase provided by TA-65, or Cenegenic's re-creation in older patients of the hormone levels that naturally occur earlier in life, entail a risk of cancer?

Telomerase is the same enzyme that stops cancer cells from dying – the basis of de Grey's WILT proposal – so isn't Andrews concerned that his TA-65 intake might inadvertently feed cancerous cells as well as healthy ones? Not at all, he insists. By keeping all cells, and especially immune cells, healthy longer, telomerase should help the body to ward off cancer, he reasons. Moreover 'at Sierra Sciences our DNA array analysis of human cells treated with TA-65 showed that TA-65 is one of the most inert chemicals that I have ever seen. All it appears to do is induce production of telomerase. So, I consider it very safe. In my opinion, it is safer than driving my car to work every day.'

At Cenegenics, I pose a similar set of questions to Beth Traylor, a proponent of bio-identical hormone treatment for herself and her menopausal female patients. She summons celebrity bio-identicals pros-elytiser Suzanne Somers, diagnosed with breast cancer in 2000, for the defence. 'Somers really has done an amazing job educating herself,' says Traylor. 'Before I knew anything about Cenegenics or bio-identical hormone replacement, I remember when she was diagnosed with her breast cancer and very shortly thereafter she went for hormone replace-ment therapy, and I thought, "Oh my God, what is she doing?" The traditional view [was that she was] pouring gasoline on a fire, [and I thought] "Oh my gosh, she'll be dead within two years". That's how we were trained. Never ever give hormone replacement therapy to a woman with a history of oestrogen receptor cancer. So I was just appalled that she did this. And she looks amazing.'

Traylor's otherwise avuncular colleague, Robert Willix, bristles when I describe 'hormone optimisation', the term Cenegenics applies to bio-identical hormone replacement and the equivalent hormone therapies for male patients, as 'controversial'. Speaking via a satellite link from Boca Raton that periodically pixelates his image and distorts his voice so that he resembles some kind of programmed Kurzweilian posthuman, Willix says that he and Cenegenics founder Alan Mintz agreed from the outset 'that what we do isn't really controversial'. The image freezes, jumps, speaks: 'So what makes controversy in medicine? What makes controversy in medicine is that mainstream medicine doesn't agree. And since they have the ability to influence the public, then they can manufacture controversy. Even if there's no evidence to support it.'

Mintz's own death during a brain biopsy has been cited by critics as a mute warning against hormone optimisation. In an essay entitled *Why Do Anti-Ageing Doctors Die?* Jay Olshansky lists proponents of diverse 'cures' and programmes who suffered untimely deaths. 'Alan Mintz – born in 1938, died in 2007 at age 69,' reads the entry for the Cenegenics founder. 'Claimed growth hormone (which he used) reverses ageing – cause of death, possible brain tumour.'[216] Weintraub describes one of Mintz's last television appearances, on the US current affairs programme *60 Minutes*:

Correspondent Steve Kroft commented that there were no controlled studies proving that the types of treatment regimens Cenegenics prescribed – and that Mintz himself was taking – actually relieved the frailties of old age. Mintz, clearly bothered, replied, 'We've never done a double-blind study on the sun, but you know and I know even on a cloudy day it's coming up every morning.' Kroft asked Mintz if he was sure the treatments wouldn't ultimately prove to be detrimental five, ten or even 15 years down the line. 'If you talk about five, ten, 15 years,' Mintz answered, 'I'm pretty comfortable.' One year later, Mintz was dead.'[217]

HEALTH GURU JACK LALANNE quipped that he couldn't die for fear of ruining his image. Mintz's death, though 'a major tragedy' for Cenegenics CEO John Adams, had a negligible impact on the reputation of the business they co-founded. '[Mintz] actually died of a brain bleed as a part of a procedure. He was having memory issues, and he kept doing test after test after test, found nothing and the doctor said, "Alan, I can do a brain biopsy." He was like, OK. He died from a procedure on the brain biopsy,' says Adams. 'I wish you could have met him, his passion for this and his dedication to it. This was just a personal passion. Not that he wasn't for profit, he understood we eventually had to make money but it took us quite a while, it took us between 1997 and our first profitable year was 2002. And a lot of money, probably to get to profitability was about $10 million. And then the total investment in Cenegenics between all the expansion and growth is north of $20 million. It's very profitable today.'

That profit remains steady at about 15 per cent of annual revenues, which, despite recent economic turbulence that saw some Cenegenics patients put their subscriptions on hold, amounted to around $65 million in 2009. Even as people felt the financial pinch, they've prioritised health and age management, says Adams; he expects Cenegenics will grow its network of 12 US centres to around 30 in the next five years, and is interested in expanding into Europe. An entrepreneur who met his future business partner Mintz at a late-night gym, Adams is an even more imposing presence than his brawny doctors, tall and with a solidity that suggests he might erode rather than age. His entire family, including his 82-year-old mother-in-law, are signed up to Cenegenics. 'You can measure somebody's passionate belief by what they would do for their own mom,' he tells me.

That seems as good a measure as any for this final section of the book, which addresses a key question for amortals: how to marry up the instinct for living agelessly with the ability to do so. The advice on healthy ageing is valid for non-amortals, too.

I DIDN'T EMBARK ON THIS BOOK as an expert in health and fitness, and make no claims to special expertise now. But my research has brought me into contact with some of the leading authorities in gerontology; I have attended numerous conferences and seminars, read widely and grappled with the science of ageing. I've observed older amortals who are weathering well and met younger amortals whose habits threaten to tip them out of their ageless, careless reverie into a slow and unnecessary decline. As I travelled, I've paid close heed to the cultural differences and economic factors that are creating a later-life health apartheid.

The primary inequity is, as ever, between richer and poorer populations. Bad, cheap, processed food, bad couch-potato habits and bad healthcare are profoundly ageing. Yet as the affluent middle classes increasingly embrace a fast-food, sedentary lifestyle and trust to the wonders of science not only to rejuvenate their cells but to clean up years of self-inflicted damage, their chances of living a long life to the full recede. America, the country that produced my vibrant grandmothers and vital parents, is slumping into premature decrepitude and Europe is following.

It all seems so *unnecessary*. Small lifestyle changes could spare many people an extended period of ill health, perhaps lasting decades. Yet you only have to spend a few days in the US to understand the challenge these small changes represent in a culture that has dulled its palate with sugar, salt and additives, atrophied its muscles by treating walking as an exotic sport and commoditised healthy habits into goods you have to pay for, through the nose.

Researchers blame American bad habits for an increasing longevity gap between the US and European countries.[218] (A visual gag, widely circulated on the internet, shows Michelangelo's David photoshopped from ideal of masculine beauty to fleshy slob. The caption reads: 'David returns to Italy after a short stay in the US.') But readers outside the States have no cause to be smug. America's most successful exports, fast food and sluggish lifestyles, threaten to turn increased longevity into a global curse. 'The biggest national weight increases among children have been in countries such as Greece and Spain, previously justly celebrated for their Mediterranean diets,' remarked one 2007 study.[219]

So, for me, the question is not only what would and should and can we do for mom – and ourselves – but how this can be applied more widely, and I'll turn to the issue of public policy later in this chapter. When it comes to advice for individuals on how to live agelessly, there's not much I'd recommend for my own mother that at 76 she hasn't already figured out for herself. A struggle with anorexia as a teenager, after the deaths, only a year apart, of both father and brother, have left her with osteoporosis which has curtailed her running. 'It wasn't doing my spine any good,' she says. She also has high blood pressure and in 2003 underwent chemotherapy and radiation therapy for colorectal cancer.

Nevertheless she is nimble and energetic, more so than many people half her age. At my request, she wrote out the routine that keeps her that way:

I play tennis twice a week (singles) for an hour each time. I do not rest or sit down during the hour. I do Pilates once a week and they let me stay two hours. I walk miles and miles. When possible, I can swim many lengths but hate indoor pools.

My diet is probably not something to hold up to scrutiny because, as with all former anorexics, it's a bit anarchic. I try to eat one main meal a day and I try to be a fish/chicken/fowl-eating vegetarian. I do love fruit and vegetables but have a dreadful sweet tooth. I also drink fizzy drinks (although not Diet Coke any more). I am a chronic nibbler although recently have been keeping raw carrots and radishes to hand).

I also do all my own housework, run up escalators and generally move my body often and vigorously. I have weighed much the same since I was a teenager – with the exception of my two-year fight against anorexia and three pregnancies.

My father, at 81, is also no slouch. Like the characters in *Cocoon* he is revitalised by regular immersions in his local pool. At least three or four times a week, he swims 32 lengths of a 25-metre pool (for the imperially minded, that's half a mile), limbering up first with a series of Pilates-influenced exercises. He was the first in our family to discover Pilates, in the early 1970s, when degenerative discs and surgery to fuse two vertebrae left him weak, inflexible and suffering from nerve damage. He has diminished sensation in his feet and sometimes stumbles. After we returned from celebrating his 70th birthday diving in Sharm, he set out to walk the 30 minutes from my house to the train station, carrying luggage that included his full scuba kit. He later felt chest pains and paid a visit to hospital where doctors diagnosed muscle strain, but also recommended blood thinners, which he still takes. He eats sensibly but has expanded inexorably around the waistline, a phenomenon he blames on his age and heritage.

The point about my parents' medical histories is that neither was dealt a perfect hand genetically and both contributed to the health problems they experienced: my mother by starving herself as a teen and eating eccentrically as an adult; my father by carrying a little more weight than is necessary, in his luggage and around the middle. But they have never invoked illness, injury or the advancing years to justify a slump into idleness. They keep physically active and remain mentally and socially engaged.

Would I like to see them signed up for the Patton Protocol or Cenegenics? No, though both programmes provide more individualised and detailed health care than anyone is ever likely to receive from a family doctor. During my consultation at Cenegenics, I was given the results of intricate bloodwork, put through monitored exercises and a series of body scans, and advised on nutrition. The results were encouraging – indeed the examining doctor Jeffrey Leake enthused that my good cholesterol (HDL) reading was 'off the scale', the highest he'd ever seen. (Nir Barzilai, the director of the Institute for Aging Research at the Albert Einstein College of Medicine in the Bronx and the director of a study seeking to identify longevity genes in humans, later told me that unusually high HDL could be a marker of exceptional longevity.)

The tests uncovered no problems, some results were rated 'excellent'; others 'good', but even good is 'sub-optimal'. Leake made that sound like a death sentence, which I suppose it is. The transition to 'optimal' would entail a fierce programme of exercise and moderate weight loss, he told me. Although my body mass index was logged at 19, towards the bottom of the normal range, one of the scans detected visceral fat, invisible from the outside, but a hazard for heart disease, diabetes, hypertension and bad cholesterol (LDL).

Leake also recommended hormone optimisation. He proposed to start me on two anabolic steroids – DHEA and testosterone – in pill and cream form respectively. 'We will monitor for possible side effects of androgen therapy which are acne, oiliness of skin, or deepening of the voice,' he emailed later. The sex hormone estradiol, like testosterone, could improve my bone density, he added. 'And if applicable – only after a comprehensive evaluation reveals an adult onset growth hormone deficiency (GHD) – we may consider supplementing with a third, growth hormone.'

I asked Leake for more information about DHEA. Produced in the adrenal glands, the hormone is thought to play a protective role against the biological changes associated with stress. We pump it out in our twen-ties and thereafter levels decline, to about 20 per cent of peak production by the time we reach our seventies. Did my DHEA reading give cause for concern? 'It was in the conventional normal range,' Leake responded, 'but I think augmenting it would be of benefit.' A month later an article in the *Daily Mail* caught my eye. 'A hormone naturally created in the body could be the elixir of life, scientists believe,' claimed the report. The fourth wave of the English Longitudinal Study of Ageing (ELSA) had picked up an apparent correlation between levels of DHEA-S, a metabolite of DHEA, and wealth. There is a correlation between wealth and life expectancy that the longitudinal study has helped to lay bare, but it's a big leap from there to pinpointing DHEA-S as the cause of the better health enjoyed by the rich. The only scientist quoted, Professor Marmot, uttered a faint 'good heavens' when I told him his comments had been framed in terms of life expectancy. 'We did not link DHEA-S to longevity. I only talk about what our research shows. I don't speculate wildly,' he said.

Clients often arrive on Cenegenics' doorstep in bad shape; commit-ment to the programme – not least to paying for it – helps to impose a discipline they may have lacked and to shed habits they may not have known were damaging. Traylor, a family doctor before joining Cenegenics, says she encountered profound ignorance about food values even in patients with college educations: 'They would come in visit after visit and their blood pressure wasn't any better and they hadn't lost any weight and their diabetes was still out of control. I remember one individual and I said, "Have you really been sticking to your diet?" "Oh yeah, doc, chicken, chicken, chicken. They know me at KFC," and I thought, oh, I didn't take the time to specify, don't make it fried. You think it's so obvious.'

Weaned off Colonel Sanders and Ronald McDonald and coaxed into the gym, converts to the Cenegenics way are likely to show clear benefits from the programme. More exercise and a better diet generally produce health improvements. And if that was all Cenegenics was selling, prettily packaged with brawny doctors and deluxe personalised health care, I'd have no hesitation in recommending its services to anyone with pockets deep enough to pay for it. But one reason Cenegenics patients often achieve such dramatic results is the same reason tiny East Germany carried off so many Olympic gold medals. Testosterone and other steroids promote muscle mass and physical strength. 'At Cenegenics our position, number one, is [hormone treatment] should never be used for athletic performance, only for health,' says Adams. 'Somebody can't walk into Cenegenics and say, "I want to take this." You have to go through an evaluation and the doctor has to determine what you need.' Cenegenics' doctors aim for 'the upper end of the normal range for a person's age. It's a very safe, healthy way to do it.'

Thomas Perls and other colleagues in the medical and scientific communities query whether long-term usage of steroids and growth hormone can ever be safe and healthy. Testosterone, for example, is implicated in 'roid rage', depressed sperm production, elevated bad cholesterol, shrunken testicles, water retention and bad skin; testosterone creams and gels have a nasty habit of transferring from the recipient, sparking a range of exotic health problems in spouses and children.[220]

In 1990, the *New England Journal of Medicine* published a study by a doctor called Daniel Rudman on the effects of growth hormone on a group of men aged 61 and above. The findings were favourable. Subjects showed marked increases in lean body mass and no apparent side effects. But such a small study, of short duration, hardly offered conclusive proof of the benefits of growth hormone, as its author pointed out: 'Among the questions that remain to be addressed are the following: What will be the benefits and what will be the nature and frequency of any adverse effects when larger numbers of elderly subjects and other doses of human growth hormone are studied? What organs are responsible for the increase in lean body mass, and do their functional capacities change as well? Only when such questions are answered can the possible benefits of human growth hormone in the elderly be explored.'[221]

As any theatre reviewer knows, a ringing endorsement can be fashioned out of the most scathing of reviews; Rudman's positive report, with its decorous note of scientific caution, was destined to be misrepresented. Instantly co-opted by the immortality industry and selectively quoted across the internet to promote growth hormone supplements, the study's provenance is usually cited as proof of its credibility: 'Remember, these startling findings were published in one of medicine's most conservative journals.'[222]

The conservative journal in question returned to the subject in 2003 with an updated look at research into growth hormone use by endocrinologist Mary Lee Vance. This time, the conclusions weren't quite so encouraging. Growth hormone changes body composition, but doesn't appear to improve function, said Vance. And then there are those niggling concerns about cancer: 'It is not known whether long-term administration of growth hormone in the elderly is potentially harmful – particularly with regard to the risk of cancer, given that older age is associated with an increased incidence of cancer.' A correlation between the development of prostate cancer and higher growth hormone concentrations 'does not demonstrate causality by growth hormone ... but it does raise concern about giving older men growth hormone.'[223]

There are alternatives to growth hormone, Vance noted. 'Going to the gym is beneficial and certainly cheaper.'

NOBODY WOULD ACCUSE the programmes and potions promoted by the immortality industry of being cheap. Bill Andrews says telomerase-activator TA-65 is safer than driving a car. It used to cost as much as a car, too, and even now represents about the same outlay as maintaining a car: from a Scion to a Porsche, depending on the dosing option agreed with your T.A. Sciences-licensed physician. Still, what price long life and rude health?

That's a calculation all of us must make as we navigate imperfect health care systems and consider available options for maintaining or improving our wellbeing in order to delay, for as long as possible, dependence on those systems. Hospital stays can fix specific problems;

hospitalisations often make us ill. Many doctors are wise; even wise doctors are not always right. My mother resisted pressure from the excellent National Health Service medical team treating her colorectal cancer to undergo a colostomy, which would have been irreversible because of the location of her tumour. They explained they couldn't be certain that chemotherapy and radiation had killed the tumour, because scans still picked up the carapace of scar tissue treatment left behind. She argued that a colostomy bag, to her, represented a fate worse than death, and insisted on exploring other options. There's an old joke about Aunt Mabel, who regrets her colostomy because she can't find shoes to match the bag, but amortal vanity gave my mother the last laugh. Her probing revealed the existence of two PET (Positron Emission Tomography) scanners in the UK, one in London, the other in Northern Ireland, expensive pieces of machinery that are able to distinguish between active cancers and scar tissue. She took the risk of waiting for an appointment and the scan indicated her tumour had succumbed to treatment. Eight years later, she is still cancer-free. The hospital has now changed its protocol, waiting longer after chemo- and radiotherapy before advising patients on whether to proceed to surgery.

My mother illustrates an important lesson for amortals and non-amortals alike. Never accept, without question, medical advice, and never more so than when you reach a vintage that could lure practitioners into false assumptions about your needs and priorities. Doctors are liable to presuppose that the over-60s assign a low priority to their physicality; fewer would imagine that sexual identity retains importance. After the age of 40, your complaint about a dodgy knee or a tennis elbow is likely to be palmed off with platitudes about what you should expect 'at your age'.

Give these inadequate responses the short shrift they deserve and push to be told what treatments your doctor would recommend to younger patients. 'Ageism in American medicine and society is a matter of life and death, as dangerous as any incorrectly prescribed medicine or slipped scalpel,' says Mark Lachs, a distinguished geriatrician and internist, in his latest book, *Treat Me, Not My Age*.[224] His observation holds true across the globe and in different health care systems.

While mainstream medicine retains its sclerotic attitudes to age, the immortality industry profits from our dissatisfaction. During a two-day conference in London in September 2010, I listened to advocates of immortalist therapies honing their sales skills on each other. The conference took place in Kensington, a London borough that perfectly illustrates the links between health outcomes and money. Health-conscious, affluent Kensingtonians live an average of a decade longer than their poorer counterparts in northern England.[225] Their wealth also makes them a prime target audience for purveyors of expensive nutraceuticals and therapies.

Zulya Maizetova, a dermatologist offering an 'integrated method of prevention and reversal of skin ageing through specific treatments to improve the body's own ability to regenerate itself', opened the conference with a eulogy to resveratrol. You might ask why a dermatologist was the organisers' choice to talk about a molecule that may or may not activate a gene that may or may not regulate the life span of mammals, possibly by mimicking caloric restriction. She told us resveratrol could inhibit cancers ('Resveratrol interacts with all three stages of developing cancer') and boost wellbeing in myriad ways. There was no mention during her segment, or a later audience Q&A, of the uncertain progress of the clinical trials of resveratrol. The compound, like telomerase, is still only available as a nutraceutical, so when I spotted its proselytiser enjoying a liquid lunch of green juice at the Kensington branch of Whole Foods, I asked her whether she was impatient for fully fledged FDA-approved properly potent sirtuin activators to become available. 'Oh no,' she said. 'I would not use such drugs. I use only natural resveratrol.'

Yet if we were happy to let nature take its course, the conference that had given Maizetova a platform earlier that day would never have taken place. The star turn of that afternoon's session was Noel Patton, the founder of T.A. Sciences. 'Short telomeres are the kiss of death,' he intoned. As the first person to take TA-65, he is, like Bill Andrews, a walking advertisement for the product. Unlike Andrews, he is a layman. 'I am not a scientist; I am not a medical doctor,' said the eponymous creator of the Patton Protocol.

Any potential credibility gap is filled by Andrews. Though Patton beat Andrews to the punch in monetising telomerase, Andrews, whose impressive curriculum vitae includes a doctorate in molecular and population genetics at the University of Georgia followed by almost three decades at five different biotech companies, latterly his own Sierra Sciences, lends his endorsement to TA-65. Not unlike de Grey's chest-length beard, Andrews's support for a competitor's product hints at a higher purpose underpinning his work. Andrews, de Grey and other notable stalwarts of the immortality industry are true believers in the humanitarian cause of vanquishing ageing. Sincere, brilliant, accomplished, they are plausible and persuasive. That doesn't necessarily mean we should invariably swallow their views or their compounds.

In September 2010, Andrews posted an exuberant tweet: 'The fountain of youth is here at last! Compound found that reverses the Aging Process in Humans!' He pasted a link to a study tracking the first 100 clients of T.A. Sciences for a year and concluding that clients' telomeres did grow longer.

Follow that link and you'll discover the findings on TA-65 not in one of the conservative journals of the medical establishment, but in a publication called *Rejuvenation Research*. The magazine is dedicated to 'cutting-edge work on rejuvenation therapies in the laboratory and clinic, as well as the latest research relevant to what these novel therapeutic approaches must do at the molecular and cellular level in order to be truly effective'. Its editor is Aubrey de Grey.

We could grow old attempting to untangle the interwoven threads of the immortality industry; it would take more than a lifetime to assess each of its products, programmes, protocols and panaceas or to analyse the individual passions that distinguish its prophets from its profit-motivated sales forces. The truth – and it's an unpalatable truth for amortals – is that no product, programme, protocol or panacea has yet been shown without a shadow of a doubt to significantly turn back the years. Some, like resveratrol and telomerase inducers, are based on serious science and may yet be proven effective. Others, as Robert Butler suggested, represent a way to make expensive urine. And there will always be treatments touted as lifesavers that might even shorten lives.

We cannot live indefinitely. We can aim to live agelessly. So as we near the end of what any confessionally minded celebrity would call our *journey*, let's take a look at the surest ways of doing so.

WHEN I ASKED MY FATHER how he keeps fit, he quoted an American folk song: 'Oh, it's beefsteak when I'm hungry / Rye whiskey when I'm dry / If a tree don't fall on me / I'll live till I die.' The lyric reminded me of two contrasting approaches to life: Herbert Grönemeyer's determination to be the tree sheltering his children, and the comical hypochondriacs of Jerome K. Jerome's *Three Men in a Boat*, who spend an evening comparing notes on manifold illnesses they have self-diagnosed. After reading medical texts in the British Museum, the narrator emerges convinced that there is only one ailment he has been spared: 'housemaid's knee'. He hurries to a doctor who writes out a prescription:

I did not open it. I took it to the nearest chemist's and handed it in. The man read it and then handed it back.

He said he didn't keep it.

I said: 'You are a chemist?'

He said: 'I am a chemist. If I was a co-operative stores and family hotel combined, I might be able to oblige you. Being only a chemist hampers me.'

I read the prescription. It ran: '1 lb beefsteak, with 1 pt bitter beer every 6 hours. 1 ten-mile walk every morning. 1 bed at 11 sharp every night. And don't stuff up your head with things you don't understand.'[226]

Nestling in a traditional song and a 19th-century novel is a formula for wellbeing more effective than any patented regimen or celebrity-endorsed nostrum available today. Nutritionists might balk at the emphasis on red meat; doctors would counsel that we restrict alcohol consumption, to 21 units a week for men and 14 for women. But the basics are sound: beefsteak (or an alternative protein source lower in saturated fat, as part of a home-cooked meal) and rye whiskey or bitter beer (a little of what you fancy), exercise (in a form that you enjoy), a healthy insouciance (think of yourself as a tree, not a delicate flower; be informed, not neurotic), sleep.

It's a simple prescription, but in common with Jerome K. Jerome's chemist, we don't always have the ability to fulfil it. One reason so many of us eat food that harms us – and isn't even tasty, although our corroded palates mislead us into thinking otherwise – is because shopping and cooking compete for our attention, and often lose, against lengthy commutes and long hours at the office and the leisure pursuits that represent our reward for the slog. Working people find it hard to fit in an exercise class once a week, much less a 10-mile daily constitutional.

Poor communities suffering high unemployment may be abundant in one commodity in short supply elsewhere: time. But such communities are less likely to use that time to do the things that will make them healthier. A large-scale study of education and obesity found 'a broadly linear relationship between the number of years spent in full-time education and the probability of obesity'. The authors added: 'The positive effect of education on obesity is likely to be determined by at least three factors: (a) greater access to health-related information and improved ability to handle such information; (b) clearer perception of the risks associated with lifestyle choices; and, (c) improved self-control and consistency of preferences over time.' [227]

As campaigning chef Jamie Oliver discovered in his quest to improve dietary habits in Britain and America, cooking is a dying art, as recondite as mental arithmetic in the age of the electronic calculator. Our governments should ensure that education systems tackle the problem. Instead they permit schools to reinforce it. Many state schools feed children cheap processed foods – an average of only $1 is spent per child per school meal in the US; a little more, around £1.50, is spent on each school meal in the UK – and domestic science is a rarity on most school timetables.[228] The children of affluent, educated parents are more likely to eat better and learn healthy habits at home, but all socio-economic groups are beginning to succumb to fast food and sloth.

Across the socio-economic range, we train kids like Perigord geese to open their gullets to food that will give them fatty livers. Children of all classes are too sedentary to use the calories they consume. They are chauffeured to and from school to keep them safe from theoretical dangers, entrenching a culture of inactivity that will most certainly harm them. Parents and offspring alike have forgotten how to walk, much less run, unless it's an awkward, flat-footed, knock-kneed sprint for a bus.

Household gadgets perform many of our chores and delivery services fill in the gaps. For all that time seems short, we're spendthrift in its use, losing hours in immobile thrall to computers and TVs. In the seductive virtual worlds of Second Life and World of Warcraft, we're supercharged athletes and ninja fighters. As we reluctantly leave our screens to make a cup of tea or answer one of the few calls of nature we're still capable of hearing, our slack muscles struggle to cope with the unfamiliar exertion. No surprise that exercise, like healthy eating, can seem a daunting prospect.

If you're lucky, you'll enjoy a long health span anyway. When Nir Barzilai inducts new participants into his centenarian research project, he asks them, 'Tell us your secret, did you eat yoghurt all your life, were you vegetarian?' He's delighted to report 'there's no vegetarians, there's no yoghurt eaters' among his doughtily long-lived subjects. Like Thomas Perls, Barzilai hopes to establish if certain genotypes are predisposed to great longevity.

But even if such genotypes are found, the genetically blessed would still be well advised to eat well and take some exercise, because health and energy are essential to enjoying life *right now*. Many people, amortals and non-amortals alike, become accustomed to low-grade discomfort and muscular weakness at increasingly young ages, forgetting the sensation of physical wellbeing and how it correlates to more elusive conditions such as happiness. Tough though it may be to balance the demands of our busy lives with the routines and habits that give us life force, the alternative is tougher.

Even the remaining enclaves in the developed world that have traditionally relied on manual labour and cuisines based on locally grown fresh vegetables and pulses and small amounts of animal protein are witnessing an erosion of the health span, as fast food and modern conveniences gain dominion. In *The Blue Zones*, author Dan Buettner reports from three such enclaves – Sardinia, Okinawa and the Nicoya Peninsula in Costa Rica – and also pays a visit to Loma Linda, a modern American town halfway between Sun City Shadow Hills and downtown Los Angeles. Though part of the LA sprawl, the otherwise unremarkable town is unusually heavily populated, like his rural destinations, with sprightly older folk, one of the so-called blue zones, 'where people reach age 100 at rates significantly higher, and on average, live longer, healthier lives'.[229]

In Loma Linda, faith – and church culture – probably boost longevity. Many residents are Seventh Day Adventists, a religion that 'expressly discourages smoking, alcohol consumption, or eating foods deemed to be unclean in the Bible, such as pork.'[230] As they grow older, they remain involved in the close-knit community, avoiding the numbing isolation that is a common feature of urban life. Buettner meets a centenarian called Marge Jetton, by this stage of her life installed in an 'independent-living facility', a retirement home, but still buzzing. She walks a mile inside the home every day and rides six to eight miles on an exercise bike. When her husband died, just short of their 77th anniversary, she might have sunk into despair. 'It took me a year to realise that the world wasn't going to come to me,' she told Buettner. 'That's when I started volunteering again, and it was the best thing to ever happen to me. I found that when you are depressed, that's when you do something for somebody else.'[231]

Jetton is proof that it's possible to carve out a way of living well within the urban world, and that's important. By 2008 half the global population had migrated to cities; in Europe and America the proportion of urbanites topped 70 per cent and that trend will only intensify.[232] Most of us aren't in a position to grow our food, farm it or hunt it; exercise isn't a by-product of our lifestyle but an optional add-on. Yet it is key to living agelessly. 'Exercise is the number one thing that could extend our life spans and our health spans as much as possible,' Bill Andrews told a sports magazine. 'I don't care what the mouse experiments say. Humans: the more exercise the better.'[233]

At 58, Andrews has completed more than 100 ultra-marathons, races of 50 miles or more. For most of us, his exercise regimen is an unobtainable dream – or nightmare. But unlike TA-65, when it comes to exercise we know for certain that something is better than nothing. Physical activity has been shown to maintain brain health and therefore reduce the danger of later-life memory problems.[234] The life span of an obese person is about a decade shorter than that of a person of healthy weight; the risk of death for an overweight person of average height increases by 30 per cent for every additional 15 kilos – and decreases by the same amount for every 15 kilos shed.[235] Being a bit less overweight and a bit more active can have a dramatic impact on health and life spans.

So if you need to lose weight, have a go, but not by relying on diet products or starving yourself. As a start, for one week only, prepare all your own food. If you frequently eat shop-bought sandwiches, ready meals, takeaways and other processed foods, your palate will be attuned to sugary, salty fare. Cut out added sugar and salt from your diet as far as possible, and you'll start to rediscover your taste buds. In remarkably short order, it becomes as unpleasant to consume fast foods as it seems desirable to habitués to eat them. I'm a dedicated carnivore so I don't plead for vegetarianism though it offers potential health benefits to us (and the planet). Nor would I recommend any austere regimes. Resveratrol was discovered by scientists trying to replicate, in humans, the life-extending effects of calorie reduction in laboratory rats. Some human lab rats aim for the same effect by subsisting on diets of steamed vegetables. That would certainly make life *feel* longer.

Kick smoking – if you must kill yourself slowly, there are more interesting ways to do it – and you'll be catapulted into a whole new world of flavour.

And add movement to your daily routines. Unless it's raining or I'm late, I never take a tube journey in central London of less than three stops and, like my mother, I walk or run up escalators.

You might consider taking Vitamin D, essential to the growth and maintenance of bones. It's the only vitamin that a decent diet doesn't always supply in sufficient quantity. Our bodies synthesise it when ultraviolet rays strike our skin, but that may not be much use to those of us living in northern climes and following medical advice to slap on protective creams if ever the clouds should part.[236] However, a recent study questioned the idea that most of us are vitamin D-deficient, so swallowing tablets daily, as I do, may just increase the value of your pee.

Thomas Perls provided another health tip, for men only. The male of the species isn't as proficient at surviving as his female counterparts. Indeed, only 15 per cent of centenarians are men. Some researchers believe this disparity is down to the female talent for social integration – we have better support networks and remain more engaged.[237] Another theory about why women 'win the longevity marathon', as Perls puts it, is that we menstruate every month for four decades or so, losing iron in the process. Iron 'plays a very important role in our cells' ability to produce free radicals', Perls explains.

> And free radical damage is a very important part of ageing and maybe being relatively iron deficient for a significant period of time could be an explanation in part for why women delay the onset of heart disease and stroke by about ten years compared to men …
>
> So I do something weird – I menstruate every eight weeks by donating a unit of blood to the blood bank. I'm B-negative, which

is a fairly rare blood type, so I do it because of that. But it may not be an entirely altruistic act.

I include this tip as an extremely optional, if socially useful, element of my advice on living well and agelessly. But there's one further lifestyle change I believe is essential, and it's a lesson learned from Britain's royals. If you fall off the horse, get back on the horse. If you eat too much or badly, drink to dribbling excess, smoke a crafty fag or play couch-potato for a week: get back on the horse. Don't set targets you're bound to miss or use one slip as an excuse to abandon all attempts at healthy living. Keeping fit and active is essential if, in the amortal words of Mick Jagger, you aim to just keep going while you can, doing what you like. And if that's not incentive enough, do it for your country and community. As the population ages, increasing the pressures on health care and the public purse, staying amortally ageless for as long as possible is a social service.

ONE FORM OF EXERCISE is guaranteed to make everyone feel better: using our powers as citizens and consumers to lobby for changes to the systems and policies that sabotage our ability to live agelessly. 'It is not enough for a great nation merely to have added new years to life,' declaimed John F. Kennedy, in a 1963 address to Congress. 'Our objective must be to add new life to those years.' Here's why America is still failing in that objective and Europe is doing little better.

- Ageism isn't a marginal problem. It's the dominant attitude in industrialised countries.
- We are all implicated. We reinforce prejudices about age by accepting the deification of youth.
- Policy-making – at government and institutional level – is piecemeal and incoherent.

- Politicians are too craven to tackle the habits that increase the risk of those diseases or to regulate more strictly the industries encouraging those habits.

Let's just look at one aspect: food. Agribusiness and its cheerleaders argue that industrialised food production and manufacture helps to alleviate poverty (pointing out that the recipients of its largesse are getting taller as well as wider) and is essential to feed the world's expanding populations. The counter-argument isn't straightforward. Without economies of scale and reforms to food subsidies, healthy produce is likely to remain an expensive luxury.

Nor are voters often to be found demanding that our indulgences be curtailed. There's nothing more surely guaranteed to rile the American electorate than an increase in the price of petrol or to dismay British voters than the threat of higher taxes on booze. On the face of it, you might think taxpayers are happy to subsidise their fellow citizens to get sick.

One underlying problem is that many of us have lost the ability to distinguish between food that is good and food that is addictive. The breakfasts and lunches served during the Age Boom Academy under-lined the way in which even the best-informed people who seek to eat healthily are let down by their own corrupted palates. I'd sit there every day watching prominent health experts chowing down uncom-plainingly on the foodstuffs creating many of the problems they were working to address.

At the start of each day, our generous hosts provided platters of pastries, muffins and fresh fruit. At lunch there would usually be a wild rice salad and a selection of sandwiches. By American standards, these were healthy meals. But the pastries and muffins and sandwich breads were loaded with sugar, the sandwiches filled with insipid processed meats, limp cheeses and salty mayonnaise; the rice salad was studded with dried cranberries; the sweet, blemish-free strawberries and pineapple chunks yielded only the faintest of flavours apart from generic 'fruit'.

I had first begun to understand America's eating disorder some years before, when I travelled to Chicago for my uncle's funeral. In his later years, he and his friends established an informal social club, the Romeos – Retired Old Men Eating Out. They had been particularly fond of the all-you-can-eat lunches at a suburban Chicago roadhouse with a bucolic name that suggested wholesome, farm-fresh produce, so that's where my aunt chose to hold Uncle Bud's wake. Mourners occupied one corner of the barn-like eaterie, while the remaining tables remained open to the regular clientele.

Dishes were arranged by continent – the Americas, Europe, Asia, Salad – and each tub and tureen of full-fat cuisine sat next to a 'low-fat' or 'lite' version. The larger the regular diners – and many of them were spectacularly large, with shelf-like hips and buttocks that appeared to have been borrowed from yet larger beings – the more inevitably they'd choose the 'lite' versions, the larger the portion they'd ladle on to their plates and the more often they'd return for further helpings.

I disliked the food, but found myself returning again and again to the buffet, trying this dish, that continent, in search of the one commodity in all this apparent variety that proved elusive: flavour. Flavourless, over-sweetened, oversalted food first turns us into Jewish mothers: it's no good, we complain, and the portions are too small. So we eat more and remain unsatisfied. And soon we lose the ability to discern what real flavours are.

We have the option to reverse that process and I hope readers will take from this book inspiration to push for change, on a personal level and as consumers and voters. Ageless living, without improvements to the way we age, is more likely than not to end badly. And we can improve the odds of not just long life but good long life simply by eating better.

To some ears that may sound like 'let them eat quinoa', the battle cry of the pampered middle classes. There's a widespread reluctance to advocate healthier eating for fear of appearing to ignore economic realities confronting poorer sections of society. The alternative is to accept the status quo and a health divide that already sees wide variations in the life expectancies of the poorest and the richest. Such longevity gaps are pronounced in the United States and Britain, two countries with glaring disparities in income, health care and education between their elites and their underclasses. Americans at or above the 95th income percentile are likely to live nine years longer than those at or below the 10th percentile.[238] There's an even larger gap in disability-free life expectancy, a full 17 years, between the UK's richest and poorest.[239]

Low-cost foods are cheaper than healthier options because they're less nutritious and because of a complex set of subsidies and tax regimens. Craig Sams, author of *The Little Food Book* and co-founder of the organic chocolate brand Green & Black's, supplies the following punchy summary:

> Governments have subsidised large-scale monoculture, which uses more agrichemicals, because they are subservient to agribusiness lobbying. Large-scale monoculture produces corn, soybeans, rapeseed and cottonseed. All are sources of cheap fat that is hydrogenated to compete with natural solid fats (though this route to 'market' is being replaced by biofuels). The resulting 'cake' or residue from oil pressing is virtually free for the processor, so can be sold as animal feed at an artificially low price. Hence cheap chicken and pork and feedlot beef.
>
> Hormones, constant antibiotic consumption throughout the animal's life and confined exercise-free conditions produce animals that are sexually confused, have degraded immune systems, and are fat and lazy.
>
> You are what you eat.

A WORLD I RULED would dine well and be a little more flexible, thanks to the provision of Pilates for all. Though I've practised Pilates since the mid-1980s, I'm not exactly the most compelling spokesperson for this form of exercise. The ease with which classmates decades my senior stretch and extend and balance and bend gives more eloquent testimony to an exercise technique that encourages flexibility as well as strength. When Pilates enthusiasts ask me what they should be doing to live agelessly, my first response is: 'You're already doing it.'

A German national called Joseph Pilates, interned by the British as an enemy alien during World War I, invented the system. (Aficionados will know that many of the machines incorporate springs to create weight resistance. They may not realise that Pilates improvised his early equipment from the scant materials available, including bedsprings.) Long favoured by dancers and athletes, the technique gained wider popularity once celebrities locked on to its benefits. A teacher at my studio was lured away by Madonna; sharp-elbowed divas pushed their way into our quietly companionable classes; gyms and community halls launched Pilates courses, often taught by instructors with no more than a weekend's training in the discipline. (By contrast, a teacher certified by Britain's Pilates Foundation trains for a year and logs 450 hours of study just to be able to give mat-work instruction; to teach the full studio class, using Pilates equipment, requires up to 24 months and 1,200 hours of study.)

The initial rush has subsided but teaching standards remain patchy. And Pilates – properly taught Pilates – could hardly be described as a cheap option. Ninety-minute studio classes at my central London haunt cost £25 – you could buy four packets of cigarettes for that. Not that classes are the preserve of rich celebrities. Classmates are a diverse bunch, hailing from six continents, ranging in chronological age from teens to eighties, from plebeian to patrician, working, retired, unemployed or 'resting', united by prioritising Pilates over other uses for their time and money. A regular for some 20 years, Brighton-born Barbara Giffin, the daughter of a farm worker, describes herself as 'an ordinary working person'. She left school at 15, became an office junior, did a stint as a chambermaid in a Swiss hotel, and then moved through various secretarial jobs. Redundancy money from the last of these, at Britain's Race Relations Board, covered the cost of training as a hairdresser, her original ambition.

She deploys her styling skills at a day-care centre and retirement homes and remarks that the physical condition of the older people she meets in the course of her work is 'scary … You have to keep fit to be healthy,' she says.

Cost and availability mean Pilates isn't a universal option. But a form of exercise that maintains mobility – whether walking, circuit training, yoga, swimming, a martial art – will keep you limber longer. With her chic deep-russet, blunt-cut bob and toned body, Giffin provides few external clues to her chronological age. Many of her friends are in their forties and fifties. She shudders at the idea of a Saga holiday 'where it's all old people. You want to mix with people doing the same sorts of things as you are.' And she's startled to find herself preparing to celebrate her 70th birthday. She has no plans to quit working or scale back on leisure pursuits that include frequent line-dancing weekends. 'I was talking to somebody and they were saying they were looking forward to their retirement, saving it all up for retirement and they would go away on a trip,' she says. 'But they weren't even fit enough to enjoy their cruise and they'd waited all this time, they'd waited until they were too old to enjoy it. You never know what's going to happen so you should think about what's happening in the here and now.'

in conclusion
THE INEVITABLE CONCLUSION

'Nothing of him that doth fade,
But doth suffer a sea change
Into something rich and strange.'
William Shakespeare, *The Tempest*

'A good thing never ends.'
Mick Jagger

'It seems more of a beginning than an ending.'
Eternal Reefs marketing slogan

GRANDMA JANE, THOUGH FIERCE, was also a giggler. When her best friend, a sculptor more imperious even than she, worried how long a proposed replacement hip would last, my grandmother spluttered. 'You're 89, Lillian,' she said. 'How long do you need it to last?'

Americans see 89 as the ideal age to die, according to a recent poll.[240] My grandmother may have laughed at the notion that her 89-year-old friend might outlive a brand new prosthetic, but like Lillian she did not accept, at 89, that her dancing days were over or that life – and the enjoyment of life – must come to an end. Nor did her view change at 90, 91,

92, 93, 94, 95, 96 or any time up to the moment of her death, aged 97. Elina Makropulos exhausted the possibilities of the world, but for amortals – enthralled by our changing universe and agents of enthralling change – those possibilities appear limitless. We assume ourselves to be capable of doing all sorts of things that convention tells us are unfeasible or inappropriate: founding empires as teenagers, forming attachments at any age, producing kids when we're old enough to be grandparents, diving when we're old enough to be great-grandparents. Sometimes reality douses us in cold water. At other times, and increasingly, reality yields to our influence.

Only in her final years, after her car accident, did my grandmother seem frail, but that wasn't her view of herself. My cousin Adam reminded me of an incident that took place a year or so before she died. Against every prediction of the doctors who reset her shattered bones, she was back living independently in her apartment on the eighth floor of a Chicago condominium. One of her neighbours became concerned that she hadn't seen Jane for a few days and when neither doorbell nor phone elicited a response, alerted paramedics. The ambulance crew arrived with a contingent of policemen, as is routine in such cases, to discover Grandma asleep in her bed. She awoke and, seeing the cops hovering over her, asked, 'Am I under arrest?'

As far as her family knows, Jane's only crimes were committed in the kitchen (she was a shockingly poor cook). But to her last day she conceived of herself as a wanted person: someone with enough spark that the authorities might mistake her for a criminal and with enough to contribute that she could engage with the world on her own terms and not, as so often happens with older people, as a supplicant. And for almost a century, that amortal self-image prevailed.

Then something changed – cells senesced, life began to ebb. Medical staff gave us a photocopied sheet headed 'Signs and Symptoms of Approaching Death'. Jane was already in what they called the 'pre-active phase', restless, devoid of appetite, short of breath. By the time she tumbled into the 'active phase of dying', she had ticked off all the common symptoms but two: she had no inclination to 'tie up unfinished business' and refused to acknowledge her fate. There was no sense that she was ready to go; no comforting glimmering of serenity. Nothing in her life became her like the living of it. The leaving of it was quite another matter.

Rather like the trade-off described in the theory of antagonistic pleiotropy between the characteristics that confer vigour in youth yet can curdle old age, the amortal lust for life stems from impulses that also make us peculiarly unsuited to cope with frailty and death. Writing this book forced me to focus on the science of ageing and to recognise, if not viscerally to accept, that mortality is inescapable. Despite also having pondered the potential pitfalls of immortality, I would still urge my husband, family and friends to drink elixirs or open their veins to restorative swarms of nanobots if I thought that would grant them even a few additional years. Instead I cling to the hope that by eating well and taking exercise, engaging and being engaged, they will at the very least challenge Jeanne Calment's record for longevity.

That is a goal to which any healthy human can aspire, assuming he or she has access to the fundamentals of life and the modern health and sanitation systems that have already extended our life spans. The blind watchmaker has saddled some of us with defects likely to thwart that ambition; accidents will happen; we inhabit a fractured, fractious planet in which violence is distributed as blindly as the genes for ataxia. Those eventualities are largely unpredictable and unavoidable, but the rest is down to us.

As we've seen, stretching the health span to match the life span depends in part on establishing certain virtuous cycles of physical maintenance. Attitude is also decisive, and amortals have plenty of attitude. In our assumptions of agelessness and blindness towards age, we crisscross a fine line between resilience and denial, optimism and absurdity. Yet to paraphrase Marilyn Monroe, it's better to be absolutely ridiculous than absolutely boring – or *bored*. As the work of psychologist Ellen Langer affirms, how you feel often becomes who you are. Boredom and its ugly sisters – detachment, isolation, rigidity – can drain life of joy, as surely as sickness and poverty.

This book has attempted to define and describe amortality and its energetic offspring, to explain a little of who and why we are and how we come to be overturning long-held assumptions about age and ageing. Unwitting revolutionaries, we have the potential to take that revolution in better and worse directions. Nothing will stop us from remodelling the family unit or leaping age barriers buoyed by love or lust. What matters is the quality of the relationships we form, the quality of the parenting we provide. We will not generously step aside for younger talent, but our compulsion to keep working, to remain productive, may provide at least partial relief from the economic strains of a greying population. Amortality is a product of a world that has normalised certain narcissistic traits, favours individualism over collectivism, has lost faith in God and public life. Yet, as Richard Flint so clearly demonstrated, amortals have the capacity for an enlightened self-interest, for a recognition of the inter-dependence of individual wellbeing and the common good.

Richard never shook his fear of death – as for many amortals, it was the combustion engine that powered him – but his inexorable illness encouraged him to make conscious decisions about how best to use the life he had left. That is an approach his fellow amortals would do well to emulate. Unacknowledged terrors can drive us in all sorts of directions and into all sorts of behaviours. Anxiety is debilitating. 'The thing of which I have the most fear is fear,' said Montaigne.[241] A deep dread of mortality disfigured the first decades of the essayist's life and only after a riding accident brought him close to death was he able to control that fear, to 'stare at the sun', in Jason Pontin's words. Finally well in his skin, Montaigne could joke about death. 'If you don't know how to die, don't worry,' he wrote. 'Nature will tell you what to do, on the spot, fully and adequately.'[242]

Amortals have to take that on trust. In the meantime we can try to live well and with some meaning, look to our own health and the health of our wider communities, challenge ageism and help by example to re-define age. If those aspirations seem too grand, we might just try to be a little less annoying to those closest to us: to temper our amortal impulse towards deliciously distracting drama and chaos. We could even force ourselves to plan for needs that might change over time, no matter how ageless we feel.

I can't claim to be leading by example. I fill every moment, but not necessarily with purpose. I doubt I'll ever be able to afford to retire. This book forced me to squint at the sun, but I looked away as fast as I could.

I did, however, find an acceptable conclusion — not, of course, that any amortal accepts the necessity of a conclusion. But if we can't achieve immortality by not dying, it seems that a number of companies including US-based Eternal Reefs offer to guarantee us immortality after death, by mixing our ashes into man-made reefs that divers place on the seabed. These start as comical-looking structures, inverted concrete tubs riddled with holes, but will gradually be transformed by the ocean environment, the dead core overlaid by new and pulsating growth and all around a kalei-doscope of light and movement. We'd still be at the centre of the action, still employed. It sounds reassuringly like amortal life.

ten questions towards a diagnosis

ARE YOU AMORTAL?

Tick the answer that most closely matches your immediate response.

1. **The difference between the age you are and the age you feel is:**
   a) More than 10 years.
   b) Up to 10 years.
   c) I feel the age I am.
   d) No idea. Age is an irrelevance.

2. **Describe your typical Sunday:**
   a) I often have to catch up on work but I also find time for friends.
   b) I usually have a lazy day and watch TV.
   c) Church, household chores and family pursuits.
   d) Hard to say, but just as busy as the rest of the week.

3. **The late thirties and forties are the best ages to have babies:**
   a) I agree, and I/my friends have done just that/are planning to do that.
   b) I'm not sure that's true. It's probably better to have kids when you have more energy.
   c) I disagree. It's unfair on the kids who have older parents.
   d) I haven't got round to thinking about babies.

4. **Your friend's new lover is 25 years younger than your friend. You:**
   a) Don't think the age difference matters. They're soul mates.
   b) Understand the attraction but the age gap means the relationship is unlikely to last.
   c) Think 'there's no fool like an old fool'.
   d) Hadn't noticed.

5. **You are permanently stressed and worried. You turn to:**
   a) Therapy. I start by fixing myself.
   b) Retail therapy. It always makes me feel better.
   c) Prayer. It always makes me feel better.
   d) Stress? The only thing that makes me stressed is having nothing to do.

6. **Your ideal holiday would be:**
   a) Action-packed. An adventure.
   b) A mixture of relaxation and sight-seeing.
   c) I like to spend quiet time at home.
   d) I prefer work trips. They're a better way to get under the skin of a country.

7. **Your fitness routine involves:**
   a) Guilt. I belong to a gym but I rarely go.
   b) I exercise/play a sport but I'm not as fit as I used to be.
   c) At school/college I played a vigorous sport.
   d) I don't really need to exercise because I'm always running to the next appointment.

8. **When you think about retirement you:**
   a) Shudder. I never want to stop working.
   b) Wonder if I'll ever be able to afford to retire.
   c) I am looking forward to my golden years.
   d) I haven't really thought that far ahead yet.

9. **The following statement best describes your attitude towards getting old:**
    a) I don't intend to get old the way people used to.
    b) It comes to us all, I suppose …
    c) I look forward to the dignity and wisdom of age.
    d) I haven't really thought that far ahead yet.

10. **Every life ends in death. Discuss:**
    a) Maybe, but science is on the point of finding ways to make us live longer.
    b) That's true but I'd really rather not think about it.
    c) And death is the beginning of eternal life.
    d) I haven't really thought that far ahead yet.

ANSWERS:

Mostly As

Bona fide amortal: You have strong amortal inclinations and are already living agelessly, at least in some respects.

Mostly Bs

On the way to amortality: You have latent amortal tendencies that may well develop in future.

Mostly Cs

Mortal soul: You have significant immunity to amortality and are unimpressed by many of its manifestations.

Mostly Ds

Amortal to the max: You're so detached from external concepts of age that you probably don't even realise how agelessly you live.

notes

INTRODUCTION

1 Author's dive log, Ras Caty, 16.4.99 'Painted moray, big tuna, confused divers. Pa lost a weight and aborted dive, later referred to buddy as "incestuous halfwit". Sergeant Pufferfish was so happy to find a dive watch he'd lost earlier that he kept tapping it. Charlotte and I thought he wanted to return to the boat.'

2 US National Institute on Aging

3 Office of National Statistics, figure for 2007

4 'Calls to raise age of criminal responsibility rejected', BBC Online, 13 March 2010

5 'Child Poverty in Perspective: An Overview of Child Wellbeing in Rich Countries', Unicef, Innocenti Research Centre, 2007

6 Ibid

7 Record Numbers of Britons Ended Their Lives at Dignitas Last Year, Martin Beckford, *Daily Telegraph*, 22 February 2010

8 '10 Ideas Changing the World Right Now: Amortality', Catherine Mayer, *TIME*, 12 March 2009

9 *Passages: Predictable Crises of Adult Life*, Gail Sheehy, E.P. Dutton & Co, 1974, 1976, Chapter 2: Predictable Crises of Adulthood

10 Piers Morgan, *Life Stories*, Simon Cowell, broadcast 6 March 2010

11 Hugh Hefner in interview with Renee Montagne, *The Long View*, NPR, broadcast 23 April 2007

12 Mick Jagger: 'My upbringing kept me stable', Martyn Palmer, *Sunday Telegraph*, 23 May 2010

13 'Dennis Hopper's last interview: His accomplishments, divorces and career', Bob Colacello, *Vanity Fair*, August 2010

14 'Why Are We Here? And Why Is It So Terrible?' Woody Allen in interview with Adam Higginbotham, *Seven* magazine, *Sunday Telegraph*, 20 June 2010

15 Department of Economic and Social Affairs, Population Division, United Nations

16 The Economist Intelligence Unit for GE's healthymagination, 2010

17   'Remeasuring Aging', W.C. Sanderson and S. Scherbov, Science Policy Forum, *Science*, 10 September 2010

PART ONE

18   '2010 Report of the 2009 Statistics: National Clearinghouse of Plastic Surgery Statistics', American Society of Plastic Surgeons

19   'International Survey on Aesthetic/Cosmetic Procedures Performed in 2009', International Society of Aesthetic Plastic Surgery

20   '2010 Report of the 2009 Statistics: National Clearinghouse of Plastic Surgery Statistics', American Society of Plastic Surgeons

21   Ibid

22   'International Survey on Aesthetic/Cosmetic Procedures Performed in 2009', International Society of Aesthetic Plastic Surgery

23   *The Disappearance of Childhood*, Neil Postman, Part 1, Chapter 2: The Printing Press and the New Adult

24   Ibid

25   Ibid, Part 1, Chapter 4, Childhood's Journey

26   *Teenage: the Creation of Youth 1875–1945*, Jon Savage, Part 7, Chapter 29, The Arrival of the Teenager

27   *Arrested Adulthood: the changing nature of maturity and identity*, Chapter 1: Maturity transformed: the rise of psychological adulthood, James Côté, New York University Press, 2000

28   Ibid

29   'Births and Deaths in England and Wales 2009', *Statistical Bulletin*, October 2010

30   'Social Trends', Office for National Statistics, July 2010

31   'Generation Gap in Values, Behaviors As Marriage and Parenthood Drift Apart, Public Is Concerned about Social Impact', Pew Research Center, 1 July 2007

32   '2010 Del Webb Boomer Survey', released 13 April 2010, conducted by Survey in November and December 2009

33   *The Culture of Narcissism: American Life in An Age of Diminishing Expectations*, Afterword: The Culture of Narcissism Revisited, Christopher Lasch

34   'American Religious Identification Survey 2009', Principal Investigators: Barry A. Kosmin and Ariela Keysar

35   http://people-press.org/

36   'The limited in vitro lifetime of human diploid cell strains', Leonard Hayflick, *Exp Cell Res*, 1965

37   'The SENS Challenge', Jason Pontin's blog, 28 July 2005, www.technology review.com

38   'Is Defeating Aging Only a Dream?', Jason Pontin, *Technology Review*, 11 July 2006

39   I refer in this book to 'immortalism', over de Grey's objections to the phrase. In a written exchange several months after our first meeting, he complained that the word suggests his aim is 'zero risk of death from any cause, something that is technologically unachievable ... by blurring the distinction between

something controversial and something impossible, one invites people to assume that the controversial thing is also impossible and is only being discussed for entertainment.' He emailed again: 'People are so scared of ageing that the only way they cope when forced to confront it is to pretend (to themselves) that they aren't scared of it at all, and thereby to put it out of their minds. That's why they trot out excuses for ageing that they'd be embarrassed to use to quieten a child on any other topic. And the range of excuses is broad, incorporating all kinds of reasons why ageing is a good thing after all on balance, but it also incorporates all kinds of dumb reasons for believing that there will never be anything we can do about ageing anyway, so let's just live with it. And use of the terminology of the impossible is a particularly insidious way of doing that, because it insinuates the idea of ageing's immutability into the mind without actually saying it and thus having to defend it. People WANT to believe that ageing is immutable, so that they aren't preoccupied by it – so they use, and like to hear/read others use, terminology that helps them to presume that it is.' So to be clear: de Grey does not foresee the death of death, but the possibility of substantially extended life.

40 *The Singularity Is Near: When Humans Transcend Biology*, Ray Kurzweil, Chapter 1: The Six Epochs

41 Cover endorsement for *The Singularity is Near: When Humans Transcend Biology*

42 The self-parking Toyota Prius went on sale in Japan at the end of 2003.

43 This is a reference to terror management theory, which is explored later in the book.

44 'Small molecule activators of sirtuins extend *Saccharomyces cerevisiae* life span', A. David, K. T. Howitz et al. *Nature* 425, 191–196, 2003

45 *Horizon*, 'Don't Grow Old', BBC 2, broadcast 9 February 2010

46 J. C. Milne et al. *Nature* 450, 712–716, 2007

47 'Health benefits of red-wine chemical unclear: Sceptics continue to ask whether resveratrol really can delay the effects of ageing', Lizzie Buchen, *Nature*, 19 January 2010

48 Ibid

49 'Doubts Build on Glaxo's Anti-ageing Drugs', Matthew Herper, *Forbes*, 26 January 2010

50 Glaxo Halts Development of Sirtris's Resveratrol, Albertina Torsoli, *Bloomberg News*, 2 December 2010

51 'Public never warned about dangerous device', Christine Willmsen and Michael J. Berens, *Seattle Times*, 19 November 2007

52 'Seven Warning Signs of Bogus Science', Robert L. Park, *The Chronicle of Higher Education*, 31 January 2003, posted on www.quackwatch.org

53 'Compounded hormone therapies: unproven, untested – and popular', *Endocrine Today*, 25 March 2008

54 'Anti-Aging Products: A Global Strategic Business Report', Global Industry Analysts, Inc, January 2009

55   US Department of Health & Human Services

56   'Chronic Care: A call to action for health reform', AARP, March 2009

57   *Counter Clockwise: Mindful Health and the Power of Possibility*, Chapter One, Ellen J. Langer, Ballantine Books, 2009

58   'Mindful Health and the Power of Possibility', Ellen J. Langer, essay in *Longevity Rules*, ed. Stuart Greenbaum, Eskaton

59   *Problems of the Self: Philosophical Papers 1956–1972*, Chapter 6: The Makropulos Case: reflections on the tedium of immortality, Bernard Williams, Cambridge University Press

60   Ibid

61   'Europe's Extraordinary Makeover', Catherine Mayer, *TIME*, 5 March 2006

62   'Food mixers are not on the menu, thanks: Kristin Scott Thomas on why turning 50 has opened new doors in French cinema – where beauty doesn't fade with age', Elizabeth Day, *Observer*, 4 July 2010

63   'Koppel vs. Letterman: A Little Perspective Please', James Poniewozik, *TIME*, 4 March 2002

64   'Bruce Forsyth: Hasn't he done well?' Brian Viner, *Independent*, 11 September 2010

65   'Selina Scott: Why I believe the BBC is guilty of blatant ageism and sexism', *Daily Telegraph*, 14 July 2010

66   'Learning Productive Aging as a Social Role: the Lessons of Television', George Gerbner, Greenwood Publishing Group, Inc., 1994

67   'Definitions and Descriptions of Age', George L. Maddox, *The Meanings of Age, Selected Papers of Bernice L. Neugarten*, University of Chicago Press, 1996

PART TWO – CHAPTER I

68   'Biological clock ticks for men too', *New Scientist*, 5 November 2005

69   *Menopause*, Kerstin Rodstrom, October 2003

70   Ibid

71   UK Office for National Statistics, 'Births in England and Wales by Characteristics of Mother 2009', *Statistical Bulletin*

72   'US National Vital Statistics Reports', Volume 57, Number 7, 7 January 2009

73   'The effect on human sex ratio at birth by assisted reproductive technology (ART) procedures – an assessment of babies born following single embryo transfers', Australia and New Zealand, 2002-2006. J. Dean, M. Chapman, E. Sullivan. BJOG 2010.

74   'Factors associated with fathers' caregiving activities and sensitivity with young children', *Journal of Family Psychology*, Vol. 14 (2), Jun 2000

75   'With a baby boy and a new album, Sheryl Crow says: "I Want To Experience Life"', James Kaplan, *Parade*, 2 March 2008

76   'It's a Little Bit Funny', John-Paul Flintoff, John Harlow and Miles Goslett, *Sunday Times*, 2 January 2011

77   'We want to spoil him with love': Sir Elton John and proud partner David Furnish reveal their joy following the birth of their son Zachary – and the

heartbreak after trying to adopt two Ukranian orphans, Interview by Melanie Bromley, *OK!*, 25 January 2011

78 'Romania's Princess Lia becomes a mother at 60', *Daily Mail*, 25 January 2010

79 *Larry King Live*, segment aired 14 July 2000

80 *Data in Focus*, Eurostat 2009

81 'Baby Gap: Germany's Birth Rate Hits a Historic Low', Tristana Moore, Time.com, 23 May 2010

82 Ibid

83 'One and Done', Lauren Sandler, *TIME*, 19 July 2010

84 'Baby Gap: Germany's Birth Rate Hits a Historic Low', Tristana Moore, Time.com, 23 May 2010

85 *The Youth Pill: Scientists at the Brink of an Anti-Aging Revolution*, Chapter 3: Hagrid's bat and the sabre-toothed sausage, David Stipp, Current, 2010

86 *Arrested Adulthood: the changing nature of maturity and identity*, Chapter 1: Maturity transformed: the rise of psychological adulthood, James Côté, New York University Press, 2000

87 Ibid

88 'Two Decades of Terror Management Theory: A Meta-Analysis of Mortality Salience Research', Brian Burke et al, *Personality and Social Psychology Review*, May 2010

89 'The Pill at 50: Sex, Freedom and Paradox', Nancy Gibbs, *TIME*, 22 April 2010

90 'One and Done', Lauren Sandler, *TIME*, 19 July 2010

91 Office for National Statistics. In 2007 26 per cent of all households were single-child families.

92 *The American Journal of Psychology*, 1915, copyright University of Illinois Press

93 'Only Children and Personality Development: A Quantitative Review', Denise F. Polit and Toni Falbo, *Journal of Marriage and Family*, Vol. 49, No. 2, May 1987

94 'Nuclear Implosion', Catherine Mayer, *TIME*, 26 September 2006

95 'We want to spoil him with love': Sir Elton John and proud partner David Furnish reveal their joy following the birth of their son Zachary – and the heartbreak after trying to adopt two Ukranian orphans, Interview by Melanie Bromley, *OK!*, 25 January 2011

96 'Social Trends', Office for National Statistics, July 2010

97 'Italians "slow to leave the nest"', BBC, 1 February 2005

98 'I just want to be their friend', Jane Gordon, *Sunday Telegraph*, 18 July 2010

PART TWO – CHAPTER 2

99 'Facebook Fuelling Divorce, Research Claims', *Daily Telegraph*, 21 December 2009

100 'Princess for a Day', Rebecca Mead, *Guardian*, 7 August 2010

101 'Generation Gap in Values, Behaviors: As Marriage and Parenthood Drift Apart, Public Is Concerned about Social Impact', Pew Research Center, July 2007

102 'Breaking Up is Hard to Do, Unless Everyone Else is Doing it Too: Social Network Effects on Divorce in a Longitudinal Sample Followed for 32 Years',

Rose McDermott, James H. Fowler and Nicholas A. Christakis, *Social Science Research Network*, 18 October 2009

103 'Population and social conditions', Monica Marcu, *Data in Focus*, Eurostat 2009

104 'Divorce Rate Lowest for 29 Years', BBC, 28 January 2010

105 'Generation Gap in Values, Behaviors: As Marriage and Parenthood Drift Apart, Public Is Concerned about Social Impact', Pew Research Center, July 2007

106 Ibid

107 'Youth Risk Behavior Survey', The Centers for Disease Control and Prevention, 2003

108 'Child Poverty in Perspective: An Overview of Child Wellbeing in Rich Countries', Unicef, Innocenti Research Centre, 2007

109 *The Mirror Effect: How Celebrity Narcissism is Endangering Our Families – and How to Save Them*, Chapter 8: The Most Vulnerable Audience: Teens and Young Adults, Drew Pinsky and S. Mark Young, HarperCollins, 2009

110 'Sexual Desire, Erection, Orgasm and Ejaculatory Functions and Their Importance to Elderly Swedish Men: A Population-based Study', Asgeir R. Helgason et al, *Age and Ageing*, 1996

111 *Almost Like a Whale: The Origin of Species Updated*, Chapter 4: Natural Selection, Steve Jones, Doubleday, 1999

112 'Understanding human ambivalence about sex: the effects of stripping sex of meaning', Jamie L. Goldenberg, Cathy R. Cox, Tom Pyszczynski, Jeff Greenberg, Sheldon Solomon, *Journal of Sex Research*, November 2002

113 Ibid

114 *Straw Dogs: Thoughts on Humans and Other Animals*, Chapter 3, The Vices of Morality: A Weakness for Prudence, John Gray, Granta Books, 2002

115 'Modern dating myths dispelled as study reveals cougar women do not exist … but aging men still hopeful of young, attractive partner', University of Wales Institute, Cardiff, 16 December 2009

PART TWO – CHAPTER 3

116 Republished with *Let's Welcome the Extraterrestrials* in one volume, as *Intelligent Design: Message from the Designers*, The Raelian Foundation, 2005

117 *The God Delusion*, Chapter 10: A much needed gap? Richard Dawkins, Black Swan, 2006

118 Ibid

119 *Straw Dogs: Thoughts on Humans and Other Animals*, Chapter 2: The Unsaved: The Grand Inquisitor and the Flying Fish, John Gray, Granta Books, 2002

120 American Religious Identification Survey 2008, Principal Investigators: Barry A. Kosmin and Ariela Keysar

121 Ibid

122 *How to Live: A Life of Montaigne in one question and twenty attempts at an answer*, Chapter 1: Q: How to Live? A: Don't Worry about Death, Sarah Bakewell, Chatto & Windus, 2010

123 *Conversations about the End of Time*, Umberto Eco, Stephen Jay Gould, Jean-Claude Carriere, Jean Delumeau, Penguin Books, 1999

124 http://www.scientology.cc/en_US/index.html, Kelly Preston, Scientology Celebrity Center International website

125 'Ringo's Rhythm Without Blues', Catherine Mayer, *TIME*, 12 December 2007

126 '"Clone baby" parents bar tests', BBC Online, 8 January 2003

PART TWO – CHAPTER 4

127 *Panorama*: 'The People's Princess', interview with Martin Bashir, BBC, first broadcast 20 November 1995

128 'Get Off the Couch', Frank Furedi, *Guardian*, 9 October 2003

129 Ibid

130 Coverline, *Hello!* 26 August 2008

131 *The Dick Cavett Show*, ABC, 20 October 1971

132 *Therapy Culture: Cultivating vulnerability in an uncertain age*, Chapter 5: The diminished self, Frank Furedi, Routledge, 2004

133 Ibid, Introduction

134 Ibid

135 'At her stunning home in the south of France, Brigitte Nielsen reveals all about her dramatic transformation – inside and out', interview by Dawn Emery, *Hello!* 26 August 2008

136 Ibid

137 *Affluenza: How to be successful and stay sane*, Are you infected with affluenza? Oliver James, Vermilion, 2007

138 'Praying "Aids Mental Health"', BBC Online, 12 November 1999

139 *Therapy Culture: Cultivating vulnerability in an uncertain age*, Chapter 4: How did we get here? Frank Furedi, Routledge, 2004

140 'After Drug Treatment: Are 12-Step Programs Effective in Maintaining Abstinence?' Robert Fiorentine, *The American Journal of Drug and Alcohol Abuse*, Vol. 25, No. 1, 1999

141 *Break the Mirror*, Nanao Sakaki, Blackberry Books, 1996

142 'Better or Worse: a longitudinal study of adults living in private households in Great Britain', editors Nicola Singleton and Glyn Lewis, Office for National Statistics, 2003

143 'Non-fatal suicidal behaviour among adults aged 16–74 in Great Britain', Howard Meltzer, Deborah Lader, Tania Corbin, Nicola Singleton, Rachel Jenkins, Traolach Brugha, Office for National Statistics, 2002

PART TWO – CHAPTER 5

144 'Men Become Richer After Divorce', Amelia Hill, *Observer*, 25 January 2009

145 'The Old Age "Offenders": Generation of Elderly Turned into Criminals', Paul Bentley, *Daily Mail*, 3 April 2010

146 *Losing My Virginity: The Autobiography*, Chapter 5: Learning a lesson, Richard Branson, Virgin Books, 1999

147 'The Andrew Davidson Interview: Richard Branson', *Management Today*, 1 August 2002

148 'Richard Branson Beats Jesus in British Role Model Poll', Reuters, 28 February 2008

149 *Losing My Virginity: The Autobiography*, Chapter 21: 'We would have about two seconds to say our last prayers', Richard Branson, Virgin Books, 1999

150 Ibid

151 'Escape of the Bankrupt', Nick Leeson, *Guardian*, 19 September 2008

152 'Former Convict Now Poker Pro', Donna Romano, www.gambling911.com, 11 January 2006

153 *Coningsby*, Book 3, Chapter 1, Benjamin Disraeli

154 'The Fading Future of Italy's Young', Jeff Israely, *TIME*, 10 April 2006

155 'L'image du travail selon la Génération Y. Une étude intergénérationnelle', *Revue Internationale de Psychosociologie*, December 2010

156 'The kids are alright but they need help', Stefan Stern, *Financial Times*, 22 February 2010

157 'UK's oldest councils', report published by Partnership, 17 August 2010

158 'The Effects of Retirement on Physical and Mental Health Outcomes', Dhaval Dave, Inas Rashad and Jasmina Spasojevic, NBER Working Paper Series, March 2006

159 'Why the Notion Persists that Retirement Harms Health', David J. Ekerdt, *The Gerontologist*, Volume 27, Issue 4, 1987

160 'Health Change in Retirement: A Longitudinal Study among Older Workers in the Netherlands', Hanna van Solinge, *Research on Aging*, May 2007

161 'Meryl Up Close', Martyn Palmer, *Good Housekeeping*, 1 August 2008

162 *A Vindication of the Rights of Woman: with strictures on political and moral subjects*, Chapter 3, Mary Wollstonecraft, 1792

163 'Attractiveness and Income for Men and Women in Management', Irene Hanson Frieze, Josephine E. Olson, June Russell, *Journal of Applied Social Psychology*, July 1991

164 'Woody Allen's Fourth London Film is an Elegant Return to Form', Jason Solomons, *Observer*, 16 May 2010

165 Ibid

166 'Cannes: Tamara Drewe to the rescue!' Richard Corliss, Time.com, 17 May 2010

167 Ibid

168 *Disney's World*, Chapter 22: The Wounded Bear, Leonard Mosley, Stein and Day, 1985

169 Ibid, Chapter 23: Finis

PART TWO – CHAPTER 6

170 'Modern Living: Man on the Cover: Del Webb', *TIME*, 3 August 1962

171 *Crazy Age*, Jane Miller, edited extract in the *Guardian*, 26 August 2010

172 'Walls Come Down on Age for Over-55 Communities', Haya El Nasser, *USA Today*, 22 March 2010

173 Ageless Marketing: Strategies for reaching the hearts and minds of the new customer majority, Part One, Chapter 1: Why Marketing Stopped Working, David B. Wolfe with Robert E. Snyder, Dearborn Trade Publishing, 2003

174 *microMARKETING*, Chapter 1: The next big thing is lots and lots of small things, Greg Verdino, McGraw Hill, 2010

175 'Cognitive age: a useful concept for advertising?' Nancy Stephens, *Journal of Advertising*, 1 December 1991

176 Ibid

177 'Who is buying the iPad, and will they also buy an iPhone?' Roger Entner, The Nielsen Company, NielsenWire, 4 August 2010

178 *Ageless Marketing: strategies for reaching the hearts and minds of the new customer majority*, Part One, Chapter 1: Why Marketing Stopped Working, David B. Wolfe with Robert E. Snyder, Dearborn Trade Publishing, 2003

179 Ibid

180 Ibid

181 'Scion sales will near 100,000 in 2011: CEO', Reuters, 31 March 2010

182 'Scion moves to expand its lineup', Mark Rechtin, *Automotive News*, 9 August 2010

183 'Showroom Showdown: Honda Element vs Scion xB', Dan Lienert, *Forbes*, 5 January 2005

184 *microMARKETING*, Chapter 3: From Mass Communications to Masses of Communicators, Greg Verdino, McGraw Hill, 2010

185 'Social Media and Technology Use Among Adults 50+', Jean Koppen, AARP Research & Strategic Analysis, June 2010

186 'Fastest-growing demographic on Facebook women over 55', www.insideface book.com, 2 February 2009

187 'After 5 funky years, Toyota's Scion now finds itself in a funk', *Automotive News*, 8 August 2008

188 Scion sales down 20 per cent, but 'we have the exact customer we want', Jonathon Ramsey, AutoBlog, 14 January 2011

189 'Neuromancer at 25: What It Got Right, What It Got Wrong', Mark Sullivan, PC World, 1 July 2009

190 *Zero History*, Chapter 41: Gear-Queer, William Gibson, G.P. Putnam's Sons, 2010

191 'Gap's Comeback Strategy: Jeans for Life', Mike Duff, *BNET Retail*, 11 February 2010

192 'Ashlee, Halle and More Help Gap Launch Premium Denim Under $60!' Shruti Dhalwala, People.com, 7 August 2009

193 *Ageless Marketing: strategies for reaching the hearts and minds of the new customer majority*, Part One, Chapter 3: Second-half customers seen through a new consciousness, David B. Wolfe with Robert E. Snyder, Dearborn Trade Publishing, 2003

194 'Activity Holidays – UK – February 2010', Mintel

195 'Benchmark Study Values Adventure Tourism Market at $89 Billion', George Washington University in association with the Adventure Travel Trade Association and Xola Consulting, 3 August 2010

196 *Sport Diving: the British Sub-Aqua Club Diving Manual*, Stanley Paul, 1988

PART THREE – THE APPLIANCE OF SCIENCE

197 Manuscript in the collection of the Royal Society

198 'China's Growing Cell Phone Market', Sumner Lemon, *International Data Group*, 29 May 2007

199 *Problems of the Self: Philosophical Papers 1956–1972*, Chapter 6: The Makropulos Case: reflections on the tedium of immortality, Bernard Williams, Cambridge University Press

200 *Holy Fire*, Chapter 2, Bruce Sterling, Phoenix, 1996

201 *Gulliver's Travels*, Jonathan Swift, original publication 1726

202 'In power to 120 years old: Putin, Berlusconi joke at summit', AFP, 11 September 2010

203 'Caloric restriction and aging: an update', Edward J. Masoro, *Experimental Gerontology*, Volume 35, Issue 3, May 2000

204 'Genetic Signatures of Exceptional Longevity in Humans', Paola Sebastiani, Nadia Solovieff, Annibale Puca, Stephen W. Hartley, Efthymia Melista, Stacy Andersen, Daniel A. Dworkis, Jemma B. Wilk, Richard H. Myers, Martin H. Steinberg, Monty Montano, Clinton T. Baldwin, and Thomas T. Perls, *Science*, 1 July 2010

205 'Editorial Expression of Concern', *Science*, 12 November 2010

206 'Position Statement on Human Ageing', Authors: S. Jay Olshansky (School of Public Health, University of Illinois at Chicago), Leonard Hayflick (University of California at San Francisco) and Bruce A. Carnes (University of Chicago/ National Opinion Research Center); Endorsers (alphabetical order): Robert Arking, Allen Bailey, Andrzej Bartke, Vladislav V. Bezrukov, Jacob Brody, Robert N. Butler, Alvaro Macieira-Coelho, L. Stephen Coles, David Danon, Aubrey D.N.J. de Grey, Lloyd Demetrius, Astrid Fletcher, James F. Fries, David Gershon, Roger Gosden, Carol W. Greider, S. Mitchell Harman, David Harrison, Christopher Heward, Henry R. Hirsch, Robin Holliday, Thomas E. Johnson, Tom Kirkwood, Leo S. Luckinbill, George M. Martin, Alec A. Morley, Charles Nam, Sang Chul Park, Linda Partridge, Graham Pawelec, Thomas T. Perls, Suresh Rattan, Robert Ricklefs, Ladislas (Leslie) Robert, Richard G. Rogers, Henry Rothschild, Douglas L. Schmucker, Jerry W. Shay, Monika Skalicky, Len Smith, Raj Sohal, Richard L. Sprott, Andrus Viidik, Jan Vijg, Eugenia Wang, Andrew Weil, Georg Wick and Woodring Wright. *Scientific American*, 13 May 2002

207 Ibid

208 'Free Radical Shift: Antioxidants may not increase life span', Kate Wilcox, *Scientific American*, 7 May 2009; 'The free radical theory of aging', Nathan C. Nelson, Department of Physics, Ohio State University, Columbus, OH 4320

209 'The 2009 Nobel Prize in Physiology or Medicine – Press Release', Nobelprize.org. 23 Sep 2010

210 *Long for this World*, Part II: The Hydra, Chapter 9: The Weakest Link, Jonathan Weiner, Ecco, 2010

211 *Holy Fire*, Chapter 2, Bruce Sterling, Phoenix, 1996

212 'Telomerase reactivation reverses tissue degeneration in aged telomerase-deficient mice', Mariela Jaskelioff, Florian L. Muller, Ji-Hye Paik, Emily Thomas, Shan Jiang, Andrew C. Adams, Ergun Sahin, Maria Kost-Alimova, Alexei Protopopov, Juan Cadiñanos, James W. Horner, Eleftheria Maratos-Flier and Ronald A. DePinho, *Nature*, 28 November 2010

213 'Long May He Run', Pete Gauvin, *Adventure Sports Journal*, 8 July 2010

214 *Transcend: Nine Steps to Living Well Forever*, Part 2, the Plan: Chapter 12: Supplements, Ray Kurzweil & Terry Grossman, Rodale, 2009

215 *Selling the Fountain of Youth: How the anti-ageing industry made a disease out of getting old – and made billions*, Chapter 9: Anti-Ageing Goes Mainstream, Arlene Weintraub, Basic Books, 2010

216 'Why Do Anti-Ageing Doctors Die?' S. Jay Olshanksy, essay in *Longevity Rules: How to Age Well into the Future*, edited by Stuart Greenbaum, Eskaton, 2010

217 *Selling the Fountain of Youth: How the anti-ageing industry made a disease out of getting old – and made billions*, Chapter 6: The invention of the male menopause, Arlene Weintraub, Basic Books, 2010

218 'International Differences in Longevity and Health and Their Economic Consequences'; Pierre-Carl Michaud, Dana Goldman, Darius Lakdawalla, Adam Gailey, Yuhui Zheng, NBER Working Paper Series

219 'Overcoming policy cacophony on obesity: an ecological public health framework for policymakers', T. Lang and G. Rayner, Department of Health Management and Food Policy, City University, The International Association for the Study of Obesity, *Obesity Reviews*, 8, 2007

220 *Selling the Fountain of Youth: How the anti-ageing industry made a disease out of getting old – and made billions*, Chapter 6: The invention of the male menopause, Arlene Weintraub, Basic Books, 2010

221 'Effects of Human Growth Hormone in Men over 60 Years Old', Daniel Rudman et al, *New England Journal of Medicine*, 5 July 1990

222 www.alternative-doctor.com

223 'Can Growth Hormone Prevent Aging?' Mary Lee Vance, *New England Journal of Medicine*, 27 February 2003

224 *Treat Me, Not My Age: A Doctor's Guide to Getting the best Care as You or a Loved One Gets Older*, Introduction, Mark Lachs, Viking, 2010

225 'Tackling inequalities in life expectancy in areas with the worst health and deprivation', Report by the Comptroller and Auditor General, HC 186 Session 2010–2011, 2 July 2010

226 *Three Men in a Boat*, Jerome K. Jerome, first published 1889, Bibliolis Classics, 2010

227 'Education and Obesity in Four OECD Countries', Franco Sassi, Marion Devaux, Jody Church, Michele Cecchini, Francesca Borgonovi, OECD, 15 June 2009

228 'Jamie's Platform for Change: Why America Needs a Food Revolution Now', www.jamieoliver.com

229 *The Blue Zones – Lessons for living longer from the people who've lived the longest*, Preface: Get Ready to Change Your Life, Dan Buettner, National Geographic, 2008

230   Ibid, Chapter 4: An American Blue Zone

231   Ibid

232   'Human Population: Urbanization', Population Reference Bureau, 2010

233   'Long May He Run', Pete Gauvin, *Adventure Sports Journal*, 8 July 2010

234   'Physical activity predicts gray matter volume in late adulthood', Professor Kirk Erickson et al, *Neurology*, 13 October 2010

235   'Obesity and the Economics of Prevention, Fit not Fat', OECD, 2010

236   'Vitamin D Deficiency', Michael F. Holick, *New England Journal of Medicine*, 19 July 2007

237   'Social Integration and Longevity: An Event History Analysis of Women's Roles and Resilience', Phillis Moen, Donna Dempster-McClain, Robin M. Williams, *American Sociological Review*, August 1989

238   'Unequal America, causes and consequences of the wide – and growing – gap between rich and poor', by Elizabeth Gudrais, *Harvard Magazine*, July–August 2008

239   'Fair Society, Healthy Lives: The Marmot Review – Strategic Review of Health Inequalities in England post 2010'

PART THREE – IN CONCLUSION

240   'Growing Old in America: Expectations vs Reality', Paul Taylor et al, Pew Research Center, 29 June 2009

241   *Essays*, Book I, Michel de Montaigne, 1580

242   *How to Live: A Life of Montaigne in one question and twenty attempts at an answer*, Chapter 1: Q: How to Live? A: Don't Worry about Death, Sarah Bakewell, Chatto & Windus, 2010

bibliography

Allen, Woody, *Getting Even*, First Vintage Books, 1978

Athill, Diana, *After A Funeral*, Jonathan Cape, 1986

Athill, Diana, *Stet: An Editor's Life*, Granta Books, 2000

Baker, Nick, *Groovy Old Men: A Spotter's Guide*, Icon Books, 2008

Bakewell, Sarah, *How to Live: A life of Montaigne in one question and twenty attempts at an answer*, Chatto & Windus, 2010

Berg, Adriane, *How Not To Go Broke at 102: Achieving Everlasting Wealth*, John Wiley & Sons, 2008

Bower, Tom, *Branson*, Fourth Estate, 2001

Branson, Richard, *Losing My Virginity*, Virgin Books, 2009

Bright, Randy, *Disneyland: Inside Story*, edited by Lory Frankel, Harry N. Abrams for the Walt Disney Company, 1987

Buettner, Dan, *The Blue Zones: Lessons for Living Longer from the People Who've Lived the Longest*, National Geographic, 2008

Butler (MD), Robert N., *The Longevity Prescription: the 8 Proven Keys to a Long, Healthy Life*, Avery, 2010

Chopra, Deepak, *Ageless Body, Timeless Mind*, Rider, 1993, 2003

Côté, James E., *Arrested Adulthood – The Changing Nature of Maturity and Identity*, New York University Press, 2000

Critser, Greg, *Fat Land: How Americans Became the Fattest People in the World*, Houghton Mifflin, 2003

Cunningham, Hugh, *Leisure in the Industrial Revolution*, Croom Helm, 1980

Dahmen, Nicole S. and Raluca Cozma (eds), 'Media Takes: On Aging', International Longevity Center USA and Aging Services of California, 2009

Dawkins, Richard, *The God Delusion*, Bantam Press, 2006

Eco, Umberto, Stephen Jay Gould, Jean-Claude Carriere, Jean Delumeau, *Conversations about the End of Time*, Penguin Books, 1999

Eskapa, Ben, *Bizarre Sex*, Quartet Books, 1987

Fairley, Josephine and Stacey, Sarah, *The Anti-Ageing Beauty Bible*, Kyle Cathie, 2010

Furedi, Frank, *Therapy Culture: Cultivating Vulnerability in an Uncertain Age*, Routledge, 2004

Gibson, William, *Zero History*, G.P. Putnam's Sons, 2010

Gladwell, Malcolm, *The Tipping Point: How Little Things Can Make a Big Difference*, Abacus, 2010

Goldacre, Ben, *Bad Science*, Fourth Estate, 2008

Gray, John, *Straw Dogs: Thoughts on Humans and Other Animals*, Granta Books, 2002

Greenbaum, Stuart (ed.), *Longevity Rules: How to Age Well into the Future*, Eskaton, 2010

Haeberle, Erwin J., *The Sex Atlas*, Continuum Publishing, 1981

James, Oliver, *Affluenza: How to be Successful and Stay Sane*, Vermilion, 2007

Jennings, Luke, *Blood Knots*, Atlantic, 2010

Jerome, Jerome K., *Three Men in a Boat*, first published 1889, Bibliolis Classics, 2010

Jones, Steve, *Almost Like a Whale: The Origin of Species Updated*, Doubleday, 1999

Kessler, David A., *The End of Overeating: Taking Control of Our Insatiable Appetite*, Penguin Books, 2009

Kurzweil, Ray, and Terry Grossman, *Transcend: Nine Steps to Living Well Forever*, Rodale, 2009

Kurzweil, Ray, *The Singularity is Near: When Humans Transcend Biology*, Duckworth, 2009

Lachs, Mark, *Treat Me, Not My Age: A Doctor's Guide to Getting the best Care as You or a Loved One Gets Older*, Viking, 2010

Langer, Ellen J., *Counter Clockwise: Mindful Health and the Power of Possibility*, Ballantine Books, 2009

Lasch, Christopher, *The Culture of Narcissism – American Life in An Age of Diminishing Expectations*, W.W. Norton, 1979, 1991

Layard, Richard, and Judy Dunn, *A Good Childhood: Searching for Values in a Competitive Age*, Penguin Books, The Children's Society, 2009

Layard, Richard, *Happiness: Lessons from a New Science*, Penguin Books, 2005

Lewis, Wendy, *Plastic Makes Perfect – The Complete Cosmetic Beauty Guide*, Orion Books, 2007

Mezrich, Ben, *The Accidental Billionaires: the Founding of Facebook: A tale of sex, money, genius and betrayal*, Doubleday, 2009

Mosley, Leonard, *Disney's World*, Stein and Day, 1985

National Health Insurance: Lessons from Abroad – A Century Foundation Guide to the Issues, Century Foundation Press, 2008

Neugarten, Dail A. (ed.), *The Meanings of Age: Selected Papers of Bernice L. Neugarten*, University of Chicago Press, 1996

Palmer, Sue, *Toxic Childhood: How the Modern World is Damaging Our Children and What We Can Do About It*, Orion Books, 2006

Pinsky, Dr Drew, and Dr S. Mark Young, *The Mirror Effect: How Celebrity Narcissism Is Endangering Our Families – And How To Save Them*, HarperCollins, 2009

Pollan, Michael, *Food Rules: An Eater's Manual*, Penguin Books, 2010

Postman, Neil, *The Disappearance of Childhood*, Vintage, 1994

Poundstone, William, *Priceless: The Hidden Psychology of Value*, Oneworld, 2010

Sams, Craig, *The Little Food Book: An Explosive Account of the Food We Eat Today*, Alastair Sawday Publishing, 2003

Savage, Jon, *Teenage: The Creation of Youth 1875–1945*, Chatto & Windus, 2007

Sheehy, Gail, *New Passages: Mapping Your Life Across Time*, Ballantine Books, 1995

Sheehy, Gail, *Passages: Predictable Crises of Adult Life*, E.P. Dutton & Co., 1974, 1976

Shelley, Mary W., *Frankenstein or the Modern Prometheus*, Boston, 1869

Sport Diving: the British Sub-Aqua Club Diving Manual, Stanley Paul, 1988

Sterling, Bruce, *Holy Fire*, Phoenix, 1996

Stipp, David, *The Youth Pill: Scientists at the Brink of an Anti-Aging Revolution*, Current, 2010

Strawson, Galen, 'Against Narrativity', *Ratio* (new series), XVII, 4 December 2004

Swift, Jonathan, *Gulliver's Travels*, Wordsworth Classics, 1992

Twenge, Jean M., and W. Keith Campbell, *The Narcissism Epidemic: Living in the Age of Entitlement*, Free Press, 2009

Verdino, Greg, *microMARKETING: Get Big Results by Thinking and Acting Small*, McGraw Hill, 2010

Voltaire, *Candide*, 1759. Edited by Stanley Appelbaum, Dover Publications, 1991

Weiner, Jonathan, *Long for this World: The Strange Science of Immortality*, Ecco, 2010

Weintraub, Arlene, *Selling the Fountain of Youth: How the anti-aging industry made a disease out of getting old — and made billions*, Basic Books, 2010

Williams, Bernard, *Problems of the Self: Philosophical Papers 1956–1972*, Cambridge University Press, 1973

Wolfe, David B., with Robert E. Snyder, *Ageless Marketing — Strategies for Reaching the Hearts and Minds of the New Customer Majority*, Dearborn Trade Publishing, 2003

acknowledgements

This book owes its existence to the Gods of Placement — and Time Warner's European public policy chief Carolyn Dailey — who seated me next to the illustrious literary agent Ed Victor at what she billed as an opinion formers' lunch in October 2009. 'So what books have you thought of writing?' Ed asked, and within a few minutes we were discussing amortality. By the following January he had persuaded Miranda West, at that stage senior commissioning editor for Vermilion, to take on the project. Only a few weeks after signing me to Vermilion, Miranda handed in her notice and left the country, but to my enormous relief agreed to edit my book on a freelance basis. Her input has been invaluable.

Huge thanks also go to my colleagues at *TIME*. Lev Grossman, who moonlights as a writer of seductively dark fantasy novels, commissioned my original meditation on amortality, for *TIME*'s March 2009 cover package *10 Ideas Changing the World Right Now*. Michael Elliott, *TIME*'s deputy managing editor and international editor, has been a friend and mentor since we worked together at *The Economist* back in the Pleistocene era. He agreed to my book leave even though it fell immediately after parliamentary elections in the main territory I'm employed to cover. *TIME* associate editor Jumana Farouky and the rest of *TIME*'s editorial team in London selflessly covered for me, not least on a few occasions after my return to work when the strain of finishing a book and doing my real job threatened to tip me into madness. Daphné Vanden Borre and Tracy Chan in the

TIME & Fortune creative department in London contributed design ideas and moral support.

Deputy international editor Bobby Ghosh and his wife Bipasha were outstanding and generous hosts among a string of outstanding and generous hosts who put me up during the research process and/or put up with me during the writing process, when I proved myself the worst kind of house guest, antisocial, unhelpful and always hogging the broadband. I sometimes added insult to injury by pushing my hosts or fellow guests to be interviewed for the book. Special mentions – and apologies – go to Sara Burns and Richard Sayer, Nicky and Luke Jennings, Florian Haertel, and family members including Bill Agee and Kirsten Burgess Agee, Adam Bezark and Kristen Simental-Bezark, Laura and Skip Mandracchia and Angus Deayton and my sister Lise.

My other sister Cassie helped to inspire this project. One of my closest elective family members, Charlotte Grimshaw, mentioned briefly in the book, not only provided substantial input but was also my diving partner during the Red Sea trip with my father. She has long encouraged me to write long-form and some years ago suggested a theme, about women's later-life reinvention, that set me thinking about amortality.

The Age Boom Academy, run by the International Longevity Center and sponsored by the *New York Times*, was a fantastic resource. My appreciation to Biz Stone and the rest of the Twitter team for creating and maintaining a research tool that remains widely undervalued. (Props, too, to Tim Berners-Lee, for kicking off the revolution that made Twitter possible and contributed so much to amortality.) Twitterati William Gibson and University of Maryland's Allen Stairs took time to dig out exceptionally useful research materials and brainstorm for me. On the research front, I was also given significant assistance by Alec Howe and Patrick Lodge at Breaking Trends™.

Helping me to make sense of the tidal wave of information was Catriona 'Katy' Watts, the best researcher I've ever encountered.

Four people allowed themselves to be suckered into reading early drafts of the book and giving me their unvarnished opinions. They did so with grace. I am indebted to Gary Stix, senior writer at *Scientific American*; Peter Gumbel, friend, former colleague and all-round genius; Jef McAllister, my amazing predecessor as *TIME*'s London Bureau Chief, whose shoes still seem unfeasibly big, and the lovely Beth Mitchell, an incisive mind and fellow Pilates enthusiast.

The following people gave me great leads, ideas and support: Maggie Alderson, Anoushka Boone, Josephine Fairley, Veronica Grant, Sabrina Guinness, Susy Hutchence, Dominique Jansen, Martine Johnson, Wendy Lewis, Tim Livesey, Cindy Palmano, Mary Schiffer and Sian Williams.

My gratitude goes to all of my interviewees, my step-parents, my godchildren (even better than the real thing), and my husband (again, and profoundly). But above all, I thank my parents, and not only for tolerating my incessant questioning but for raising the questions in the first place.

index

about the author

Catherine Mayer is London Bureau Chief for *TIME* magazine. An award-winning journalist and former President of the Foreign Press Association, she was a staff writer at *The Economist*, deputy editor of *Business Traveller* and *International Management*, and a correspondent for the German news weekly *FOCUS*. She was born in Wisconsin, educated in the US and Europe and has a degree from Sussex and Freiburg universities. Married to a rock musician, she lives in London. And in hope.

© Adam Lawrence